Start Smart™
Your Home-Based Business

D0916110

Bernadette Tiernan

Macmillan Spectrum
an imprint of
Macmillan • USA

Macmillan General Reference
A Simon & Schuster Macmillan Company
1633 Broadway
New York, NY 10019

START SMART ™ is a trademark of Start Smart Productions, LLC

Spectrum, MACMILLAN and colophons are registered trademarks of Simon & Schuster Inc.

Manufactured in the United States of America

10   9   8   7   6   5   4   3   2   1

Library of Congress Cataloging-in-Publication Data
Tiernan, Bernadette, 1951–
        Start Smart!: Your home-based business
    Bernadette Tiernan.
            p.   cm.
        Includes bibliographical references.
        ISBN 0–02–860330–3
        1. Home-based businesses—Management—Handbooks, manuals, etc.
    I. Title
    HD62.38.T54   1996
    658'.041—dc20   96-21526
                                                                 CIP

Book design by Margaret D. DuBois

Contents

Dedication

*To my husband Bill
and our children
Katherine, Billy, and Caroline*

There's No Place Like Home

Current Trends

Growth in the number of home-based workers in the current decade has exceeded even the most advanced projections. Trend-watchers who predicted that more people would work at home during the 1990s must be surprised at *how fast and how wide-spread* this growth is. We are in an era of entrepreneurship, characterized by dramatic increases in the number of women-owned businesses and highlighted by home offices.

Working at home is the reality of this decade. Today 36 percent of the labor force works at home. It has been predicted that by the year 2000 the number will reach 50 percent.

In 1980 there were 5.7 million full-time home-based businesses, according to the American Home Business Association in a 1988 *U.S. News & World Report* survey. At that time it was predicted that there would be 20.7 million home-based businesses by the mid-1990s. In actuality, the number of Americans doing full- and part-time income-producing or job-related work at home is expected to soar by the end of this year, according to IDC/LINK Resources, a New York research firm. According to the IDC/LINK Home Office Market update, between second quarter 1994 and second quarter 1995 the work-at-home universe expanded by three million households to 39 million, a growth of 7.6 percent over a 12-month period.

The largest segment of the work-at-home population, according to LINK, is defined as "primary and part-time self-employed homeworkers," which includes home-based businesses, self-employed freelancers, and contractors. This category represents 58 percent of the universe and numbers about 26.7 million workers.

According to LINK Resources, corporate after-hours workers include company employees who bring work home from a conventional job after normal business hours and who use any combination of PCs, modems, fax devices, and/or multiple phone lines.

Telecommuters are defined as salaried employees who normally would go to the office to work but now spend two to three days working at home or off-site from the company during normal business hours. Telecommuting provides an opportunity for businesses to meet the needs of talented people. Like other new workstyle options such as flex time and job sharing, it offers a new benefit for employees.

The growing trend toward home-based business is projected to continue into the next millennium.

Factors Influencing Growth

Three major factors have caused a dramatic increase in the rate of growth in the number of homeworkers in the United States:

1. The need to have more flexibility in lifestyle is widely accepted as the chief force spurring growth. Often these lifestyle and workstyle decisions are influenced by family—particularly child-rearing—demands.

2. Technology advancements have changed offices enormously by making personal computers, computer networks, software, fax machines, cellular phones, and overnight delivery services accessible and affordable to virtually any business.

3. Environmental clean-up efforts, like the Clean Air Act and other state and federal government regulations, almost force large corporations to seek alternatives to traditional five-day workweek commuter schedules in order to comply.

Additional factors have contributed to the dramatic and sustained increase in home-workers. The recent wave of corporate layoffs and downsizings has sent more people into self-employment than ever before, redefining expectations of security and success. For many professionals who suddenly find themselves out on their own, a home-based office can offer the ideal place to reconstruct a career.

It is no secret that low overhead costs are an important advantage of home-based business. For a rapidly growing number of entrepreneurs, a home-based business poses far less risk than signing a conventional office or building lease. Not that entrepreneurs are adverse to risk. In fact, few entrepreneurs today face the first stages of their new business fearlessly. For most start-ups, some degree of risk—financial, psychological, logistical, emotional—is evoked from the very beginning. Anxiety is a state many entrepreneurs grow accustomed to. But while legends of entrepreneurial risk-takers abounded in the 1980s, in the more cautious climate of the 1990s, the economy will not support ill-planned business dreams and whims.

For some small-business owners, their home-based business is temporary. It is the first step in a process that will culminate in building their own office building. For others, there is no place like home—ever. They may ultimately build or buy a bigger home for their base, but they have resolved never to commute again.

New Attitudes Toward Home-Based Business

The influx of former corporate employees into the world of home-based business has created a distinct and fascinating attitudinal shift. This influx, including women and

Growth of Work-at-Home Universe in millons, 1994–1995		
Individuals	**1994**	**1995**
Primary self-employed	12.7	12.9
Part-time self-employed	12.7	13.8
Corporate after-hours	9.0	11.5
Telecommuters	8.8	7.9
Total Individuals	43.2	46.1
Households	**1994**	**1995**
Primary self-employed	10.6	11.0
Part-time self-employed	9.8	12.0
Corporate after-hours	7.7	10.0
Telecommuters	7.9	6.0
Total Homeworker Households	36.0	39.0

Figure 1-1. Dramatic increases have occurred in the number of home-based workers, beyond projections of experts *(Source: IDC/LINK 1995 Home Office Market Update, New York)*

minorities who "hit the glass ceiling," men and women who parachuted from the executive ranks before their time, and employees of all types in search of a new work-style, has influenced more than the *number* of home-based workers. Their predominance has also affected the *prestige* of home-workers.

The raging popularity of home-based business today is the result of a "paradigm shift," a break with traditional thinking. Because paradigms influence the way we view the world, we are forced to reexamine old viewpoints. Suddenly everything looks different.

Traditional home-based workers have always included writers, editors, lawyers, and other professionals. Our towns and cities were perfectly comfortable with these occupations at home and designed zoning laws and local ordinances accordingly. But advancements in technology have changed all that. The scope of home-based business now includes virtually *any* service or product that space permits, even if zoning does not (see chapter 3). The landscape of home-based business looks different today and will continue to change into the next millennium.

Today streamlined high-tech equipment and state-of-the-art CD-ROM databases replace traditional cumbersome storage areas in many home-based businesses. It is now possible to access the information superhighway in seconds, reaching resources that once took hours to locate. Home-based businesses have access to almost unlimited computer databases—everything that is available to large companies but at far lower overhead cost. Today technology and networking can provide a home-based business with immediate access to urban and suburban clients throughout the nation—and the world—without a painful commute or expensive travel arrangements.

"Small-time entrepreneurs have seized multi-billion-dollar markets from well-heeled businesses," wrote John Naisbitt and Patricia Aburdene in *Megatrends 2000*. "Individual entrepreneurs are playing larger roles in the world economy." Home-based businesses now enjoy the release that new technologies have provided, empowering individual entrepreneurs.

The new trend toward virtual corporations, a method to expand potential service and/or product offerings, further increases the capability of even the smallest business to aim for a larger share of the market. Home-based businesses can create links with companies with manufacturing and production capabilities to open new markets. (Virtual corporations will be covered in detail in chapter 8.)

Everything suddenly looks *very* different. The paradigm shift to home-based business has created a climate in which working from home is perceived from a new perspective, with a new and improved image.

Growth of Women in Business

In 1995 the National Foundation for Women Business Owners (NFWBO) released a report that is still widely quoted today. These statistics bear repeating:

- ◆ There were an estimated 7.7 million women-owned businesses in the U.S. in 1995.

- ◆ Women-owned businesses employ 35 percent more people in the United States than the 1994 Fortune 500 companies combined worldwide.

- ◆ Women-owned businesses provide jobs for over 11 million people.

- ◆ While the largest companies in the United States were reducing their numbers of employees, 25 percent of women-owned businesses were adding employees.

- ◆ Women-owned firms with 100 or more employees expanded at six times the rate of all firms from 1991 to 1994.

Another significant statistic reported by the NFWBO study concerned the stability of women-owned businesses. Most women-owned businesses not only were stable, but also offered stable employment for a growing number of workers. Over 40 percent have been in business 12 years or longer, and they were less likely than other businesses to grow or decline rapidly. These businesses operate in every sector of the economy.

While many women did rise up through the ranks of the corporate world in the last decade, others grew tired of seeing their reflections in a glass ceiling and of being denied access to positions in the top levels of the corporate workforce. Thus, many women who reached a career plateau in middle management decided to leave. Women who assessed their own bright potential to find only dismal prospects in working for corporations have now created a whole new world of work.

The glass ceiling phenomenon is certainly not the only driving force behind the dramatic increase in the number of women-owned businesses. Many women in need of a career change—regardless of their position—leave in search of a workstyle that harmonizes with their lifestyle. In some cases their decisions come when boardrooms and babies' rooms do not blend in a way in which they feel comfortable. These decisions have been recorded and analyzed in the media and have been agony for the individuals involved. But as part of this new direction, the number of self-employed women working full-time at home tripled between 1985 and 1991, from 378,000 to 1.1 million, LINK reported.

Where Do Entrepreneurs Get Their Ideas?

According to a recent study in the *Harvard Business Review*, "How Entrepreneurs Craft Strategies That Work," entrepreneurs rely on something more than forecasts, trends, or inventions when they start a business. This research indicated that most new ventures are started to solve problems the entrepreneurs have personally dealt with, either as employees of another company or as customers. Here are the ways entrepreneurs have come up with their ideas:

71 percent: Replicated or modified an idea encountered through previous employment

4 percent: Discovered a product or service through systematic research for opportunities

5 percent: Swept into the PC revolution

20 percent: Discovered a product or service serendipitously:

Built temporary or casual job into a business (7 percent)

Wanted product or service as an individual consumer (6 percent)

Happened to read about the industry (4 percent)

Developed family member's idea (2 percent)

Thought up during honeymoon in Italy (1 percent)

This research offers encouraging news for home-based business start-ups. You don't need to venture into unfamiliar territory to start a successful home-based business. In fact, your opportunities for success may be even better if you stick with what you know. So don't get discouraged if you don't have an invention or new product to offer—there are plenty of opportunities to take an existing product or service and improve it. By staying tuned in to business, economic, and social trends, you will have a good sense of the products and services most likely to appeal to the market.

What the Trend-Watchers Predict

Some of us eagerly anticipate each wave of new releases from trend forecasters. Like readers of horoscopes, we want to know where we might be headed before we arrive. The forecasts serve as our map. Other individuals prefer to find their own road and surge ahead, ignoring the fickle barometer of forecasting. "Even if you do not endorse the direction of a trend," according to John Naisbitt and Patricia Aburdene in *Megatrends 2000,* "you are empowered by your knowledge about it." According to their analysis, you "may choose to challenge the trends, but first you must know where they are headed."

Try the following warm-up exercise (Figure 1-2). Fill in the blanks for "What's New?" with the response you can identify from your own research, observations you have mentally noted, reports from multiple media sources, and personal conversations with friends and family. Then fill in the "What's You?" column.

How far from "trendy" are you? When does it matter? The answers are different for everyone. Take cars, for example. If you have frequent customer contact by car and drive clients around, your car choice is more important than if you don't. And if you are in a business where you need to be perceived as "state-of-the-art" in everything, your image is *really* critical. (More on this topic in chapter 6.)

But whether you prefer the textbook-style prose of researchers John Naisbitt and Patricia Aburdene or the conversational colloquialism of Faith Popcorn, you need to feel the pulse of the leaders lest you rapidly become a follower. What are the gurus predicting?

Trend forecaster Faith Popcorn, founder of BrainReserve and best-selling author of *The Popcorn Report* (Doubleday, 1991) and *Clicking* (HarperCollins, 1996), identified a set of trends that she predicted would influence marketing, businesses, consumers, and lifestyles. She defined, for example, the phenomenon of Cashing Out, "where men and women leave the corporate rat race in search of a better quality of life." In her books,

About Today's Trends

	What's New?	What's You?
Colors	_____	_____
Food	_____	_____
Job	_____	_____
TV Shows	_____	_____
Cars	_____	_____
Radio Station	_____	_____
Sports	_____	_____
Hobby	_____	_____
Books	_____	_____
Leisure Activity	_____	_____
Special Interest	_____	_____

Figure 1-2: Personal Survey About Today's Trends

Popcorn provides very specific details and direction about trends that can be applied to your own business. Her books are a must-read to create your own "map." Figure 1-3 summarizes the "top trends" selected by Faith Popcorn's BrainReserve Trend Bank.™

In *Megatrends 2000,* the assessment of trends is more expansive and theoretical. "By identifying the forces pushing the future, rather than those that have contained the past," according to Naisbitt and Aburdene, "you possess the power to engage with your reality." Your reality, according to them, knows no boundaries. Figure 1-4 summarizes their analysis.

Jumping on each latest trend in "what's hot" could be just as hazardous to your business health as staying in a time warp. The secret to a successful application of trends to your business is in the selection of pertinent predictors. What trends affect your business today and in the future? Try a short form of "Trend Analysis" for your business or business idea. Answer the questions in figure 1-5 for your current business, or for the business ideas you are considering.

New Directions for Small Business

Globalization, the rise of new technologies, and the development of new markets affect the whole American economy, and small businesses are claiming a larger piece

BrainReserves "Top Trends"

Cocooning
The need to protect oneself from the harsh unpredictable realities of the outside world.

Fantasy Adventure
Modern age whets our desire for roads untaken.

Small Indulgences
Stressed-out consumers want to indulge in affordable luxuries and seek ways to reward themselves.

Egonomics
The sterile computer era breeds the desire to make personal statements.

The Vigilante Consumer
The consumer manipulates marketers and the marketplace through pressure, protest, and politics.

Staying Alive
Awareness that good health extends longevity leads to a new way of life.

99 Lives
Too fast a pace and too little time forces us to adapt to multiple roles.

Cashing Out
Working women and men, questioning personal/career satisfaction and goals, opt for simpler living.

Down-Aging
Nostalgic for their carefree childhood, baby boomers find comfort in familiar pursuits and products of their youth.

Save Our Society
The country rediscovers a social conscience of ethics, passion, and compassion.

Wildering
A new appreciation of man as primal being, a return to the great outdoors; capturing the pioneer spirit by testing physical and mental limits.

Clanning
Belonging to a group that represents common feelings, causes, or ideals; validating one's own belief system.

Pleasure Revenge
Consumers are having a secret bacchanal. They're mad as hell and want to cut loose again.

Icon Toppling
A new socioquake transforms mainstream America and the world as the pillars of society are questioned and rejected.

Female Think
A new set of values that shift marketing consciousness from a hierarchical model to a familial one.

Anchoring
Our society looks back to ancient practices to prepare itself for future challenges.

Figure 1-3: Top Trends from the BrainReserve Trend Bank,™ *One Madison Avenue, New York, NY 10010*

The Millennial Megatrends: Gateways to the 21st Century

1. Booming Global Economy of the 1990s

2. Renaissance in the Arts

3. Emergence of Free-Market Socialism

4. Global Lifestyles and Cultural Nationalism

5. Privatization of the Welfare State

6. Rise of the Pacific Rim

7. Decade of Women in Leadership

8. Age of Biology

9. Religious Revival of the New Millennium

10. Triumph of the Individual

Figure 1-4: Millennial Megatrends from Megatrends 2000. *Text © 1990 by Megatrends, Ltd. By permission of William Morrow & Company, Inc.*

TREND ANALYSIS

Identify four trends that impact your business today.

1. _____

2. _____

3. _____

4. _____

List three trends that could affect your business in the future.

1. _____

2. _____

3. _____

Figure 1-5: Trend Analysis

of the action. There are a number of predictions that all the trend-watchers seem to agree on. Industries that have gained momentum in the 1990s and are projected to continue to grow into the next millennium are technology and information management, health care, servicing the small and home-based business market, and education and training. Products and services that save us time are also still on the rise, as well as Kids and Kid Stuff to meet the needs of the new miniboom.

There are many individual business ideas that arise from these growth industries. Technology and information management are driving us into the next millennium at a rate that sometimes exceeds our grasp, although many are slow to admit that. We may need more computer capacity than we own for specific tasks, or our need to access data from many sources may sometimes exceed our capacity. Consider also that the major corporations that have downsized and reengineered haven't eliminated computer and data-processing services, but instead are more willing than ever to farm out this work to small businesses.

Businesses that tie in with health care in *any* way have been growing steadily. In our aging population, the number of people age 35 to 59 now exceeds the number of 18 to 34-year-olds. More of us live longer than ever before. As a nation, we are increasingly preoccupied with our own health and confronted with the increasing medical needs of our aging parents. The most obvious connections to health care are home health care providers, physical and occupational therapy, and medical billing services. Tangentially, businesses with a focus on nutrition can thrive as well.

The home-based and small-business market itself generates the need for products and services that cater to it. Last year, *Entrepreneur* magazine rated Mailboxes, Etc., number seven in its listing of the top ten franchises. Many home-based businesses use Mailboxes, Etc., facilities for post office boxes, fax machines, copy machines, and last-minute supplies. But other providers of home-based business needs will be home-based themselves. This is a $401 billion market, according to *Entrepreneur.*

Education and training businesses will play a critical role in escorting us into the next decade. We all need to keep pace with the rapidly changing world around us. As corporations continue to downsize, there will continue to be a need for job re-training. And programs that improve work skills—formerly a corporate human resource training department staple—may move away from internal training organizations, which can be expensive to maintain for all but the largest companies, to external resources.

Finally, because we all need a 48-hour day, and still nothing can be done about that, we need *help.* In some cases, we won't want to pay a lot for it, but in other cases we'll splurge for relief, for a break. Businesses that provide products and services that give us a break are hot.

But there's obviously more to running a home-based business than just selecting the right industry. Trend-watchers also agree that the businesses that are most likely to succeed in the future will embrace these characteristics:

Allegiances: Concentrating on Customers and Quality

The most successful businesses identify their best customers, then build long-term relationships with them. They listen to the needs of their customers and focus on providing excellent service. Small businesses have gained an edge over their corporate competitors by paying close attention to details. The little things can make a difference. Building loyalty from customers by listening to them can build allegiances that last.

Alliances: Building Links to Larger Corporations

In the past two years alone, Fortune 500 companies have reduced their payrolls by over 700,000 employees. These cutbacks offer small businesses terrific opportunities. Subcontracting in areas like accounting, marketing, and other specialty operations meets mutual needs. Job growth at business-services companies (like data-services and bookkeeping) has averaged 5 percent a year, more than three times the rate of overall job growth.

Flexibility: Responding Quickly to Changing Market Needs

Entrepreneurs and small-business owners must be smart enough to recognize mistakes and change strategies quickly. By staying on top of trends, watching the market in general, and being open to change, a small business can alter direction and avoid costly investments in equipment or technology that are outdated.

Geek Speak: Riding the Information Superhighway

The information superhighway has become a household word. Prodigy, Internet, CompuServe, and America Online are accessed even by ten-year-olds. Multimedia networking has now become a reality. It is predicted that by the year 2000, 70 percent of homes will have interactive TV (meaning that when you talk back to the television set, it listens). Use this technology whenever you can to expand your business. New technology can boost sales for companies in almost any line of work. (See chapter 5 for information on accessing the information superhighway.)

Hottest Home-Based Businesses Today

If you are trying to decide what business you should begin, and you'd like some input from the experts, these ideas are for you. Just remember that in the final analysis, the hottest home-based business for you is going to be the one that fits your talent, your lifestyle, and your financial needs.

Technology and Information Management ("Cyberspace Cowboys")

Computer Consulting Services

Computer consultants must have a wide range of expertise, including knowledge of software and hardware of all kinds, and of databases and networks. To seize opportunities, computer consultants zero in on as many services as they can, from advising their clients on the selection of appropriate hardware and software for their needs, to actual implementation and testing of systems. Technical support and training are also areas of growing need as individuals and businesses find themselves equipped with more technology than they can handle. The "800" number approach for problem resolution doesn't always work.

Software Programming Services

Software programmers possess technical knowledge to link consumers with computers through new and better user-friendly methods. With the explosion of CD-ROM usage, programmers with multimedia experience will be needed to translate not only text but also video and sound into computer code. Software programming can touch virtually every kind of business, so the opportunities are enormous. There are opportunities in customizing programs for individual use and in tailoring commercial packages to meet a company's needs.

Systems Analysts

Industries use analysts to choose a network system, link employees who work thousands of miles apart, design software, expedite billing programs, or teach employees how to debug their own hard drives. Systems analysts can zero in on a specific industry or cross over among different industries.

International Manufacturers' Agent

This may seem like an odd place to categorize this service, but it is made possible as a home-based business by today's technological and communication advances. This type of service consists of matching products with buyers worldwide.

Health Care ("Rx for Us")

Home Health Care Services

An increasing number of families throughout the country confront difficult decisions concerning long-term care for chronically ill relatives. Pressure on hospitals and medical staff to reduce costs often results in reduced hospital stays. Patients may have to leave "quicker and sicker" than in the past. Home care will substitute for prolonged hospital stays. Home health care includes a full spectrum of services that an individual or family with a serious illness must face. Services can include nursing care, but also include arrangements for medical equipment, pharmaceutical needs, progress reports for physicians and insurance, nutritional counseling, Medicare/Medicaid, and insurance billing. The range of treatments can include intravenous feeding, rehabilitation, ventilator therapy, kidney dialysis, and more. Services can be provided by a full spectrum of licensed practical nurses, home health aides, physical therapists, and live-in companions. This business, like several others described in this section, can incorporate several different components or zero in on the founder's niche.

Spin-offs:

◆ Physical therapy

◆ Nutritional programs (design and implementation)

◆ Meals-on-wheels for the homebound

◆ Billing assistance (for insurance follow-up, Medicare/Medicaid claims)

◆ Medical claims assistance (for private medical practices)

Business Services for Small Business ("Small Business Boosters")

Export Services

Everybody's talking about the great global marketplace, but small business is just at the beginning stages of jumping on this superhighway. There is a growing need for individuals who can link products and services between buyers and sellers around the world, both retail and wholesale.

Multimedia Services

Today's multimedia packages combine CD-ROM hardware and software, video cameras, photography, digitized sound boards, and more to educate, entertain, and inform. Businesses, institutions, and individuals incorporate these packages into their daily routine to learn about products, ideas, and services. The market will continue to grow as we all begin to expect multimedia packages as the norm. Big businesses that have cut back on in-house production departments and small businesses that need to appear big both have a strong need for polished, professional packages.

Marketing Services—General

Many new businesses start because the founder has a dream or an idea—not necessarily a marketing degree. And even entrepreneurs who hesitate to write a business plan will jump into marketing planning because they know they need to reach people. If you are a well-experienced marketing specialist, you can provide assistance in developing a marketing strategy, conducting market research, advertising, promotion, sales, public relations, event planning, and sales incentive programs. Not all of these functions will stand alone as a solid business opportunity, but a few will. The best follow below.

Event Planning

Conferences, meetings, conventions, and parties are staples of business and association living. Yet many companies don't keep a full-time staff involved in these activities. If you can coordinate these and other large and small events from start to finish, you're right for this work. It doesn't take a marketing degree to know how to run a great party. And lots of community volunteers gain this experience naturally in the nonprofit sector by working on local fund-raisers and school events.

Advertising and Promotions

The soup-to-nuts process of getting its business name out in the public eye confronts every small business. If advertising and promotions are in the marketing plan, most businesses need some direction regarding media options and design and implementation of the ad campaign. Should they use print? Where and how frequently? What's the cost? What should the ad look like?

Sales Incentives

This business stands alone or combines with advertising and promotion for a more complete package, depending on your ability and training. All the little giveaways that corporations and small businesses alike use to spread their name, ranging from dignified pens to silly refrigerator magnets (the range seems infinite), can be ordered and distributed through catalogs. You can have your own catalog or coordinate many, depending on which side you work for.

Public Relations

Marketing plans for small businesses often emphasize incorporation of a solid public relations campaign to keep costs within budget. Sometimes public relations programs will directly replace expensive advertising campaigns. Public relations has the extra advantage of building a positive image for a business or professional practitioner by establishing credibility.

Graphic Design

Everyone required to make a sales presentation needs professional materials. Entrepreneurs have a need for their own materials to start, then must change as their business evolves. Their image is critical. If they reserve a booth at an exhibition or a table at a conference or expo, the need escalates. Trainers and workshop presenters also need state-of-the-art materials for promoting and delivering their message.

Secretarial Services—General

Secretarial services provided for small and home-based businesses can be all-inclusive or specific. So, you can provide many services for a small number of companies (particularly important if you don't want to stray far from your home location) or concentrate on a niche. Services that will continue to be in demand are: word processing, office support staff, mailing list services, and desktop publishing.

Word Processing

Yes, in this day and age there still are people who do not use a computer. There are reports to be produced, texts to be formatted, articles to be written, and individuals and small businesses who are not trained or staffed to handle the workload.

Mailing List Services

Whether you generate mailing lists yourself or help clients use existing lists, this market keeps growing. Announcements, letters, promotional materials, inquiries, catalogs, newsletters, and more require more time and tedious attention to detail than many professional and small businesses have on hand. Consider that most companies need to keep in constant touch with their clients to ward off their competitors and you may even just double the demand.

Desktop Publishing

Desktop publishing can include everything from newsletters, brochures, training manuals, workshop handouts, other training materials, and company publications to pulp fiction. Another business that booms because of technological advancements is the production of camera-ready artwork, just like the big companies use, from your home. And with adequate volume, you can specialize in just one area.

Temporary Help Service

This service acts as an employment broker, or personnel agency, between part-time workers and businesses. The temporary help divisions of many full-service personnel agencies have grown at a faster rate than their full-time services over the past several years. Many businesses, in cost-containment efforts, prefer to add staff only as needed to handle peak workloads. Using part-time workers also helps to reduce health care costs and benefits. Add the traditional business need to cover vacation schedules and sick days, and you've got a full package of work.

Time-Saver Services and Products ("The Rejuvenators")

Gift Baskets

These businesses have taken off faster than expected. Gift baskets can include just about anything you want to work with. The business can focus on individual shoppers, business orders, or both. Whimsy and creativity can define the limits, with a practical eye to investing in supplies ahead of time.

Look-Goods

This category includes a number of the health and beauty aids, as well as nutrition programs, available commercially. It is best to stick with a brand name for recognition, so you'll want to consider a franchise opportunity or package deal. (These will be covered in further detail in chapter 3, and referrals included in the appendix.)

Education and Training ("Help")

Workshops and Seminars

This business can be worked in two different ways: for yourself, or for others, depending on your talents. First, you can package and market your own materials, using off-the-shelf or customized programs in an area you know. In the second case, you can coordinate the work of other professional practitioners, packaging, promoting, and arranging for programs conducted by others.

Spin-offs:

◆ Computer training (one-on-one or group)—"how to" use what you've already purchased.

◆ Business practices—whatever the latest is. When Total Quality Management (TQM) first hit, everyone needed to know what it was, fast. Jump on the bandwagon for the newest.

◆ Today's business environment—not environmental concerns, although that could be part of it. Like TQM, when something new hits, people need information fast. Changes in regulations, rules, strategies, players, and technology all generate grist for the workshop mill.

Kids and Kids' Stuff

Child Care Services

It would be nice to think that the child care dilemma faced by so many of today's working families has been resolved by larger educational institutions, corporations, or local programs. The fact is that the demand for safe, secure, loving child care still is there. Recent studies of child care facilities nationwide have indicated that large group settings often do not work out, particularly for very young children. A home environment is still the first choice of many parents, and this research seems to indicate that may be the best choice.

Child Care Coordinator

If you are not interested in providing child care personally, you can enter this field by putting together matches of providers and parents. Take this a step further and offer your services to small businesses and corporations that in turn can refer their employees to you. Even parents who have full-time arrangements already are bound to need back-ups during periods of illness (either the provider's or the child's), business travel, work schedule changes, and so on.

Children's Mail Order Items

Anyone who has ever marched through a mall with toddlers in tow understands why mail order for kids has such a strong appeal. Mail order services in general are booming, according to *Entrepreneur* magazine. Develop this niche and you've combined two hot elements. Clothes, educational products, toys—they all have potential. (See chapter 3 for more on mail order businesses and references in the appendix.)

Also Noteworthy ("Credentials 'R' Us")

Professional Practices

The overhead incurred by large professional practices must of course be reflected in their client billing. Logically, it follows that if you're not paying high rent for luxuriously furnished quarters and can establish your rates for your work independently, you can save clients money. Tie in with technological advances and major leaps in communication facilities, and you provide healthy competition to corporate practices. Small practices are growing, and small businesses are a natural client base. The former stigma of using a home-based provider has been dimmed. Professionals who can ride the home-based business wave include:

◆ Lawyers

◆ Accountants

- ◆ Financial Analysts

- ◆ Insurance Brokers

- ◆ Management Consultants

- ◆ Doctors

- ◆ Psychotherapists

- ◆ Career Counselors

Beware: Not So Hot

Every year different publications, from books to magazines like *Inc.* and *Entrepreneur* will publish lists of hot home-based business ideas. These are terrific reference sources as long as you examine several and do not take one opinion for the last word.

I'd like to offer a little clarification on a few of these so-called "hot" businesses that have made a couple of top ten lists lately. Based on my experience of over ten years working with start-ups and tracking their success, you can get burned by some of these businesses. On the surface, these businesses would appear to be viable—and they are, for many people. But the ratio of the "sweat factor" compared to the "income factor" feels cold. These businesses are high labor, low profit. If you truly love the nature of work involved, do not mind that the profit margin is low, can put in a lot of hours—then don't be disheartened. But remember that your painstaking hours of work may not translate into a comparable dollar reward.

Here are a few I will *strongly* caution against unless these disadvantages are not a factor for you. That's a matter of your lifestyle and financial need.

Crafts Creation

If you seek an income rather than a hobby, this is not for the faint of heart. The very features that make delicate handiwork appealing are what cause it to be a difficult and highly competitive field to enter. Crafts that are very time consuming and involve an investment in materials are also difficult to price. By the time you price your items to compensate for your time as well as your materials, you may not realize as much of a profit as you would like. So how fast can you work? Precious is in the eye of the beholder, and if you can produce quantity as well as quality you could make a comfortable living.

Specialty Food Preparation

I'll include in this category caterers working from home. As in crafts creation, part of the profit in catering results from being able to provide quantity as well as quality. Specialty chain store items can compete with you in the residential market, and unless you price yourself well you'll be in trouble. If you can hook up with a distributor (see chapter 8 on virtual corporations), your creations may stand a better chance. You'll have to really go the distance to differentiate yourself (see chapter 7 on marketing). If you are catering, remember that your work schedule—especially if you cater events—will revolve around evenings, weekends, and holidays. If you are starting a home-based business to have more time with your family, you will find endless schedule conflicts.

Cleaning Services

If you don't mind doing the work yourself, you can make a profit. However, it is a fact that you are often competing against undocumented workers and off-the-books workers. It is very expensive in today's *legitimate* business environment to hire very cheap labor. Just remember that your competition will always have the price edge while you are paying taxes and bonding fees. Many of us are currently working to improve the tax situation for small business through legislative channels, but in today's climate, we just aren't there yet. On the other hand, if you can find minimum-wage workers in your neck of the woods, and if you can work in an affluent community where cost-of-services is not a problem, your chances of making money on this venture improve. Specialize in something like carpet, floor, or chimney cleaning and you will have an edge. Industrial cleaning is another big market, but here we go again with those nights and weekends.

Errand Services for Busy People

If you hate to do these jobs for yourself, what could possibly make you enjoy doing this work for other people? We all *say* we want personal services but we don't *really* want to pay for them. Instead we expect personalized services that don't appear to cost us anything at all—from *the source.* Why pay someone, for example, to pick up your dry cleaning, when you could switch to a dry cleaner who delivers?

Professional Organizers

The value is in the eye of the beholder. Your market is enormous, but getting people to *pay* for this kind of service is different. Sounds like this would be a nice fit with some other kind of business, as an activity, not a main function.

Business Plan Preparation

The fact that entrepreneurs should write a business plan when they start a new venture or expand an existing one has no correlation to whether or not they really do. The *Harvard Business Review* study "Entrepreneurs Craft Strategies That Work" noted that only 28 percent actually write one. Generally, the small businesses who want to write a business plan are those that do need money and have to face a bank or venture capitalist. Business plans are a requirement in these situations. Think about it: if the people most likely to need help with a business plan are those who need money, what does this tell you about your potential market? A business plan takes many hours to research and write, and requires much input from the business owner.

To be compensated for your effort, you will need to charge a high fee. That's great—when you can get it. However, if you decide to edit business plans, and write them whenever possible, as part of a consulting practice that encompasses other activities—then you've got something.

The White House Conference on Small Business

Should the federal government encourage home-based business ownership? Should home-based businesses be subjected to U.S. Department of Labor and Environmental Protection Agency regulations? Should regulations governing new product development be relaxed? Should local zoning boards be prohibited from setting certain restrictions on home-based business?

These questions and over 100 small-business issues were identified in 1993 by task forces representing a cross section of the small-business community. Many of these issues are unique to home-based business. In 1995, the third White House Conference on Small Business (WHCSB) was held in Washington, D.C. Representatives of small businesses from every state participated in the conference, which was the culmination of a year-long process of state conferences, delegate elections, and appointments around the country. Figure 1-6 lists the issues that were the focus of the WHCSB.

The WHCSB is important because (since the 1980 and 1986 conferences) no significant small-business legislation has passed that was not on this agenda. Action has been taken on about half the conference recommendations. So action items resolved and recommended at the WHCSB will give you an indication of the direction home-based business can look forward to in the future.

Since the close of the 1995 White House conference, small-business advocates throughout the country have struggled to keep our small business agenda in the forefront of national priorities. Small-business advocacy groups have worked diligently to introduce legislation that incorporates the top 60 issues supported by the conference delegates. A short summary of the top twenty issues follows in figure 1-7.

Critical legislation issues raised in the twelve months following the conference included: estate tax repeal; health care reform; pension reform; tort reform; 100% health-care deductibility; increased expensing; broad-based capital gains reform; and small-business investment via capital gains tax reform. While these issues have been incorporated into various versions of the federal budget, as well as House and Senate legislation, and have finally attracted political attention, there has been limited success in tangible results.

Legislation can save these and other issues from falling by the way side of the road. Many delegates from the 1995 WHCSB have remained active in pursuit of these goals, and it looks as if their mission will continue at both the state and federal level until these recommendations become law.

White House Conference on Small Business

Agenda for the Future of Small Business

Capital Formation: Investing in the Success of Small Business

Community Development: Revitalizing Our Resources

Environmental Policy: Encouraging Environmentally Sound Development

Human Capital: Improving the Competitiveness of the Twenty-firstcentury Workforce

International Trade: Fostering Small Business Interests in the World Marketplace

Main Street: Sustaining Small Retail and Service Firms

Procurement: Balancing Public and Private Resources

Regulation and Paperwork: Reinventing Regulatory Policy

Taxation: Stimulating the Growth of Small Businesses

Technology and the Information Revolution: Leading the Way in Innovation

Figure 1-6: Agenda Items for the White House Conference on Small Business (WHCSB)

Top 20 Small Business Recommendations Voted by Delegates to the White House Conference on Small Business

1. Clarification and redefinition by Congress for the status of INDEPENDENT CONTRACTORS.

2. One hundred percent deduction for MEALS AND ENTERTAINMENT.

3. Amendment and enforcement of the REGULATORY FLEXIBILITY ACT which includes cost benefit analysis and risk assessment in all new regulations and IRS interpretation.

Continues

Continued

4. Repeal of ESTATE TAXES so that family businesses can easily pass from one generation to the next.

5. One hundred percent deductibility for HEALTH CARE costs.

6. ENVIRONMENTAL LEGISLATION pertaining to good science and realistic risk assessments.

7. Support of the PENSION SIMPLIFICATION BILL repealing current disincentives and burdensome regulations on retirement plans and IRAs.

8. Protection of INTELLECTUAL PROPERTY RIGHTS on the internet.

9. Cost benefit analysis on ENVIRONMENTAL REGULATIONS before laws are passed.

10. TORT REFORM—reform of civil justice and product liability legislation.

11. Global 1-STOP SHOPPING access to all government information and resources.

12. Provide a cooperative/consulting REGULATORY ENVIRONMENT. In other words, if and when a problem exists, fix it rather than fine it.

13. Expand, improve and make permanent SBIR (Small Business Innovation Research) programs.

14. To promote FAIR COMPETITION, prohibit government agencies and tax exempt organizations from competing with small business.

15. One hundred percent HEALTH CARE DEDUCTION.

16. Streamline regulations and vehicles for investing in PENSION PLANS and profit sharing, and provide access to private capital markets.

17. To provide ACCESS TO CAPITAL, encourage and increase small business lending by reducing paperwork and restrictions.

18. TAX EQUITY for small business.

19. SUPPORT OF THE SBA by permanent maintenance of the independent role of the US Small Business Office of Advocacy, and permanent elevation of the SBA to a cabinet position.

20. Support of a HOME OFFICE DEDUCTION BILL to allow a home office as the principal place of business even if it is used only for administrative storage or distribution.

Figure 1-7: Top 20 Small Business Recommendations Voted by Delegates to the White House Conference on Small Business

Advantages and Disadvantages of a Home-Based Business

- ◆ Emerging Workstyles and Lifestyles
- ◆ Characteristics of Entrepreneurs
- ◆ Measure Your Entrepreneurial Potential
- ◆ Enhance Your Potential for Success
- ◆ Weighing the Pros and Cons of a Home-Based Business
- ◆ Psychological Considerations of a Home-Based Business
- ◆ Physical Considerations for Space and Privacy
- ◆ Time Management Techniques That Work
- ◆ Strategies to Reduce Stress
- ◆ Preserving Family Ties
- ◆ Building Community Links
- ◆ Collaborative Couples
- ◆ Questions of Balance

Emerging Workstyles and Lifestyles

Economically, socially, logistically, physically, emotionally, and psychologically—home offices make sense. If you've ever visited Williamsburg, Virginia, or taken the Freedom Trail in Boston, you have had firsthand exposure to the origins of home-based business in the United States. Seamstresses, silversmiths, blacksmiths, pottery makers, and others who formed the basis of our early economy often worked from home. Many writers, philosophers, inventors, and statesmen generated their most brilliant works from their desks at home, using their personal libraries for inspiration or strolling through their gardens to think things through.

Considering our early American culture, it appears that long-distance daily commuting was never a preference, that it seems more like a cultural aberration forced with the invention of the automobile. As a society, we have worked in home offices far longer than we have in rented commercial space. In fact, some of the pros and cons of working at home are the same today as they were two hundred years ago. Family interruptions may offset moments of quiet contemplation; responsibilities for child care may exhaust rather than energize; and demands for self discipline may reach the limits. But still we stay.

Today the issue of home-based business is hotter than ever, and this widespread public exposure can only enhance opportunities. Traffic problems, environmental issues, and quality-of-life concerns are so important in our daily lives that we're not willing to push them aside. As a result, business and government at the local and national levels can't ignore us. Home-based business and telecommuting will be under the microscope for some time to come.

Characteristics of Entrepreneurs

In the real world of entrepreneurs, there is more to consider besides trends, demographics, and the state of the economy. Entrepreneurs also share personal characteristics that impact their success. Fundamental characteristics that entrepreneurs typically possess are:

1. **Self-confidence.** The typical entrepreneur is absolutely sure he/she cannot fail, although women entrepreneurs may not demonstrate the same bravado as their male counterparts in the early stages. While measured confidence can have a positive effect in terms of keeping your feet on the ground while your head is in the clouds, lack of confidence will work against you. In the beginning, an ego is helpful.

2. **Independence.** Most entrepreneurs like to think that they are not influenced or controlled by others. Their opinions, conduct, thinking, and actions reflect this self-reliance. And this self-reliance enables them to assume control, as well as to take responsibility for their decisions. Entrepreneurs crave autonomy and freedom of action. Unfortunately, the entrepreneurial aspirations of many families with young children are tempered by logistics issues. Parental roles as coordinators of home, children, and work do not end when they decide to start a business.

3. **Assertiveness.** The ability to articulate—and assign a high priority to—your needs and the needs of the business is an asset just about as valuable as capital. You must be able to state the goals of your business with assurance and confidence. You need to communicate effectively and emphatically. You are representing yourself *and* your business. You need to be assertive and decisive.

4. **Role Models.** Circumstances very often do play a part. Role models include parents who worked independently as professionals (lawyers, doctors, accountants, etc.). But how many entrepreneurs do you know who were groomed all their lives to take over a family business? Probably few women, although the numbers are changing now as more women start businesses. Role models help us to envision the ups-and-downs of self-employment.

5. **Risk-taking.** Willingness to take a risk and lack of fear are part of the entrepreneurial spirit. When was the last time you took a risk? Did you leave a job with an apparently secure salary to pursue your own interests and goals? Is there anything left of your home equity loan? Do you dare venture into the unknown? No one knows for certain how this venture will work out. An entrepreneur who researches the possibilities, then takes a reality-based chance, often feels personally satisfied. This means you'll need to put aside unrealistic fears of failure.

6. **Decision-making.** Entrepreneurs need to be able to seize new opportunities quickly, sometimes without the benefit of a full-scale research effort. Sometimes there isn't time for thorough analysis and planning. They are able to make decisions without every possible bit of information.

7. **Intuition.** The quality of having direct perception of truth or of fact, independent of any reasoning process, is intuition. Do you sense

things before you've been told about them? Do you often work from gut feelings? Entrepreneurs learn to trust their own keen, quick insight. It serves them well. Those who learn to recognize it and use it to help in making decisions often benefit.

8. **Negotiation.** Negotiating skills include a strong ability to step out of a situation and look at both people's points of view in an interaction. Strong negotiating skills enable entrepreneurs to get a foot in the door of the most difficult places. Much of a business start-up phase consists of breaking into new territory for sales, and a lot of the sales process involves negotiating. These skills are developed in early childhood—some studies indicate as early as age four—and can be refined throughout adulthood.

9. **Focus.** Entrepreneurs concentrate intensely on their business. The business is the core of their lives. Even when they work to achieve harmony between their personal lives and their work, they think about their company. They dream solutions to marketing problems. If they are successful, they have learned to channel this intense concentration into goal-oriented behavior.

10. **Persistence.** Entrepreneurs will continue steadfastly, in spite of opposition, to pursue their dreams against the odds. They slip in extra hours of work at crazy hours of the night while their families sleep. They will stand firm.

Measure Your Entrepreneurial Potential

Take a moment to assess your *Entrepreneurial Potential* (EP) in figure 2-1. Answer YES or NO to each of the questions. Score yourself by counting the number of YES answers.

Enhance Your Potential for Success

If your EP score was lower than 13, you lost points in one or more of the areas described below. Check your NO responses. If you examine where your weaknesses are, you can focus on development and acquire what you need, whether it's experience, knowledge, or skills. If you scored between 14 and 21, but want to build strengths in a critical area, read on.

Your Entrepreneurial Potential

Answer YES or NO to each question. Count your total YES responses to determine your EP.

YES/NO

1. Are you in need of a change? _____

2. If you decide to do something, will you do it and let nothing stop you? _____

3. Are you willing to try something new, even though it is frightening? _____

4. If people tell you something can't be done, do you have to find out for yourself? _____

5. Is pleasure in a job well done satisfaction enough for you? _____

6. Will you ask directly for what you want rather than wait for someone to notice you and just give it to you? _____

7. Do you do whatever needs to be done, without apologizing for being in charge? _____

8. Do you want to be financially independent? _____

9. Will you go to a movie alone if nobody else wants to see it? _____

10. If you believe in an unpopular cause, will you speak up for it? _____

11. Did the neighborhood(s) you grew up in have a lot of family-owned small businesses? _____

12. Was one of your parents an independent professional? (doctor, lawyer, etc.) _____

13. Was one of your parents in business for him/herself? _____

14. Was one of your grandparents the owner of his/her own business? _____

15. Were you the kind of child who was always starting things (clubs, plays, lemonade stands, etc.)? _____

16. Can you take risks with money; that is, invest it and not know the outcome? _____

17. Have you taken a risk in the last six months? _____

Continues

Continued

18. Will you try to conquer your fear when you are frightened of something? _____

19. Do you like trying new places, new foods, and totally new experiences? _____

20. Can you strike up a conversation with a total stranger? _____

21. Have you ever gone on a blind date? _____

Total number of YES responses: _____

SCORING:

7 or lower: POOR
(You'd better keep a job)

8 to 13: FAIR TO EXCELLENT
(You need development in one or more key areas.)

14 to 21: EXCELLENT
(You have an excellent chance as an entrepreneur.)

Figure 2-1: Your Entrepreneurial Potential (EP)

1. **Know yourself.** What are your personal strengths and weaknesses? How can you maximize your potential? Where do you need development?

2. **Be aware of yourself.** Assess your limitations realistically.

3. **Beware of yourself.** What's working against you?

If entrepreneurship appeals to you, improve your odds for success in every way possible. Specify your own personal development program. Explore all the available options to acquire the background, skill, or knowledge it takes. Get the training, on-the-job experience, mentoring, or private study you need. Here are a few ideas to get you started.

Self-confidence often accompanies a track record of success. Can you walk into a room full of strangers without feeling extremely uncomfortable? Are you worried that some people don't like you? Are you afraid to make a mistake? Build early opportunities to succeed by tackling assignments you are certain you can master. Don't take on your hardest sales pitch, for example, before you've practiced a bit.

Independence may be tough to negotiate. Can you get up in the morning and plan a day for yourself without checking the schedules of four or more other people (and hoping your baby-sitter doesn't cancel?) If you're a parent, can you ever give yourself a day off from parenting? Probably not. Families with young children, for example, will find autonomy the most difficult to grasp. But don't let the fact that you are hampered by logistics get you down. Children don't stay young forever, and many of us have grown healthy children and companies at the same time. Consider starting the business with "baby steps." Little-by-little a more controlled and organized pattern for working will emerge.

Assertiveness can be learned. Do you find yourself disappointed when people around you can't read your mind? Do you know when and how to ask for help? Don't despair; assertiveness can be learned, practiced, and mastered. Training in assertive behavioral techniques is widely available. Many community colleges offer American Management Association courses on this, and local community schools frequently schedule their own programs. Incorporate effective verbal and nonverbal communication skills into your repertoire quickly. Practice ahead of time for difficult encounters.

Role models can be added to your life at any time. If family or neighborhood role models were not a part of your early childhood development experience, you can adopt some. Your adoption process can consist of emulating a successful entrepreneur or can take the more practical form of securing a mentor. How many couples were groomed to perform a 24-hour juggling act, which includes doing laundry after 10 P.M.? Not many. But that's where this book can help.

Risk-taking can be difficult if you're concerned about finances, kids, family, and friends. But entrepreneurship involves a certain amount of risk. Just make sure you take educated, thoughtful risks. Sensible risks are less likely to jeopardize you personally or financially.

Decision-making is a skill you can develop. With practice you can become more confident making decisions with less information. Few decisions in life are truly irreversible. Assess your ambiguous situation and determine what the worst possible outcome of a *wrong* decision could be. Then decide. If you make a mistake, be prepared to move ahead quickly in damage control. Often the outcome of no decision is worse than the outcome of a less-than-perfect decision.

Where do you start? Work through figure 2-2 if you need a little help.

Weighing the Pros and Cons of a Home-Based Business

Your personal assessment of the advantages and disadvantages of home-based work depends on your individual and very unique lifestyle and workstyle preferences. Factor in previous positive and negative work and home experiences and top off your evaluation process with some really important private issues and, perhaps, some truly

Personal Empowerment

My goal is

_____

What's working against me? Why? List the skills, experience, people, things, and/or circumstances that could hold you back.

_____

_____

_____

_____

What can I change? Where can I get help? List the training, on-the-job experience, professionals, etc., that can help you.

_____

_____

_____

_____

What's working for me? Why? List the skills, experience, people, things, and/or circumstances that can work in your favor.

_____

_____

_____

_____

How can I maximize the use of these resources?

_____

_____

_____

_____

Figure 2-2: Personal Empowerment Exercise

nonsensible non sequiturs. Thus you arrive at a decision that may have excellent face validity or at one that makes absolutely no sense to anyone on the outside world but is totally right for you.

The considerations are varied. Some aspects of home-based business appeal to most of us, although not necessarily in the same order. We seem to agree on a number of the disadvantages. But then there is a wide gray area that is totally dependent on personal style and preference.

Pros:

- ◆ paying no office rent
- ◆ not having to commute
- ◆ enjoying a better quality of life
- ◆ being independent
- ◆ having personal control
- ◆ taking time off when you have to
- ◆ having control over your career
- ◆ creating flexible hours
- ◆ having salary control
- ◆ having more productive time
- ◆ being closer to your children
- ◆ not having a dress code
- ◆ setting your own agenda
- ◆ directing client contact
- ◆ working odd hours easily

Cons:

- ◆ no paid time off (no work, no pay)
- ◆ no wind-down time between work and home
- ◆ no support services
- ◆ potential for isolation
- ◆ no peer stimulation
- ◆ noise from kids
- ◆ no privacy from home matters
- ◆ no escape
- ◆ constant temptations
- ◆ home responsibilities to confront, by default

In the area of uncertainty, one person's advantage is another's disadvantage. Characteristics of home-based work that cross over the line between pros and cons, depending on your point of view, include:

Issues are Survival More Often Than Strategic

If you're a big-picture person, the minutiae of home-based business may drive you berserk. You'll have to remember to buy garbage bags more often than you'll change the direction of the global economy.

Technology Updates

It is up to you to stay current, by whatever means you have. Trade publications, business contacts, and networking groups are your lifeline.

Break Time When You Want It—Sometimes

Many parents working at home take a 3 P.M. break to be with their kids. Most of them arise around 5 A.M. and work late at night to compensate, but the choice is theirs.

Direct Client Contact

If you hate selling, you'll hate this responsibility. Think twice if you are not the selling type.

Setting Your Agenda

If you need direction, you'll be lost. Having your own business means being your own boss and making all the decisions.

No One to Pass the Buck To

If you're used to passing it, you could be miserable. Be prepared to accept the responsibility of being the *boss*.

Working Odd Hours

It's great to be able to follow through with a brainstorm in the middle of the night if you feel like it. But if you run your life by the clock and turn into a pumpkin instead of a race horse at midnight, you may not find flexibility to be so great.

Your Work Is Always There

If you like to pick up an extra hour here and there as you choose and like to work through the night, you'll appreciate the convenience. If the sight of your work makes you lose sleep, you're in for some hefty bags under your eyes.

There's No Place Like Home

CHECKLIST

Check each item below that describes your workstyle: AGREE?

1. I am a self-starter. _____

2. I can avoid distractions. _____

3. I don't mind spending time alone. _____

4. I can make decisions on my own. _____

5. I can discipline myself to perform unpleasant but important tasks. _____

6. I initiate projects when things are slow. _____

7. I can resist the temptation to play when I should work. _____

8. I can resist the temptation to eat from boredom or because I am near the kitchen. _____

9. I can take reasonable breaks in my work, then return to work. _____

10. I can ignore home-maintenance distractions until appropriate. _____

11. I consolidate and plan my errands to conserve time. _____

12. I can "just say no" to casual drop-in visitors. _____

13. I can control the length of unplanned drop-in visits. _____

14. I can ignore the phone if I have a deadline or need to concentrate. _____

15. I can avoid (or defer) personal phone calls when busy. _____

16. I will end phone calls after an appropriate amount of time. _____

17. I don't have to be going to a meeting to get up and go. _____

18. I can prioritize work activities effectively. _____

19. I can create and meet deadlines on a daily basis. _____

20. I can set realistic timetables for getting my work done. _____

21. I don't need feedback from others to feel secure in my abilities. _____

Continues

Continued

22. I am willing to type my own business correspondence, buy the stamps, and take it to the post office. _____

23. I have the energy and stamina to work long, unusual hours. _____

24. I can close off my office in some way at the end of the day/night. _____

25. I try not to make this arrangement an office-based home. _____

26. I limit my office space to an acceptable area of the home. _____

27. I pitch in my fair share of family/home responsibilities. _____

28. I can tune out unreasonable family demands—accurately. _____

29. I am sensitive to the changing needs of my spouse and children. _____

30. My family is supportive of my decision to work at home. _____

Figure 2-3: Checklist to Determine If "There's No Place Like Home"

Coworkers

If they enhanced your reputation, in reality or only in your mind, then it will be hard to find a substitute until you get solidly into networking (more on this in chapter 3).

Preschool Child Care

It is tempting to make a home-based business a substitute for preschool child care. But if you do, your business will reflect it. However, you can use your flexible work schedule positively to develop better child care arrangements. Your workday can usually work around the type of help you choose.

Psychological Considerations of a Home-Based Business

Why do some people seem to adjust instantaneously and joyfully to home-based work while others fumble around, lost in minutiae? Our personal psychological mix affects the way we approach this venture as much as any other major endeavor. We've already examined the psychology of all entrepreneurs. That's the base you start with. In addition, home-based work will require you to examine other dimensions of your personality in further detail.

Whether your home-based work is a psychological burden or a blessing also depends on how you handle your patterns of work. Whether this endeavor is enervating or unnerving depends on you. Workers who devise a way to give a sense of ending to each workday feel best. They close a door, cover a computer terminal, change clothes, take a walk, and so on. Most important, they decide not to take phone calls at certain times, exactly as if they were gone.

Key psychological considerations of working at home include your self-discipline, your need for structure, your ability to tune out distractions, and your need for social contact.

Self-discipline. Your energy level and your concentration will have a huge impact on the success of your business. If you become mentally or physically sloppy, your behavior will be reflected in your business right away. There is no buffer in your own business—no staff of coworkers to cover for off days. Your best bet is to stay in psychological and biological good health as best you can. Be aware of the amount you exercise, how much you sleep, what you eat. Commuting routines may have forced a walk to the train or bus that you may not require anymore. Sitting at a computer or talking on a phone all day will have a negative effect on your health if you don't consciously compensate by building in new routines for exercise and work breaks. Stay self-motivated. You are your own boss: demand of yourself that you continue to learn new skills.

Structure. Everyone has a different preference for degrees of structure vs. freedom. Those who prefer structure care greatly about the opinions and advice of others. They tend to overschedule their work, follow the rules, and interpret literally. Those who prefer to defy structure tend to avoid advice, feedback, and group norms. They seek rewards based on personal traits—what feels good. They need to create self-imposed deadlines, to adhere to self-generated schedules, and to devote time to planning just as if a boss requested it.

Distractions. Home maintenance projects, household chores, hobbies, television— almost anything can serve as a distraction and can assume a higher priority than it deserves when you face it daily. Projects around the house, no matter how mundane, can provide an antidote to intense concentration at work because at least you can see your results right away. Projects for your business invariably have longer intervals before closure.

Having young children around is a mixed blessing. If you're patient, your children and your business will mature together. Don't expect overnight growth spurts from either quarter. If you can get through the toughest early days—the infancy of your business and your kids—you can reap the benefits and expand. You'll be able to add staff, build on, or move to a larger house.

Socialization. Some people do better with lots of interpersonal contact. They thrive on phone calls, luncheons, and dinner dates. They need office camaraderie and banter to be creative, to generate ideas. They also need peer recognition and a platform to show off their talent.

Physical Considerations for Space and Privacy

No matter how large my home was, when my children were little I needed to have my office in the basement. I had to have a place where I could be far from the noise if it erupted during an important conversation. I needed soundproofing. Escape. When I first started my business ten years ago, that space was in the cellar. It offered protection from the pitter-patter of Reeboks and a door to close. I didn't have to walk past my desk all day long, and there was space to spread out my files. On the other hand, there was the dryer buzzer.

It's important to set aside some kind of space that belongs only to your business. Don't take up the whole house. A room, a floor, a closed door—anything that will preserve your sanity, and protect your family, will work. In your early days, aesthetics are less important than privacy—unless you have customers or clients visiting the office. If clients come and go from your home business, be especially careful that they do not pass through a highly trafficked family area.

You can choose to spread the business all over the house or confine it to a specific space. Those home-based businesses that *survive* have their own space. Even if you must spread out during the workday—using the kitchen or dining room table to collate papers or lay out a design, for example—be sure to clean up when the family comes back home.

Always control the basics:

- ◆ never let children answer the business line
- ◆ limit calls from family and friends during your business hours
- ◆ don't let children play with the office equipment unsupervised
- ◆ develop a signal system for your children so as to avoid interruptions during important phone calls

Time Management Techniques That Work

Patricia Aburdene and John Naisbitt wrote in *Megatrends for Women* (Villard, 1992) that self-employed people must be task-oriented as opposed to functioning under a time-clock mentality. The same amount of work can be completed in less than the standard eight-hour day by cutting out conversations with coworkers, breaks, lunch hours, unproductive meetings, and other interruptions. Commuting, the top time-waster, also diminishes energy. *Be sure you don't trade one set of interruptions for another in your home office.* Shorter work hours often enable a person to work more intensely. By designing your own workday, you may discover more opportunities to enjoy family, recreation, and a healthier lifestyle.

Everyone has peak performance hours which are characterized by clarity of thinking, creativity, confidence, and high energy. In one day, a person averages

- ◆ four hours of peak performance

- ◆ four hours of good performance

- ◆ six hours of average to low performance

- ◆ two hours of complete exhaustion

During peak performance hours, you can accomplish 200 to 500 percent more work per hour than you can during off-peak hours. Learn to arrange your work schedule to make the most of your peak performance hours.

Use peak performance hours for projects that require creativity, negotiation, learning, reading, decision-making or intense concentration. For example, make decisions so that alternatives will be clearer and more abundant. As a result, there will be less concern about making the wrong decision. Use your creative power, and ideas will flow more quickly and more coherently. Powerful words should be chosen to present well-organized thoughts. You must also have confidence in negotiating business deals. Finally, data gathering and reading should be done during peak performance hours because your mind wanders less during such hours.

Unfortunately, not all of our time is self-controlled. In Stephen Covey's best-selling book *Putting First Things First,* he wrote,

> **To think we're in control is an illusion. It puts us in the position of trying to control consequences. In addition, we can't control other people. And because the basic paradigm is one of control, time management essentially ignores the reality that most of our time is spent living and working with other people who cannot be controlled.**

In study after study of time management problems, twelve issues surface. Figure 2-4 lists these concerns and offers techniques to "Tame Terrible Time Troubles."

Tame Terrible Time Troubles: A Twelve-Step Solution

Trouble	Solution
Lack of planning	Remember that planning takes time, but saves time in the long run.
	Emphasize results, not just activity.
Lack of priorities	Write down goals and objectives.
Overcommitment	Learn to say "No."
	Put first things first.
	Develop a personal philosophy of time.
	Relate priorities to a schedule of events.
Management by crisis	Follow the planning advice.
	Allow more time.
	Expect interruptions.
	Be opportunity-oriented.
	Seek fast information for timely corrective action.
Haste	Distinguish between the important and urgent.
	Take time to get it right the first time. Avoid do-overs.
	Attempt less.
	Delegate more.
Paperwork and reading	Read selectively.
	Learn speed-reading.
	Manage computer data by exception.
	Delegate reading whenever possible.
Routine and trivia	Set and concentrate on goals.
	Delegate nonessentials.
	Stay out of your subordinates' hair. Look to the results, not details or methods.

Continues

Continued	
Visitors	Visit.
	Hold stand-up conferences.
	Suggest an alternative. (Lunch?)
	Screen. Say "No." Be unavailable.
	Close the open door sometimes.
Telephone	Screen and group calls. Be brief.
	Stay uninvolved with all but essentials.
Meetings	Make decisions without meetings.
	Make decisions even when some facts are missing.
	Discourage unnecessary meetings.
	Convene only those needed.
	Use agendas.
	Prepare concise minutes as soon as possible.
Indecision	Improve fact-finding.
	Accept risks as inevitable.
	Decide without all the facts.
	Use mistakes as a learning process.
Lack of delegation	Train.
	Allow for mistakes.
	Give credit.
	Allow for growth and challenge.
	Balance the workload.
	Reorder priorities.

Figure 2-4: Tame Terrible Time Troubles. Reprinted with permission of the publisher, from **The Time Trap**, *by Alec Makenzie, © 1990 Alec Makenzie, published by AMACOM, a division of American Management Association. All rights reserved.*

Strategies to Reduce Stress

We all have our personal weaknesses for distractions. My husband has no patience with an unmowed lawn, unweeded garden, or unvacuumed car. I can't stand to watch the laundry pile up, the rug get nappy, and the tabletops filmy. But we've taken an alternative approach that we both agree to: we hire others to do this work. Then we *both* watch the grass grow, knowing Rick will cut it on Thursday. We let the dust accumulate, confident that Marisa will take care of it on Friday. And if he takes a break to vacuum the car or if I occasionally run the washing machine and the computer printer at the same time, who cares?

Assigning home maintenance chores to someone else is a great way to clear them off your own agenda. Because there are so many tasks involved in running your business that you cannot delegate initially, you might as well delegate the routine, nonbusiness tasks around the house whenever you can.

Other sources of stress may be harder to handle. If your eyes mist at the thought of a communal coffeepot and water cooler, the transition to home-based work may be a rough adjustment. If your position was at the executive level and your exit premature, you will feel more nostalgia for the accouterments of power than if you left an entry-level position equipped with a no-frills package.

Figure 2-5 lists a few of the advantages of the executive corner office that you'll find missing in the start-up stage of your business and may never—face it—see again. Whether or not you miss these is a very personal perspective.

After a while, if you stay with your home-based business venture, you'll find you enjoy the alternatives to the power structure of corporate living. You'll learn the rules of the new game, if you give it a try:

◆ Schedule breakfast, lunch, or dinner meetings whenever you want them.

◆ Get the inside track on local gossip when you want—through community groups, business associations, and networking groups.

◆ Skip lunch and work straight through, finishing early with accountability to no one.

◆ Check in with former associates in your corporate life whenever you choose to.

◆ Keep in touch, as it suits you, with your corporate roots.

What Corporate Employees Might Miss

Influencing the work of many employees

Far-reaching decisions and programs

Clearly defined job description

On-site seminars and training

Strategic planning meetings

Spontaneous formal dining

Feedback from coworkers

Easy travel arrangements

Professional sales staff

Administrative staff

Elegant office space

Executive secretary

Prestigious address

Chain of command

Expense accounts

Office gossip

Mail room

Elevators

Status

Suits

Figure 2-5: What Corporate Employees Might Miss

Preserving Family Ties

The loss of office camaraderie is more than compensated for by gains in family and community ties. But for some people, the very concerns that drove them to forgo a corporate workstyle may drive them crazy when they first start to work at home. Left uncontrolled, the minutiae of everyday life can be the undoing of a new business.

Physical parent presence can sometimes be a cop-out. If you work at home, but the "on-air" light is always on over your office door when the kids truly need your attention, you might as well not be there. A physical presence can't compensate for a lack of emotional support. Working at home is no panacea for strained family relationships. If your children didn't listen to you before, don't expect things to suddenly change unless your behavior changes.

If you are a workaholic and you cannot make time for your family, working at home won't cure you. You'll simply be able to slip away from the family while under the same roof. You've made life easier on you because you don't have to drive to your files and equipment anymore. But you'll make life hell for your family if they now have to look at you working. When you're not home, they go about their own routine and miss you. When you are home working, they'll be forced to tiptoe around your routine, and they will probably resent you.

Some work-at-home parents feel they end up going only halfway with work and with family—neither gets their undivided attention. A home-based work arrangement can draw you closer or drive you farther apart. Very young children don't have a clue why you should ever want to be separated from them, so how on earth could they comprehend your need to work?

There is no question that interruptions from the family can present a problem. In time you'll adjust to working around them. Understand what the disruptions are and deal with them. Watch out that all distractions aren't given equal priority. You do need to ignore home-maintenance distractions during your designated work time. Schedule chores for nonbusiness hours and try to keep to the schedule you devise.

When your work becomes so overwhelming that it takes more of your time than it should, your problems aren't just between you and your family. You also have a lot more to learn about running a business. This is more than a home-based problem. If you're out of control, you have to assess your options: expand, hire, delegate, refer work to associates. We'll cover this and more about organizing your business in chapter 11.

Building Community Links

If you came from a corporation located in a different city from your residence, or commuted to any job in a remote location, you are in for another pleasant surprise. The goodwill accrued from your personal and business donations to the community of time, effort, and money now reflect back to you and your business directly. There is much more incentive to participate in local events as a business owner when your own children, school, athletic programs, hospitals, and church groups are the beneficiaries of your efforts. It is a very positive cycle. Ways in which you can tie your community interests and your business interests together will be covered in more detail in the marketing chapter.

With a home-based business, volunteer work can benefit both you and your business. The trick is to keep the volunteer work from getting out of control. You know you've gone too far when you see these symptoms:

◆ Neighbors, family, and friends drop by regularly, without calling first.

◆ Your link to your neighbors is now so solid that they are too comfortable asking you to help out with their errands, deliveries, service personnel, and so on.

◆ Community volunteer organizations regularly recruit you for very time-intensive work.

◆ Children's activities all revolve around your house.

◆ You are doing more than your fair share of carpooling.

◆ You've become everyone's helping hand.

You will need to define the point that allows you to be active and involved in community work without being overwhelmed by it.

Collaborative Couples

Just as the 1980s was the decade of the individual entrepreneur, the 1990s is turning out to be the decade of entrepreneurial couples. And what more convenient place for these couples to set up shop than in the home?

According to the Small Business Administration, husband-and-wife businesses represent the fastest growing segment of the business population. There are at least 1.8 million husband-and-wife entrepreneurial couples, according to an estimate by the National Family Business Council.

Many couples benefit from spending more time together. Their working relationships are synergistic. Other couples need to work independently, although they will still turn to one another for advice and support. Most two-career couples with children will confirm the difficulties already involved in trying to meet everyone's needs. Would joint business ownership put them over the edge? Current research suggests it won't. In fact, it suggests that couples find their relationship strengthened by working together. But the couples who succeed are the ones who start out with a solid foundation, not the ones who use the business to work out their personal problems.

If you are considering a collaborative working arrangement with your spouse or partner, take a moment to answer the questions in figure 2-6, "Questions for Collaborative Couples."

Questions for Collaborative Couples

Will your home-based business benefit or suffer from working in collaboration with your partner?

Check the statements which positively correspond to you (or say "I do").

1. Do you both feel totally committed to the importance of your service or product? ❏

2. Do you respect and support each other's talents and abilities? ❏

3. Do you derive gratification from a shared project or endeavor? ❏

4. Do you share the same goals and objectives for the business? For yourselves? ❏

5. Do you possess complementary talents, skills, and knowledge? ❏

6. Can you define separate areas of expertise, separate responsibilities? ❏

7. Do you keep your respective egos in check? ❏

8. Can you give and take constructive criticism? ❏

9. Can you relinquish control, let your partner take charge, at the appropriate times? ❏

10. Is this collaboration motivated by more than making money? ❏

11. Do you communicate openly in your marriage and in business? ❏

12. Do you trust each other? ❏

13. Can you avoid competing with each other? ❏

14. Can you combine your energy to compete together against the outside world? ❏

15. Do you share a need for independence and self-reliance in your business? ❏

16. Can you relinquish absolute control over your own ideas? ❏

17. Does working together draw you closer together? ❏

Continues

Continued

18. Do you place your relationship first? ❑

19. Are you sensitive to your spouse's need for self-esteem? ❑

20. Do you treat each other respectfully? ❑

SCORING:

Count the number of items you were able to ✔ positively. High scores indicate a healthy prognosis.

Less than 6 For better or for worse, you've both got major work to do for this business collaboration to succeed.

7–16 Let there be spaces in your togetherness. With some time, you may be able to work out your rough spots.

17–20 Pronounce yourselves a Collaboration Incorporation. You fit the profile of the most successful couples.

Figure 2-6: Questions for Collaborative Couples

Interpretation of Scoring

There are certain characteristics that researchers have found essential to success in collaborative efforts. Six components your business partnership must have are:

◆ mutual trust

◆ ability to value one another's abilities

◆ open communication

◆ preservation of self-esteem

◆ respect

◆ total commitment to the importance of your service/product

Like any other working relationship, you will need to iron out the details as you go along. Some personality types have more trouble than others letting go of complete control. However, that doesn't mean they won't ever let go.

The components that you may develop and refine as you gain experience working together include having separate areas of responsibility, accepting and offering constructive criticism, and relinquishing control.

But over time, as you adapt to the experience of working and living together and begin to see the positive results of your mutual efforts, you will move to a new plateau. Characteristics of the most effective (enduring and endearing) collaborative couples include their:

- ◆ shared need for independence and self-reliance

- ◆ motivation by more than making money

- ◆ drawing closer together through work

- ◆ placing their relationship first

Questions of Balance

For many business owners, struggling with business details and crises takes precedence over assessing their private needs for mental and physical health care. Balance sheets demand more attention than personal balance. Public relations assume a higher priority than private relationships. We often take for granted our mental and physical health and endurance. But a winter's worth of chronic illness or fatigue may be a warning signal not to be ignored. How long can we continue at a frenetic pace? What are the consequences? Every once in a while, it is important to examine our behavior and our health.

In addition to your health, monitor your *attitude*. Every time I teach a course on starting a business, or give a presentation to prospective entrepreneurs, I am reminded of what it is that I enjoy most about this phase: the personal qualities of the entrepreneurs themselves. Entrepreneurs as a whole are full of enthusiasm, intensity, creativity, and—to some extent—innocence. Nurture these positive characteristics even as you gain experience:

1. **Hold on to your enthusiasm.** If you feel it slipping, maybe your business is taking a direction you're not happy with. Or perhaps you're bogged down with bills. Lean on others with experience for a moment.

2. **Stay intense,** but don't let yourself burn out. Come up for air once in a while, please! Take a walk. See a movie. Read a magazine or novel.

3. **Use your energy wisely.** Save it for important things that help you attain your goals.

4. **Nurture your creativity.** If you're stuck in one way of thinking, shake yourself up. Rejuvenate. Maybe it's time to make a change—just for the sake of change. The minute you sit back and take your business success for granted, someone who *is* being creative will slip in and get the better of you.

5. **Maintain your innocence.** Oh sure, after you've been around awhile you learn shortcuts. But like my students in the early days of our classes, we all started our businesses with every intention of being the best and the smartest possible in what we do. So don't cut the wrong corners as you gain experience. Keep your business *ethics* intact.

Everything You Need to Get Started

◆ Defining Your Business Purpose

◆ Identifying Business Goals

◆ Start-up Business Requirements

◆ Formal Business Requirements

◆ Zoning Regulations and Local Ordinances

◆ Regulatory Requirements, Licenses, and Permits

◆ Insurance

◆ Assessing Business Opportunities

◆ Building a Solid Credit History

◆ Establishing a Relationship with Your Bank

◆ When Experts Can Help You

Defining Your Business Purpose

It is essential to get off to a good start and to avoid running off in the wrong direction. In business, you need to move ahead with a clear sense of direction. Here are a few things to check out right away.

"What is your business all about?" you will be asked by everyone from prospective customers to potential lenders. "Tell me what your company does," they will demand at receptions, conferences, and cocktail parties. You will need a concise, catchy, accurate description of your company for a variety of verbal and written responses. Spend time in the earliest days of your business development efforts working on an *excellent* business description. Ask a few trusted friends and associates to critique it. Revise it and polish it until it says just what you want it to say. Then use it in your correspondence and your conversations. It is well worth the time and effort spent to devise a description that sounds as dynamic as you envision your new business will be. Once you are satisfied that your description of your business reflects your enthusiasm and spirit, *write it down.*

Identifying Business Goals

With every new business venture, we nurture new hopes, create new plans, and foster new dreams.

Experts agree that if we can clearly define our dreams in terms of specific and measurable goals we have a much greater probability of successfully achieving what we strive for. Business goals for your new venture should consider growth or changes in the following areas:

- ◆ **Business description.** Will you increase or change the product(s) and/or service(s) you offer?

- ◆ **Scope.** Will you expand the markets you serve? What are your targets?

- ◆ **Size.** Do you plan to increase the number of people working for you? What volume of production do you hope to achieve? What level of sales will you strive for?

State your goals in terms of one-year, five-year, ten-year, and long-range increments. Use figure 3-1 as a guideline.

Business Goals

Describe your specific business goals in measurable terms as follows:

First-Year Goals:

General _____

_____

_____

Products _____

_____

Markets _____

_____

Sales _____

_____

Employees _____

_____

Five-Year Goals:

General _____

_____

_____

Products _____

_____

Markets _____

_____

Sales _____

_____

Employees _____

_____

Continues

Continued

Ten-Year Goals:

General _____

_____

_____

Products _____

_____

Markets _____

_____

Sales _____

_____

Employees _____

_____

Long-Range (or Twenty-Year) Goals:

General _____

_____

_____

Products _____

_____

Markets _____

_____

Sales _____

_____

Employees _____

_____

Figure 3-1: Worksheet for Defining Your Business Goals

Start-up Business Requirements

1. Select the best legal structure for your business. Consider: sole proprietorship, partnership, corporation (C, S, or limited liability corporation). *(See chapter 9 to help you make your decision.)*

2. Select a trade name for your business. *(See chapter 6.)*

3. Register a trade name or incorporate. *(Details follow in this chapter.)*

4. Research zoning ordinances in your municipality. Investigate interpretation and enforcement in your neighborhood. *(Details follow in this chapter.)*

5. Decide what address to use for your business. If necessary for personal or professional reasons, secure a mailing address different from your home.

6. Establish a separate business checking account. *(Other accounting and financial details are itemized in chapter 10.)*

7. Research all regulatory requirements applicable to your business.

8. Apply for all necessary permits, licenses, trademarks, patents, and copyrights. *(Chapter 14 will help you find your appropriate contact.)*

9. Apply for an employer identification number with the Internal Revenue Service.

10. Verify insurance coverage. *(See chapter 12.)*

11. Set up a basic record-keeping system.

12. Select solid professional advisors.

Formal Business Requirements

Your Legal Structure

Chapter 9 discusses the advantages and disadvantages of different forms of business organization. Review those pros and cons before you make a decision about operating as a sole proprietorship, partnership, or corporation. When you've reached your decision, don't dawdle about the paperwork. This decision has an impact in several directions, including administrative, accounting, and marketing actions.

12 Common Start-Up Mistakes and How to Avoid Them

1. Not formulating a company image. Crystallize your company image clearly before you order any marketing materials.

2. Ordering a zillion copies of your first business cards and stationery. You could change your mind—and your direction—quickly. Order the minimum you need to get started.

3. Not using temporary business cards while you wait to have a great one designed. Order black-and-white business cards to hold you over until your professionally designed cards are ready.

4. Antagonizing neighbors. Avoid noise and parking problems from the start.

5. Offering private information about your income, available funding, or other money information. Do have all this information ready if you are going for a loan.

6. Antagonizing your family. Remember you all need to live and work peacefully in this home.

7. Verbalizing doubts, insecurities, problems, concerns in public. They will come back to haunt you. Present a positive, optimistic attitude.

8. Losing touch with your bank, even if you don't need financial assistance initially. Do get to know your banker well (a challenge in this era of mergers and constant change).

9. Expecting immediate payment from customers and clients. Do set aside money for one whole year.

10. Paying for everything by cash or check. Build a solid credit history. Do run down and pay off your major credit cards so that you will have all possible credit available when you really need it.

11. Criticizing the public. Respect everyone in all interactions.

12. Avoiding professional help. Be sure to find experts to assist you. Your accountant, attorney, and insurance agent should have experience working with small businesses.

Figure 3-2: Common Start-up Mistakes and How to Avoid Them.

Incorporation

This can be handled by you or an attorney through your Department of State. Paperwork can be obtained from this department directly. You will also need to determine if anyone else is using the business name you have selected. Your state department can run a computer check for your preferred business name for a fee, and most states will check several names per phone call. (Contacts are listed in chapter 14.) Incorporation protects your business trade name throughout the state and overrides names that are registered only by county. You will also need a "corporate kit," which can be prepared for you by an attorney or purchased in standardized form. Corporate kits show that you are legitimately operating as a corporation. Corporate kits include by-laws, minutes, stock certificates, a stock transfer ledger, and a corporate seal. Many stationery and business supply stores sell these kits for less than $20.

Partnerships

You must file with the county clerk's office in the county where the business will be physically located. Fees differ by municipality, and the filing process is straightforward and simple.

Sole Proprietors and Partnerships

You should contact the county clerk of the county where the business will operate to register a trade name. The law requires that you register any name other than your own. If you are using your own name, it is recommended but not required that you register. The paperwork is minimal, and the fee in many counties is less than $50. If you do not want to incorporate, but you do want to protect your name in specific counties, you can register your business name in select counties within the state(s) where you plan to do business.

Zoning Regulations and Local Ordinances

Local zoning ordinances often prohibit home-based businesses from bringing customers to a home office. Home-based businesses are by definition located in neighborhoods or sections of neighborhoods that are residentially zoned. How does your community or the location you intend to move to view the development of home-based business?

In a community where the prevailing viewpoint is positive and home-based businesses are valued for their significant contribution to the local economy, zoning regulations and local ordinances are the least restrictive. The most positive environment is a community which encourages the development of home-based business with minimal controls and some support, whether urban, suburban, or rural. Areas defined as "mixed use" by local planners offer the warmest welcome. The least restrictive environments permit businesses in residentially zoned areas as long as the business does not create a nuisance.

At the opposite extreme are those communities which prohibit or tightly regulate most forms of home-based business. In these environments, permits are not even an issue. You may just not be allowed to operate your business *at all*. Despite the nation-wide trend in home-based business growth, many municipalities refuse to alter their local ordinances. Ridgewood, New Jersey, is one example of a village with extremely strict zoning ordinances. Tony Merlino, Zoning Officer for the Ridgewood, New Jersey, Building Department said, "Trends may not influence the culture of the town one bit." He added, "In the nine years I've been on this job, no one has challenged the home-based business restrictions. No one has applied to the zoning board for a variance."

Every community has regulations that govern the type of business you can conduct at a particular address. Local ordinances cover everything from meaningful to mundane concerns including:

- activities you may engage in

- signs (type, size, location)

- noise (how much, when)

- parking (where, how much)

- traffic (the limits)

- garages (size, location, number)

- size of office

- exterior appearance

- where (ground floor, percentage of total use)

- number of employees

- required toilet facilities

- office hours

The local zoning czar is the keeper of all pertinent information regarding rules and regulations for home-based businesses. The zoning czar is the local enforcing agency (LEA) for your town and may be part of the Building Department, Department of Buildings and Inspection, Construction Code Enforcement Division, or some similar department. This zoning officer can advise you about local ordinances that will have an impact on your business: if an ordinance prohibits it, the zoning officer can guide you through your local regulations.

If you are already in the home that will serve as your office, your first point of contact should be your community zoning officer. However, you might consider an alternative approach: try your local Chamber of Commerce first. Ask a few general questions through the Chamber of Commerce before you approach the zoning department, where you'll need to be very specific. *The practical advice offered by the most successful home-based business owners is to remain low-key.* Become familiar with the ground rules, ask as many questions as you can, and probe into specifics. Then get around and find out what's *really* going on in the local neighborhoods.

If you are moving into a new area—planning a location-driven business (e.g., bed-and-breakfast), starting over, going through a midlife crisis, divorcing—you have some flexibility about the state, city, or town to which you'll relocate. Aim for a supportive community.

There are no federal zoning laws that govern home-based businesses. Regulations are imposed at the state and local level. State laws govern the structure of local ordinances and prohibit municipalities from restricting too many activities. New Jersey, for example, has state regulations which have traditionally been among the strictest land use codes in the country. The state of New Jersey specifies what a municipality can and cannot deny. A municipality cannot deny individuals from establishing

◆ group homes (for example, foster children) with fewer than 12 children

◆ model homes within a development

◆ special-purpose schools accredited by the State Department of Education. These shall not be subjected to more stringent regulations than those imposed on individuals within the community.

◆ community residences for the developmentally disabled

◆ community shelters for victims of domestic violence

Towns must permit these facilities to exist, but requirements are the same as for single-family residences. A municipality can deny almost anything else it chooses or restrict activity into separate zones for commercial, professional, and residential use.

If you are contemplating a move or need to find out how much flexibility you will have within a particular community, start by contacting the:

1. State's Office of Planning and Economic Development for general regulations.

2. Town's Local Enforcing Agency (LEA). If several towns are grouped together in an interlocal agreement, you will be informed.

3. Municipal Building Department (or town hall) and ask for the local building code from the Department of Buildings and Inspections or Construction Code Enforcement.

If you are moving, your most effective strategy may be to have a realtor investigate this information. A realtor can also discern the difference between reality and fantasy. In many municipalities where home-based businesses are technically not permitted, they flourish by keeping a low profile. In Ridgewood, New Jersey, local zoning ordinances permit only doctors and lawyers to operate a business in their homes. These ordinances are as old as the village itself. On the other hand, in next-door Midland Park, you may run virtually any kind of business out of your home. But watch out if you violate the local sign, noise, or parking regulations.

In reality, home-based businesses exist in abundance in some of the most restrictive municipalities as a form of "underground economy." If municipalities were to recognize this, fees from permits could serve as another source of revenue. However, the ordinances remain unchallenged because, for the most part, these businesses are service providers—accountants, distributorships, consultants, instructors—who do not flaunt their address and maintain strict control over noise, parking, and traffic. They are good neighbors. According to Tony Merlino, Ridgewood's zoning officer, "The only way a home-based business will be detected is if somebody notifies the police. Then it is up to the police to pursue it or not." What might cause a call to the police? "Cars, noise, traffic . . . that's what irritates neighbors the most," he said. So accountants, computer consultants, telemarketers, piano teachers, swimming coaches, craftspersons, and many others thrive as they would in any other, less restrictive community.

Considerations About Zoning Restrictions

1. Are you going to run a high vs. low profile business? Do you need a sign in order to identify your business? How large, bright, high, and attention-grabbing must that sign be to accomplish your goal?

2. Is it necessary for clients/customers to meet with you at your home office or could you go to them? How many people do you expect to visit you at one time?

3. What are your neighbors most sensitive to (e.g., traffic, noise, etc.) and when (evenings, weekends, daytime)? Can your business operate effectively within these parameters?

4. What image should you project to your clients and prospects? If you think your position as a home-based business will work against you with prospective clients, secure an outside business mailing address. Rent a post office box or Mailboxes Etc. address. Arrange to use a friend or colleague's small-business office mailing address.

Figure 3-3: Considerations About Zoning Restrictions

Questions to Ask About Zoning and Local Ordinances

1. What are the official zoning regulations for home-based business?

2. Are any home-based businesses not allowed?

3. Is a permit or license required? If yes, how much does it cost? How do you apply for it? Who approves it? Perhaps you can request a zoning variance or special exemption permit, then seek the approval of your neighbors.

4. Has anyone ever challenged your local zoning/permits/license arrangement? What was the result? Some business owners have succeeded in changing local zoning laws through organized appeals to local officials. However, this is *never* a speedy solution.

5. Does anyone monitor home-based businesses? What is the local procedure? What is the penalty for violations of your local ordinances? (It could be closure, fines, and/or payment of back taxes.)

6. What aspects of home-based businesses (e.g., number of employees, lighting, parking or traffic problems, hours of operation) are the most critical concern of this municipality?

Figure 3-4: Questions to Ask About Zoning and Local Ordinances

The town of Midland Park, New Jersey, grants approval to operate in residential areas with a zoning certificate. Strict controls or "quiet laws" are enforced concerning noise. No construction is permitted on Sunday. Local businesses are permitted only one truck (a pick-up truck, that is) as long as it is not visible from the street at night. According to the town building inspector, "The local sign ordinance is enforced to a T. I'd be thrown out of office if it wasn't."

If you are buying a new home, it is important to consider means to accommodate business growth. Can you use a loft in your garage? Are there restrictions about finishing basements? What are the guidelines for additions? Don't let yourself get trapped in a location that you might rapidly outgrow with no options to expand.

Finally, if you will need to hold meetings with three or more people and your home office is inappropriate for this purpose, locate conference room facilities right away. In some situations, business lunches or dinners at a local restaurant will serve your purpose. In other cases, you may be able to borrow or barter for a private conference room in an office suite complex or in the facilities of another small business.

Regulatory Requirements, Licenses, and Permits

Municipal concerns extend beyond zoning. Contact the main office of your municipality or town to identify:

- ◆ Municipal tax obligations

- ◆ Local mercantile licenses and requirements

- ◆ Registration requirements

Many occupations and business activities are regulated by state boards through license, permit, charter, or registration requirements. These boards are licensed by each state's Division of Consumer Affairs.

States often require some form of registration, license, or certification for specific professions, occupations, and business activities. The Office of Business Advocacy in your state can help to answer any questions regarding licensing and registration requirements.

Insurance

Call your insurance agent before you start your business. Describe the type of business you will run. Your insurance agent will question you about how this business will operate. If the agent is competent, this question-and-answer drill will determine if any action needs to be taken right away.

Key questions your insurance agent will ask when you first start your business are:

- ◆ Will anyone (customers, clients) be coming to your home for business reasons?

- ◆ Will you receive deliveries at home, particularly packages marked with a company name?

- ◆ Will you have expensive business equipment on hand right away?

- ◆ Will you have any workers in your home (including part-time)?

Your most important immediate concerns are liability issues. "You don't have to be as concerned about loss to the business," said Audrey Kessler of Personal Lines Insurance Brokerage, Inc., in Lyndhurst, New Jersey. "At least property is measurable," she explained. "If you have a fire, you can calculate the cost of your loss. Liability is scary because it can run into hundreds of thousands of dollars." (Chapter 12 provides further details about insurance coverage for you and your business.)

Assessing Business Opportunities

Should you start your business from scratch or buy into an existing operation? If start-up efforts seem to overwhelm you and you have money to invest at the outset, you should consider the options of franchises, mail order, vending, and distributorships.

Franchises

Franchisees today employ more than seven million workers in a half million small businesses in more than sixty different industries. The purpose of franchising is to allow individuals to enter established business operations to achieve a mutually beneficial relationship in an entrepreneurial environment, according to the American Franchise Association (AFA). The AFA is the largest franchise trade association in the country, representing more than 13,000 franchised outlets and more than 6,400 individual franchisees. The better known—McDonald's, 7-Elevens, and Jiffy Lubes—are Main Street rather than home-based business concerns. But franchising remains one of the hottest growing areas for new business, with new home-based entrants to the market evolving.

Franchisees have the opportunity to function as entrepreneurs without the start-up hassles of figuring out how to distribute goods and services. Prepackaged marketing materials and sales strategies move franchisees quickly into their customer base in the best of cases. In the worst cases, franchisees are led falsely into the wrong markets in the wrong location with inadequate support and ironclad contracts. Some precautions to take when considering any franchise opportunity include the following:

- ◆ **Watch out for the franchise contract.** Make sure that you don't end up in a contract that gives you fewer rights than any employee. Have the franchise contract reviewed by an attorney experienced in franchise law. You probably decided to go into business on your own to control your own destiny. Don't turn your future over to a franchiser without protection.

- ◆ **Be prepared for significant costs up-front.** You'll have the huge advantage of national brand marketing and guidance, but you may pay from $5,000 to $35,000 for this luxury. Of course that doesn't include the cost of advertising, equipment, and training. But at least in a home-based business you won't have the extra lease or mortgage cost. Watch out for royalties, which can snatch 2 to 8 percent of your gross sales.

- ◆ **Don't expect easy rewards.** Success as a corporate executive won't necessarily guarantee franchise glory. You must still make the same transition from the security of corporate life to the hard, cruel world of long work hours with a reduction in income. Franchises have a certain appeal to former top executives with golden parachutes who have a few dollars to deal with, but the price may be higher than what appears on paper.

◆ **Be wary of any new or unfamiliar franchise system.** Investigate it with a vengeance. It could backfire.

Dealers and Distributors

A quick and easy overview is available in *Entrepreneur* magazine's list of Business Opportunity 500®. This listing identifies dealers and distributors by type and includes information about products, capital requirements, training, support, and more. Scanning this list will give you some ideas about start-up costs. To identify home-based distributorship opportunities, you will need to scan the product and service descriptions. The service categories most conducive to home-based business are: advertising services, apparel, and business systems.

Building a Solid Credit History

Long before you calculate the actual and projected costs to run your home-based business, start getting your act together regarding credit. Every little mistake you ever made will come back to haunt you when you apply for loans, so *watch out*. (See chapter 6 for specific strategies involving credit cards.) But in your earliest preparation stages, *clean up your major credit cards*. Get the balance down as far as you can. If possible, pay off the entire balance for a few months in a row. The larger the amount, the more likely you will receive the following good news:

> **Because you have been such a (faithful, responsible, trust-worthy, financially dependable) customer, we are pleased to inform you that we have extended your credit limit to (some delightful increment of thousands of dollars). Thank you for using our ABC credit card.**

If you can achieve this result with multiple cards, all the better.

Find out what your credit history looks like before you actually need to seek a loan or new credit. Make sure there are no surprises on your credit report. Order a copy of your own credit record from a credit reporting bureau like TRW before you need to have someone else request it because you're completing an application. TRW provides one report a year free of charge; other bureaus may charge only a minimum fee for a report. If you have an opportunity to review the credit report first, you can clear up errors (and there *definitely* may be errors) and come up with a good explanation for the 60- to 90-day payment cycles that appear too often.

When starting their own businesses, many women are surprised to find that none of their individual credit history is reported. Despite the advances women have made in business, married women often have no credit record in their own names. And without a solid credit history, even very successful businesswomen need cosigners for business loans and mortgages. That's because most credit reporting agencies report joint accounts under the husband's social security number. In addition, a woman's personal earnings-and-saving history may be nonexistent if she has consistently filed joint tax returns and maintained joint checking or savings accounts. These two cost-effective moves may have unfortunately killed her credit track record.

Women planning to start a business must both request their credit history reports and take immediate action to establish their own credit records. This will entail supplying the credit bureau with such data as bank account numbers and former addresses. Women must tell credit bureaus to set up individual credit files for them.

Establishing a Relationship with Your Bank

Do *not* wait until you need financial help to get to know your local banker. Introduce yourself now to the local vice president(s) who one day might be reviewing your loan application. Make sure that key bank personnel know that you are a good customer, with your personal, business, and retirement accounts, children's savings accounts, and your mortgage and home equity firmly entrenched in their establishment.

In today's world of consolidations, mergers, and corporate takeovers, yesterday's neighborhood bank is tomorrow's megabank affiliate. The people who *used* to know you could be gone in a moment's notice. So while the banks are reengineering, you should be reintroducing yourself, over and over. There is nothing worse than desperately needing a fast favor—a loan pushed through quickly, a credit line increase, a cash advance—only to have a brand-new bank officer say, "Now can you spell that name again for me." There just isn't the same sense of urgency when *you* go in cold and try to get *them* to turn up the heat. On the other hand, as a well-known and respected customer, you'll stand a much better chance of getting excellent service.

When Experts Can Help You

Early in your business planning, establish a resource list of experts to help you through the maze of decisions you will make on a daily basis. Don't wait until you have an emergency to look for an accountant, lawyer, and business consultant. Check these individuals out in advance so that when you need them you know where to turn.

Some people find it helpful to interview professionals before selecting them. A brief interview can be set up at which you can explain your business and discuss fee arrangements. As a start-up home-based business, you will probably find that a fee for services will work best to start. You can keep your costs under control by discussing in advance what you need and what your limits are. If you can benefit from the regular services of a consultant or specialist, work out a retainer arrangement.

In a retainer arrangement, your consultant should define the average number of hours per week or month that will be devoted to your business, and the products or services that will be provided during that time. A minimum amount of time should also be allocated for you and the consultant to meet on a regular basis to track progress and identify up-coming projects. You should be actively involved in this process and designate follow-up activities that meet *your* needs.

Be as prepared as possible before meeting with an attorney, accountant, or consultant. You can significantly reduce your cost and gain the most benefit from their services when you've done some research ahead of time. How to prepare will be discussed in detail in later chapters. For starters, just remember not to set up any meetings with experts with a blank look on your face and a blank check in your pocket.

Figure 3-5 lists business experts you may want to recruit as your business demands it. Do your homework; prepare specific questions; then solicit their help.

How Experts Can Help You

Experts can help you in a number of different ways. The following list identifies many of the business functions the experts can perform for you. Remember, not all these services require professional training. Perhaps you will choose to handle some of these activities yourself. It always depends on your own expertise and experience. Just be sure to do your homework first.

Lawyers
- help you select your business structure form and/or file partnership or incorporation papers
- assist you with protection of intellectual property rights
- keep you on track when you set up agreements, sign leases, and so on.
- can assist with licenses
- help you sue

Continues

Continued

Accountants

◆ assist in the S Corporation or LLC decision about your business structure

◆ keep you on track with the forms and filing requirements of your business

◆ work out your estimated taxes and your schedule for payment

◆ complete and file your income taxes

Bookkeepers (optional)

◆ handle all the paperwork connected with your monthly income and expenses

◆ bill your customers/clients

◆ could be talked into handling collections for you

Insurance Agents

◆ make sure your home has adequate insurance protection

◆ make recommendations about additional coverage as your business grows or changes

◆ assess the need for commercial policies—when you add employees, add business functions, and so on

Management Consultants

◆ assist you in writing a business plan

◆ work with you to structure your business and keep you focused on goals and growth

◆ teach you how to plan and organize your business

◆ help you design jobs and hire the appropriate people as required

◆ coach you in managing and developing yourself and your staff

Marketing Specialists

◆ help you create a comprehensive marketing strategy for your business

◆ write a marketing plan with you

◆ implement your marketing strategy (Note: any or all aspects can be handled by one or more people), including advertising, public relations, sales, and marketing

- design advertisements and select media placement

- write press releases and follow up with media

- develop sales campaigns and create sales strategies

- make your name a household word

Graphics Designers

- provide special artwork (or even the semi-special if you're not used to using the computer-assisted design on your own system)

- create a logo and letterhead for your stationery, brochure, and business cards to make a powerful positive statement about you and your business

Printers

- for business cards, stationery, brochures, your holiday greeting cards—you'll be amazed at how many things you can by at great rates through your local printing company

- work out some good deals and you might not have to buy or lease a copier

- for special occasion color presentations, your printer will probably have a color copier

- for when you need copies of meeting handouts that look first class, and you have second-class equipment, they're a lifesaver

Figure 3-5: How Experts Can Help You

Designing and Equipping
Your Home Office

- ◆ Privacy Considerations
- ◆ Acoustics and Accouterments
- ◆ Ergonomics
- ◆ Carpal Tunnel Syndrome (CTS)
- ◆ Layout and Furniture
- ◆ Lighting Considerations
- ◆ Professional Design Assistance

Privacy Considerations

When you consider your need for privacy in setting up your office, first determine whether or not people will come in to see you. While an attic nook or spare bedroom may seem to offer the quiet you need, if you plan to meet with clients in this office it just won't work. It is best if you don't have to guide your clients through your home to get to your office. If clients—or employees, for that matter—will come to your office, the closer it is to an exterior entrance, the better.

There is no better route to privacy than a door to close off your office—it keeps you out of your family's way, as well as out of sight. It can also act as a psychological transition point. When you are *in* the office and the door is closed, you are indicating "this is serious stuff." When you are *out* of the office, the closed door can symbolize the end of your workday. But what if you don't have a room of your own available in the house? What if the most quiet and isolated place is the basement, where you share your work space with a washing machine and dryer, ten thousand tiny plastic blocks, the furnace, and the hot-water heater. Can you manage?

Amy H. Horner and Maura Barrett, interior planners for the furniture dealership Danker, Sellew & Douglas in New York City, offer some creative advice to create privacy for a home office in a way that is space-efficient and cost-effective. Without carpentry work, you can make your own "room" with moveable panels, they suggest. "Using 'systems' or modular furniture, you can create a workstation, reconfigure it as your needs change, or move it around," recommends Barrett. "Trackable-acoustical panels act as a boundary wall, give visual privacy, and absorb noise within the panels." These panels are made of fabric and sound-absorbing material. You can start with a small area, then add panels to expand your work area as needed.

"You can also maximize your space by hanging things (like shelves) from the panels instead of taking up valuable floor and desk space," adds Horner. The panels have different looks and can be ordered in a wide range of sizes (from a minimum height of 30 inches to a maximum of 8 feet) and prices. These are self-supporting and require no construction work. They can be ordered with or without a door.

How much space do you really need for one person to work effectively? Barrett suggests that a 6-foot by 8-foot area would provide enough space for an individual worker and equipment. If you will meet with one other person, the additional space for a visitor's chair (allowing at least 30 inches) would make an 8-foot by 8-foot area your best bet, according to Horner.

Pat Ziv, founder of PVZ Space Planning and Design, suggests that the more you plan the details of your office in advance, the better use you can make of space. When planning in advance, always consider the number and placement of electrical outlets, the adequacy of the power supply for equipment, air conditioning, and so on, and the

Ziv's Points to Ponder Before Building

1. Plan the layout of your office as you design the room. Watch out for window placement, wall space, and electrical connections.

2. Brace walls so that you can use wall-hanging bookshelves.

3. Free up floor space for your heaviest pieces of furniture and equipment.

4. Consider frequency of use to determine where to place equipment and storage space.

5. Design for flexibility. Give yourself options and opportunities.

6. Accentuate acoustics. Build extra soundproofing (special insulation) into the walls and use acoustical interior design.

7. Furniture—your equipment is your most important concern, so be sure the furniture fits the equipment. "Your overall productivity is more important than the look of the furniture," says Ziv. But if you plan ahead, you should be able to have the best of both.

Figure 4-1: Ziv's Points to Ponder Before Building

number of telephone lines you will need. Additionally, if you plan to upgrade, add to your equipment, or add new telephone lines, be sure that there will be enough space to do so.

If you are building an office from scratch, Ziv suggests that you take a few precautions. See figure 4-1 for details.

Acoustics and Accouterments

Designing a new room or buying trackable-acoustical panels for better sound quality are not your only options. You can also incorporate acoustical considerations into your interior-design scheme. Some materials used to furnish and decorate your room will also act as sound absorbers. Ziv recommends that to keep your office as quiet as possible, there are various items that can be used. Fabric-covered tackboards can be color-coordinated to match your decor. Wall hangings and window treatments should also be considered. Finally, carpeting is extremely helpful as a sound absorber.

Ergonomics

Ergonomics or human engineering is the application of physiological and anatomical principles to the workplace. The design of devices, systems, and working conditions that are compatible with the physical requirements of workers applies to the home worker just as to the corporate employee. Proper equipment and furniture design can not only make you feel more comfortable and let you work more efficiently, but can also prevent the occurrence of repetitive stress disorders such as carpal tunnel syndrome (CTS).

There are industry standards that govern the design and production of office equipment and furniture, but companies follow these standards to different degrees. Your work surface, for example, should be 28 inches high.

As you design your office, ergonomic considerations are most important in the selection of your chair, desk/workstation, computer monitor, and computer keyboard.

Ergonomics is assuming a greater role in the design of equipment, but there are precautions you will need to take to protect yourself with even the best design.

Periodic changes in activity may be what you need to be more productive and to avoid costly disability in the long run.

Carpal Tunnel Syndrome

In today's high-tech offices, employees around the country—home-based, corporate, and professional—are spending hours a day using a keyboard. The dramatic increase in reports of carpal tunnel syndrome, the most well-known of the hand, arm, shoulder, and neck ailments collectively known as repetitive stress injuries, is believed to be the result of using poorly designed equipment. It is exacerbated by today's work habits.

Typing on computers is not the same as typing on typewriters. On typewriters, there is a natural pause for the carriage return about every 15 seconds, forcing our hands to rest. These micropauses prevent the injuries that computer users experience after typing hundreds of words per minute on a daily basis.

The "carpal" (meaning wrist) tunnel is exactly that—a narrow tunnel in the center of the wrist formed by bones and a ligament. Tendons and a major nerve are contained in this tunnel. This nerve conducts sensation from the hand, up the arm, to the central nervous system. When the nerve is compressed at the wrist, the hand and fingers are affected. Injury to the nerve is first felt as numbness and tingling in the thumb or index finger, often waking the person up at night. If ignored, symptoms become progressively worse until the grip weakens and there is difficulty holding objects and performing tasks such as buttoning clothing. The pain, experienced as the syndrome worsens, can be mild or severe, periodic or constant.

Who is at risk? Individuals whose work is hand-intensive and whose jobs require repetition of certain movements involving the wrist, especially secretaries and administrative assistants, data processors, receptionists, and cashiers. Home workers who do not have the formal interruptions of a corporate office routine are likely candidates because they often take fewer breaks.

Dr. Areta D. Podhorodecki is a leading authority on the prevention of CTS and other repetitive motion injuries. She founded St. Marks Rehabilitation Associates to focus on the diagnosis and treatment of CTS and other disorders. An Australian-born specialist, Dr. Podhorodecki is attending physiatrist (doctor of physical medicine) at St. Vincent's Hospital and Medical Center in Manhattan and assistant clinical professor at New York Medical College. She has lectured around the country on physiatry for over a decade, stressing the importance of proper diagnosis and preventive techniques.

Preventing Carpal Tunnel Syndrome

Change positions and tasks
A five-minute stretch every hour plus micropauses every 15 minutes or so reduce muscle fatigue and strain. Job or task rotation is also effective.

Correct posture
Sit straight back in a chair with good back support and keep your chin up and neck vertical. Avoid the "neck forward" position as in craning to read your computer screen. Such extreme positions cause neck/shoulder pains and even severe headaches.

Use elbow/wrist supports at the keyboard
Keep hands/wrists in a straight line to decrease risk of carpal tunnel syndrome.

Adjust your chair
Your feet should be resting on the floor or a foot rest. Sit right against a back rest that fits against the curve of your back, such as a lumbar roll.

Check your desk height
It is important that your desk is at a comfortable height.

Get medical attention early
If you become symptomatic, early medical attention is imperative. Proper diagnosis and treatment can heal symptoms faster and prevent future chronic problems.

Figure 4-2: Preventing Carpal Tunnel Syndrome

"Accurate diagnosis and early treatment are imperative in dealing with CTS and avoiding surgery," warns Dr. Podhorodecki. "Foremost among the diagnostic procedures is the electrodiagnostic study which stimulates the nerve with a mild electric shock. The speed of the response in the fingers is registered on a computer screen. This gives a definitive answer. Often, symptoms of tendonitis mimic those of CTS." Dr. Podhorodecki urges, "The patient should find a rehabilitation specialist or a neurologist to conduct the test."

Figure 4-2 lists Dr. Podhorodecki's recommendations for preventing repetitive motion injuries.

According to recent studies, disability claims resulting from carpal tunnel syndrome have increased 467 percent in the last five years. CTS has financial repercussions as well as painful physical symptoms. For both insurance carriers and employers, the costs of disability payments, medical treatment, and absenteeism are growing at an alarming rate. On the other hand, preventive measures are often simple and inexpensive to implement. In a home-based business, where reduced costs and increased productivity are vital, don't take chances yourself.

Layout and Furniture

Buy your equipment first; then determine your office furniture requirements.

An L-shaped work area is the most efficient for an individual worker. The basic components of a standard work area, according to Barrett and Horner, are:

- ◆ work surface
- ◆ shelves for storage (preferably overhead to conserve floor space)
- ◆ center drawer (for your most frequently used items)
- ◆ main work surface (size determined by the nature of the work you do)
- ◆ keyboard space

Barrett adds panels and a "pedestal" or small storage piece that could fit under a table or desk to the "must have" list.

Your work surface has to be solid enough to support your daily needs. If your equipment includes a computer, be sure to select a surface strong enough to handle the weight. Furniture designed for computers usually works best, allowing you to position your terminal and keyboard for easy access.

It is tempting, when you are trying to keep your start-up costs to a minimum, to find the least expensive alternatives whenever possible. While you will be certain not to scrimp on your telecommunications or computer systems, you may decide to cut expenses on furniture to keep your bottom-line costs low. One word of caution: If you buy discount furniture, be sure you check out the quality. If you decide that low cost is preferable no matter what, then find the lowest-cost pieces that will at least last until you've assembled them. I am a firm believer in starting smart and not getting in over your head. If your budget allows for little furniture, but you need a few essential pieces, simply keep in mind these guidelines from Danker, Sellew & Douglas:

1. Check the quality of the furniture by testing it out.

2. See how much *weight* each piece will hold, not just the physical dimensions. Much of the equipment you will use on a daily basis is heavy. Unless your furniture is specifically designed to hold equipment, it may bow under the weight.

3. Test the piece to be sure it works. Do the drawers open and close smoothly? Are the file drawers wide enough to hold files?

4. Are the basic ergonomic requirements met? You don't have to be a human factors engineer to know whether or not your knees fit comfortably under a desk.

5. Check out the warranty. Larger manufacturers will warranty parts for 10 years to life. If all you want is a year of use while getting started, knowing you'll replace and upgrade later, then just be sure you hold onto your receipt and charge the purchase to a major credit card. Otherwise you could be stuck if the piece breaks.

The size of your office may depend on how much space you can lay claim to in your home. You may not have much control over it and may end up in an area that is not as large as you would like. Just remember that where you do have control is in the layout of the work area. The layout should be driven by the nature of the work you do. Barrett and Horner suggest that you think through the activities that you perform in a typical day, then develop a list of the things that would help you do the work more efficiently. "Walk through your work," suggests Barrett, "to figure out what you use most often and where you spend the most time." Your two most important considerations, according to Pat Ziv, are (1) your work surface, and (2) your access to it.

In a very small office, Ziv recommends that you maximize use of the space with the following ideas:

1. Use wall space wherever possible, with shelving bracketed to the walls to leave floor space open for furniture and equipment.

2. Design the work surface to be ready for work. Piles of paper strategically placed around a desk will be difficult to control for even the neatest individual.

3. Organize your files based on frequency of use.

4. Place materials you use often within arm's reach.

5. Store reference materials, support documents, and correspondence files that are not of immediate concern farther away from your desk and computer.

6. Keep a wide-open work space where you can readily get to work.

7. Stay neat. Throw out material you don't *really* need.

Barrett and Horner recommend that you think through the best type of overhead storage for your needs. *Open storage* is fast and easy to access, but will usually look messy. *Doors* or lockable doors will keep your area neater, dust free, and secure.

An extra bonus of overhead storage is that it can support lighting. Your task lighting can be attached to the underside of the storage unit to allow additional open space on your work surface.

Even an award-winning office design will fall apart if you don't keep it organized once you set it up. Use the space that you have efficiently and don't clutter it up. You'll find yourself feeling cramped and claustrophobic even if you have a spacious office unless you consistently file papers when you're finished, throw out unimportant items, keep your work logically organized, and have easy access to information you need for work.

Chairs

Probably the most important office accessory for your overall comfort and performance is your chair. You must try out your chair, according to Ziv, before you purchase it. Ziv says, "Consider whether you need a 'managerial' or 'operator' style." Barrett suggests, "Make sure it fits *you*." "Let's face it," she points out—"everyone has different requirements." We come in all shapes and sizes. No matter what size you or your chair are, look for wheels; office chairs usually have casters (see below). Wheels make life easier when you need to reach for other equipment, files, coffee cups, and so on.

There are ergonomic laws about chair design, one of which is that it must be flexible. Adjustable chairs are preferable so that you can alter the height of the seat. Manual adjustments (e.g., the chair screws up or down) are just as good as hydraulic.

Additional features to look for include:

- ◆ lift

- ◆ swivel tilt mechanism

- ◆ back lock

- ◆ extra lumbar support (a bonus)

- ◆ adjustable back height

- ◆ arms, no arms, adjustable arms (for your wrists)

Note that cantilever (short) arms are easier to push under the average desk or work station.

Most chairs come with carpet casters. Specify hard-floor casters if necessary when you are ordering a chair. Ziv recommends gluing down the carpet for comfort. You really don't need a plastic carpet liner under the chair (these usually get caught in the chair legs or wheels).

Lighting Considerations

When you plan lighting for your office, Ziv recommends that you consider two distinct requirements: task lighting and general illumination.

Task Lighting

You must be able to see your work clearly. Consider your office function first, and aesthetics will follow. Some manufacturers have a fluorescent tube mounted under a shelf over the work surface. This seems to be the best form of task lighting for a typical desk arrangement.

Other aspects of your office have to be taken into account. If you have a dark work surface (e.g., hardwood cherry desk), your eye has to make the transition to white paper. This can cause discomfort after extended work intervals. Barrett and Horner suggest avoiding any shiny finish, like laminates and highly polished wood, on your work station because they create glare. Also watch that your lighting doesn't create glare on your computer screen. According to Barrett and Horner, you don't need task lighting when you are working at a computer. General illumination should be adequate.

General Illumination

Three basic types of light are used for general illumination:

Fluorescent Lighting

Today fluorescent lighting is color corrected and is the least expensive form of lighting. Barrett and Horner suggest that fluorescent lighting is best. It is evenly distributed with little glare. It doesn't create "hot spots." Fluorescent lighting is available in "cool" and "warm." Warm lighting produces the least amount of glare when you are working with a computer.

Incandescent Lighting

This type of lighting provides a softer look on people. If you are using overhead lights, you can vary intensity by controlling the wattage.

Halogen Lights

These lights are bright and are very color correct (white correct) and therefore are a popular choice for businesses that deal with color, like graphic design, interior decorating, and the like.

General lighting can be made most flexible with a dimmer switch for different needs, time of day, and weather conditions.

Finally, oddly enough, visual discomfort can also result from poor air circulation, according to Barrett. Even if you have carefully selected your lighting, you may have other considerations as well.

Professional Design Assistance

If you are the type of person who generally has difficulty organizing things, organizing your office will be no easier for you. And if you don't enjoy decorating and furniture shopping, you probably won't enjoy equipping your office either. Fortunately, there are professional designers and planners who can help you through this startup phase. They can help you select the best furniture and finishes for your needs. Most furniture stores and dealers offer design assistance.

Many home-based workers think of furniture dealers as a resource for the corporate office where quantity is a requirement. That isn't the case. Furniture dealerships will gladly work with individuals as well as with larger companies. They offer interior planning services, personal attention, high-quality furniture at a full range of costs, and secondhand furniture for reduced cost. It may be to your advantage to purchase a high-quality, secondhand piece of furniture through a dealership instead of an inexpensive lower-quality piece that is not warranted, does not have a service guarantee, and may not endure.

Assessing and Meeting Your Technological Needs

- ◆ Taking Advantage of Technology
- ◆ Telephone Communications
- ◆ Fax Machines
- ◆ Copiers
- ◆ Computers
- ◆ Printers
- ◆ Software
- ◆ CD-ROMs
- ◆ On-line Services and the Internet
- ◆ World Wide Web (WWW)

Taking Advantage of Technology

Today even the smallest home-based business can sound and look as sophisticated as any large corporation by taking advantage of equipment and services that technological advancements have made available at low cost. This chapter will show you how the technological components of your home office can enable you to do more than simply survive. (See chapter 8 for strategies on image building.)

Depending on the nature of your business, the quality of your business equipment at start-up varies. A first step for one business and upgrade for another will be defined differently. This decision applies to almost every piece of office equipment you will need. Basic needs vary, so *you* should clarify your requirements, business objectives, and the true daily use.

Before making any major purchase of equipment or investment in new technology, analyze the benefits versus costs. Ask yourself if this investment will enable you to:

◆ work more effectively

◆ increase your productivity

◆ attract new customers

◆ reduce staff requirements

◆ influence your corporate image

◆ enhance customer relations

The amazing thing about the technological advances of the last decade is that a single individual can be more productive than ever before, stay in touch with clients, respond quickly to customer requests, resolve problems efficiently—and stay sane. Home-based businesses have the resources available to provide the same quality products and services as larger companies.

Telephone Communications

Communications companies are wildly competing for small-business owners' attention and budgets. Take the time to learn what's available and to understand how each service and product can benefit your business. You probably won't need to duplicate exactly what's in a corporate office. Start simple and add features, services, and equipment as your business grows. If you are on a very tight budget and your household does not have heavy telephone traffic (e.g., you don't have children, you live alone, your spouse works outside of the home), you may be able to get by with one phone for a short time.

Although the coaxial cable used for cable television has a much greater bandwidth (capacity) than the telephone lines, the cable system does not currently provide 2-way communications. Regional and long distance providers will be the best source for a variety of services in the near future.

But even at the basic level, take full advantage of all the services you can use with one consumer telephone line for a minimal extra cost per month. You'll need several of the following services to enhance your capabilities if you have a single telephone line:

Answering Machine

If you decide to use an answering machine instead of a voice-mail service, don't buy the least expensive one. A basic unit with the capability of checking calls from outside your office is the simplest arrangement. Think through your whole strategy for equipment before you buy one, however. Some integrated phone/fax machines come equipped with an answering machine.

Call Waiting

Your incoming callers will not receive a busy signal when you're on the phone, and you will hear a special signal to indicate you have another call. You can talk to the second caller by putting the first call on hold, handling two calls on one line at the same time. If you don't want your calls interrupted for a certain time interval use a tone block feature to turn off call waiting.

Three-Way Calling

You can hold conference calls, local and long distance, with two different locations at once. The simplification and speed of information exchange offers you a tremendous advantage. (Just be careful that you have *really* disconnected your third party on the call before you start to talk about him behind his back.) But if you decide to have two telephone lines, a telephone with a built-in conference button will enable you to accomplish the same thing without the additional monthly service fee. Three-way calling handles everything on one telephone line—perfect for beginners.

Call Forwarding

You can reroute your calls to a remote telephone number of your choice—including your mobile phone. The incoming caller never knows the call has been forwarded, and you never have to miss an important call. (Imagine the possibilities of *this* feature— a personal favorite of everyone from the insatiable sun worshipper to the frenetic workaholic.) If you are working outside of your office for any extended period of time, this feature is a real blessing. Calls can be transferred to a business associate for coverage if you can't be interrupted.

Speed Calling, Repeat Call, Return Call, and Priority Call

Speed Calling: Store up to 30 different telephone numbers of the people you talk to most often, then dial them with the touch of one or two buttons. Repeat Call: Your phone can continuously monitor a busy number every 45 seconds for up to 30 minutes, with no impact on your own incoming or outgoing calls. A special ring alerts you when the call finally gets through. Return Call: Whether or not you answered your last phone call, this feature automatically redials the number of the last caller until the call gets through, for up to 30 minutes. Follow-up calls are simplified with this, and if a call got away before you could pick up the phone, you can try to get it back. Priority Call: Up to six caller phone numbers can be programmed "high priority" and can be assigned a different ring. Combined with call waiting, this ensures that you will only interrupt your call of the moment for important calls.

Caller ID

If you want to screen your calls and decide which to answer immediately, this is the feature for you. If you know who is calling before you answer the phone, you can prepare yourself to handle the call more effectively. With caller ID, you give yourself time to gather your notes and collect your thoughts before answering the phone.

Voice Messaging Services

You can communicate without conversing as your business grows if you build in flexibility directly on your phone line. You don't need to buy additional telephone equipment or extra lines. The extra attraction of voice messaging services over an answering machine is that the service takes messages when you are on the phone, too. This provides your customers with greater access to you and no busy signal.

Call Answering

The answering machine without the equipment, call answering services handle all incoming calls, whether you are on the phone or out of the office. With most forms of this service you will use a password to retrieve your messages. You have the capability with some local services to add "mailboxes" for several other people to receive and retrieve messages. This can work for children, family, and employees.

Voice Mail

A more sophisticated form of call answering service, voice mail enables you to edit messages and forward them to other voice mailboxes. Voice mail is a great enhancement if you have employees who don't work in your office all the time. Everyone can remain in contact with one another, working their own hours in the locations best suited to your company's needs. Voice mailboxes can also be set up to activate a pager when messages are received.

Second Telephone Line

Recognize when the time has come to install a second telephone line. You won't need to install a business telephone right away unless your business will benefit from a Yellow Pages listing. If you are a consultant who would not advertise, or if the business is in your name and can easily be found in a phone book or via directory services, the Yellow Pages listing will be less important for you. Business line rates are higher, both monthly and by volume. There is no doubt that the advantages are tremendous, but you have to be able to absorb the costs. Many home-based businesses never install a business line and work with consumer lines even as they grow.

Before you put in a business line, additional consumer lines offer tremendous advantages. Get several lines as soon as you possibly can. Three lines can give you a real boost: one line for the family, with call waiting and the features most needed for busy personal lives; one line dedicated to business calls; one line for your modem or fax modem.

Multi-line Telephones

With the use of simple equipment like two-line phones, you will be able to perform more complicated tasks with ease through the equipment instead of through the telephone network. You can set up conference calls with ease (just remember to block call-waiting whenever you use three-way or conference call features). Two-line phones also enable you to put one call on hold when another comes in. Speed call and redial are now common features on most phones.

Wireless Communication Services

It is important to stay in touch with your office even when you're on the road. If you work alone and don't have a secretary or associate to track you down, learn quickly how to use technology to build your links to your clients. Your clients and customers won't want to wait long for a response from you. Wireless services give you an extra edge. Pocket-size portable phones, car phones, and pagers keep you in contact wherever you are.

You will purchase your cellular phone and service separately. Sometimes phones are given away free as part of a service sign-on incentive, but the phone is the least of your expenses. What adds up is the monthly bill. Shop around for the best cellular service for you. Compare monthly charges, per-minute charges, roaming fees, duration of peak and off-peak hours, and penalties to see which company offers the best deal.

Cellular Phones

Watch for best buys in services and equipment when you first connect. You'll need to think about your calling patterns in order to make any sense of the packages offered by the various cell phone services. The two most popular cellular phones are mobile car phones and pocket-size portable phones. Mobile car phones have the best transmission range but can't be removed from the car, which is a big disadvantage. Portables are lightweight but have the least transmitting power. If you use a portable in your car, be sure to get a charger for your car as well. Batteries can run down quickly with a few long calls.

Business Telephone Lines

This costs a little more than regular consumer lines, but you will have the advantage of a listing in the Yellow Pages and in the telephone directory's business section. With business telephone lines comes the potential to handle a high volume of calls, faxes, and data transmission, to add on multiple lines, and to lease sophisticated phone-answering systems.

Leasing Phone Answering Systems

As your business grows, you may need a more sophisticated phone answering system to handle a variety of functions. For a monthly fee, your company can lease a phone answering system that will enable callers to place credit card orders, check on the status of pending orders, or request sales or promotional information.

Some customers may complain about not having a business representative to talk to, but these systems free you and your staff to focus on customer service for the serious buyers.

Business Telephone Systems

If your business continues to grow and you hire several employees, you'll need to upgrade to a more sophisticated system. Work with a telecommunications consultant to identify the best configuration for your needs and to learn how to establish the most cost effective system. Some services to consider are Toll-Free Numbers or a High Capacity Digital Service.

Toll-free number encourages customers to call and call again. In fact, the more calls you receive, the lower the rate you pay. Your charges are based on the total volume of calls. This is a great service to provide when you advertise your business.

If your business involves the transmission of data (like inventory control, credit information, etc.) you may need high-volume, high-transmission lines, and you may want to consider High-Capacity Digital Service. There are various alternatives available, and a communications expert can guide you through the alternatives, including:

◆ Networking Services

◆ Local Area Networks (LAN)

◆ Wide Area Networks (WAN)

◆ Integrated Services Digital Network (ISDN)

Fax Machines

What did we ever do without them? How did anyone ever meet a deadline? The fax machine makes it possible to transmit fast and accurate hard copy documents any time of the day or night. Considering how many entrepreneurs use this modern marvel at odd hours, your best bet is to have the capability to send and receive faxes at any time, i.e., a dedicated fax line or phone/fax equipment that receives both and stays on 24 hours a day. Even if you choose to purchase a fax modem, you'll need a separate fax machine to receive incoming transmissions from systems that are incompatible with yours. You will also need it to transmit copies of documents, graphs, or illustrations that are not stored on your computer.

Fax Broadcast, Fax Waiting, and Fax Mailbox

Fax broadcast enables you to broadcast the same message to multiple locations at the same time. You can send your customers pricing information immediately, release time-sensitive material on time, and send charts, graphs, and pictures in a cost-effective manner. If your business entails heavy fax traffic, fax waiting and fax mailbox will be essential start-up components. Other businesses can manage for a time without these more advanced features.

Copiers

Desktop copiers generally cost between $550 and $1,000. The more expensive models are faster and have automatic paper feed functions. How often will you need to use a copier? Some fax machines have a copy function built in, suitable for occasional copying and adequate if fax paper quality will suffice. For high-volume copying, like meeting handouts, student materials for class, a mass mailing—any periodic projects that you'd hate to spend time on anyway—you might be best served by going to a copy shop or printer.

Computers

For the uninitiated, a quick review of basic computer components is provided below. *Home Office Computing* magazine offers regular updates and reviews of all the newest equipment and software. Before you go computer shopping, check out the newest models and the pros and cons of each by researching magazine articles and by questioning other home-based business owners. You can usually save money by purchasing your entire computer system at once. Often the software you need to get started will be offered at a special rate if you buy it at the same time that you buy your peripherals.

If you need to read the following paragraphs to gain a better understanding of computer components, that's a *sure* sign you should bring an expert with you before you purchase anything. You'll be an easy target for techno-speaking sales reps. Don't get in over your head, but don't scrimp in the areas that will affect your productivity and performance. Joanne McBet of Shakespeare Computer & Graphics strongly recommends that home-based businesses invest in powerful tools from the start. "Don't start with the minimum, or you'll spend much more time at your computer than you need to."

Central Processing Unit (CPU)

Your CPU is the power of the machine. Speed is one of your most important considerations when your make your selection. Every time you scroll through pages of a word processing file or use a spreadsheet, you will feel the impact of the speed of your computer. As software packages become more advanced, they require faster microprocessor speed. Speed is measured in megahertz (MHz), and the minimum you'll be interested in is 75 MHz.

RAM

Random Access Memory, or RAM, is a type of computer memory. RAM temporarily stores data while your computer processes it. RAM is measured in MBs (megabytes). You will need a minimum of 4MB, but 8MB is recommended. You can use more powerful software with larger amounts of memory. Many basic Windows-based word processors, for example, will require 16MB RAM to run effectively. Go for as much as your budget can afford because it will increase the range of software you can use in the future.

Chip

A small piece of semiconducting material on which an integrated circuit is embedded. The Pentium chip is the newest and most powerful. Predecessors go by three-digit numbers—486, 386, 286. Standard Microsoft Windows™ will only run on a 386 or better. Go for the newest you can possibly afford. Technology changes so quickly that if you start a half-step behind, there is no way you'll catch up.

Disk Drives

Disk drives read data from or write data onto disks. Long-term electronic copies of your work are stored on your hard disk drive. A hard disk drive helps you work faster. Costs increase with higher capacities. In today's fast changing world, go for as much as you can afford.

Monitor

The quality of your monitor is most important if you will be viewing the screen for extended periods of time. Look for a monitor that will support the smallest dots per inch (dpi .28 or less) and that has a high refresh rate (70 hertz or better). You could get by with a monochrome (either green or amber) monitor, but there are now so many well-priced color monitors there is no reason to.

Keyboard, Mouse, and Mousepad

If you know you will doing a lot of word processing on your computer, using the keyboard for extended periods of time, go for the most ergonomically correct keyboard you can afford. A mouse is an essential element of minimal cost that controls the movement of the cursor or pointer on a display screen. The mouse is used in conjunction with a keyboard and in some cases with a scanner. A mousepad provides traction for moving the mouse accurately on smooth surfaces.

Scanner

Do you input much data from other printed sources? Would you like to store photographs or illustrations? Scanners get better and better all the time, just like all other computer components. In some businesses, a scanner is a must. If your budget permits, a scanner can save you time. A scanner, for example, will enable you to send copies of information not created by your computer through your fax-modem. Printer/scanner/copier combinations are a new technology that could save you money.

Surge Protector

Surge suppressors provide protection to your electronic equipment from power spikes caused by such things as electrical storms and local power problems. Even a small power outage can "crash" your system, so consider an uninterrupted power supply (UPS) if you plan to use your computer for long hours.

Modem

This device enables a computer to transmit data over telephone lines. You will need a modem if you want to dial on-line services and databases or if you want to access the internet. A computer modem with fax capability is only slightly more expensive (about $10) than a standard modem and is well worth the price even if you have a separate fax machine. The increasingly common fax modem, which sends documents directly from your computer without printing a hard copy first, saves time by automatically transmitting long documents. Some communications software can receive faxes directly into the computer to be printed out from there.

Portable, Laptop, or Notebook Computers

The cost of portable computers varies widely, ranging from as low as $400 to as high as $4,000. A notebook model with a 486 microprocessor and four megabytes of RAM might cost around $1,000, but lighter computers with better screen quality cost more. Watch for new releases and better prices almost daily. If this is your primary computer, you may want to invest in a full-size monitor and mouse for office use.

Multimedia Computers

These computers are souped up with a built-in fax modem, CD-ROM drive (see below), color monitor and sound capability, and are equipped with mega-memory. The cost of a multimedia system will depend on the quality of the sound components—speakers and sound card—and the speed of the CD-ROM. Try to buy the components as part of a computer package, but no matter what, experts recommend that you buy the sound card, CD-ROM drive, and speakers together.

Back-up Options

Hard drives can fail, so it is essential to back up your data on "DAT" tape (Digital Audio Tape) or on a "removable" disk.

Printers

Of course, you will need a printer capable of high-resolution text and graphics if you are doing any desktop publishing. But today so many businesses use laser printers for correspondence that if you don't, you run the risk of having your materials look tacky. All letters to clients should be of high quality.

Laser Printers

Laser printers give a professional finish and top-quality look to documents, papers, graphics, and presentations. Laser printers offer the clearest, cleanest look. No matter what kind of paper you use, the quality of the print is consistent. In addition, laser printers are fast. If you print large quantities of paper at once, the savings in your time will be well worth the additional cost of a high-speed laser. You can't beat it for quality, performance, price, ease of maintenance, and support. Speaking of maintenance, a laser-printer toner will last about 4,000 pages and costs a little more than $100.

Ink-jet Printers

These printers are much less expensive than laser printers. If you produce only a few hundred pages a month, this may be your best bet. Ink-jet cartridges cost about $25 and last for about 250 pages.

Dot-matrix Printers

Dot-matrix printers will suffice if cost is your primary concern and the appearance of the documents you produce is of little consequence. Printer ribbons cost about $10.

Color Printers

These printers are more expensive than black-ink printers (about twice the price). You can go a long way without owning a color printer.

Software

The disk operating system is the basis for choosing all other software to run on your computer. Microsoft's DOS has been the standard operating system for IBM-compatible computers. Macintosh computers require Macintosh software at this time, although there may be a day when IBM and Macintosh computer operating systems are interchangeable. Some individual software programs to consider are:

Word Processing

Word processing applications are used to create, edit, and print documents. Microsoft Word,™ WordPerfect™ (for IBM-compatible and the Apple Macintosh), and Ami Pro™ from Lotus (for IBM-compatibles only) are three popular programs.

Windows

This graphical user interface makes DOS user-friendly. Windows 95™ is an updated DOS, designed to be even "friendlier," but with some mixed results at the time of this book's publication.

Spreadsheets

These are numeric programs that can help you to track/analyze your business. The most popular spreadsheets are Microsoft Excel,™ Lotus 1–2–3,™ and Borland's Quattro Pro.™

Accounting and Personal Finance

The most popular personal finance software today is Quicken from Intuit Corp. Many accountants recommend it for small businesses. More expensive software is available if your needs become more complex.

Integrated Packages

Combination applications packages are available to help you. Microsoft Works, for example, includes word processing, filing, spreadsheet, and record-keeping functions in a single package. Microsoft Office combines Word,™ Excel,™ Power Point™ (for preparing presentations), and cc: Mail.™ Lotus SmartSuite™ is another popular combination. Both are available for IBM-compatibles and Power Macs. If you work with an organization that has E-mail, request a remote user name and a password to stay connected.

CD-ROMs

A CD-ROM is a type of optical disk capable of storing large amounts of data. The most common CD-ROM size is 600MB. The disk can integrate sound and pictures, creating a multimedia effect. Buy a CD-ROM drive if you are purchasing a new computer. External CD-ROMs are easier to install than internal, but internal CD-ROMs cost less and take up less space.

On-line Services and the Internet

The five largest on-line services today have over five million subscribers logging on for everything from electronic mail to managing their businesses. The five largest services are America Online, CompuServe, Delphi, Genie, and Prodigy. It has been predicted that by 1998 there will be 13 million subscribers.

Components you'll need to get on-line include:

Computer	a 386 will suffice (but go for a 486 if you can)
Modem	2400 baud is adequate (don't buy that, but if you already have it you could live with it to start)
	9600 baud runs most commercial on-line services
	14,400 baud is your best bet if you are buying a modem now—faster, more expensive, and powerful
Phone Line	use your fax line if it won't interrupt service; a dedicated phone line is better
On-line Service Subscription	use the service that best meets your needs.

America Online, CompuServe, and Prodigy each offer a wide range of features, with electronic mail, news, reference materials, and bulletin boards.

America Online (AOL)

AOL seems to be the current front-runner in consumer appeal, passing Prodigy and tying CompuServe in membership. It is easy to use with a pleasant layout and a human-like interface. Content includes

Reuter news service

Business Week

The New York Times

Investor's Business Daily

Prodigy

Prodigy charges extra for features like on-line newspapers and investment services, but has a good reputation for news, personal finance, and children's features.

CompuServe

This service is both extensive and expensive. It includes: basic news, stock quotes, entertainment-oriented features, newspapers, and magazines, including *Fortune, People,* and *Sports Illustrated.*

Specialized databases, like medical journals and computer magazines, are available at extra cost. Using on-line services to market your business will be covered in chapter 7.

Internet

Thirty million people are on the Internet, the government-sponsored international network. Your home office can be transformed into a global information center with access to millions of resources by using the Internet. All you need is an Internet account from an Internet provider (such as Delphi), knowledge of E-mail, and access to Gopher software. The Internet provides access to:

1. Government resources, including census data, current legislation, commerce department activities, trade, and contract opportunities.

2. An on-line business reference library, including foreign currency exchange rates, industry statistics, and more.

3. Free publications in the Electronic Newsstand and free access to selected articles from more than 100 magazines.

4. Entrepreneur's discussion group to ask a question or seek a solution to a problem, share tips on business contacts, software and more.

5. Advice for new Internet users is found in a file, "Where to Start," which answers the most frequently asked questions.

World Wide Web (WWW)

The World Wide Web is a service on the internet that allows users to publish, search for, and retrieve text, pictures, and sounds. One by one, the major on-line service providers are offering access to the Web, enabling millions of personal computer users to join in.

Some estimates report that the Web grew over 100,000 percent last year. This is easily understood when you consider that the Web had an estimated one to three million users before Prodigy, Microsoft, and other on-line consumer services connected millions more users to it. The Web holds hundreds of thousands of "pages" of narrative and/or graphics on computers all over the world, linked to other pages on the

Internet. *Hyperlinks* let you select different pages or topics with specific underlined or colored words. You can download a file to your computer, do an information search, or access video or audio files.

The Line on On-line Services

System	Phone	Great for	Approx. Cost*
America Online	(800) 227-6364	Electronic forums, online publications	$9.95 month/5 hours $2.95 ea. add'l hr.
Prodigy	(800) 776-3449	Electronic forums, sports, education, references	$9.95 month/5 hours $2.95 ea. add'l hr.
CompuServe	(800) 848-8990	Business databases, electronic forums	$9.95 month/5 hours $2.95 ea. add'l hr
Genie	(800) 638-9636		
Delphi	(800) 544-4005	Full Internet access	
Dialog	(800) 334-2564	Various databases include business files	
Dow Jones News/Retrieval	(609) 452-1511	Investment business databases	
Lexis/Nexis	(800) 543-6862	News and legal databases	
Westlaw	(800) 328-0109	Legal databases	
Microsoft	Coming soon	Watch for details	
AT&T Business Network	(800) 967-5363	Business, reference, export hotline	5 hours free for AT&T users $2.50 ea. add'l hr.

* Note: Frequent user rates vary. Check your local contact for details. For most services, monthly payments provide unlimited use.

Figure 5-1: The Line on On-line Services

Financing Your Venture

- ◆ Making an Honest Assessment
- ◆ Seeking Financial Help
- ◆ Types of Financing
- ◆ Credit Cards
- ◆ Safeguards

Making an Honest Assessment

Undercapitalized and hustling for money, too many entrepreneurs fall short of their expectations in the first year. Optimistic about their vision of success, confident in the value of their products and services, they open their doors with a smile and get ready for some hard work. And they usually know it will take hard work. What they don't know is that there may be no correlation whatsoever between cash flow and intense concentration on the business.

Your cash flow may have nothing to do with your focus. It's all about other people's money; if other people don't pay you on time, you're in trouble—unless you have a backup. This chapter is all about identifying and securing the money you'll need to give yourself some breathing room.

Start-up and First-year Costs

Do a careful estimate to determine how much money you'll need to get your business off the ground. Since your estimate will be your best guess, make sure you make it an educated one. When you get busy with customers, you *really* won't have time to stop and calculate all this. Do it as soon as possible. It will be much easier on you if you make your mistakes with a pencil and paper than with your checkbook.

Your early expenses fall into two general categories: start-up capital and working capital (start-up costs and stay-up costs). Start-up capital includes money used for purchases of equipment (e.g., computer, telephones, fax machines), supplies, furniture, fees, and so on. Working capital includes your routine business operating expenses.

Cash Flow

Debra Lessin, C.P.A., founder of D.J. Lessin & Associates, Inc., in Chicago, suggests that you estimate your monthly billing and monthly cash receipts to determine what your cash flow situation will be. "Don't expect your customers to pay you in thirty days. Be glad if they fit the sixty- to ninety-day limit," she cautions. If you base your cash flow projections on prompt payments, you'll always end up short. There are many day-to-day business expenses that we take for granted and pay by cash. Trips to the post office, stationery and office supplies, cab fare, tolls, and other auto expenses are usually paid out-of-pocket. When you're busy, these expenses accumulate rapidly. In addition, your vendors will need to be paid in a timely manner to keep your business in good standing. Often you will need to pay for materials and labor before you've ever made a sale.

When you are trying to concentrate on operating your business, negotiating with clients, pitching a new account, it is unnerving to have to stop and figure out how to

Checklist of Start-up Expenses

Item / Expense	Cost
registration fees	_____
licenses, permits, other miscellaneous fees	_____
legal expenses	_____
accountant fees	_____
office supplies (from staples to everything else)	_____
office equipment (miscellaneous)	_____
machinery	_____
cost of goods	_____
stationery	_____
brochures	_____
business cards	_____
furniture (desk, chair, shelving, etc.)	_____
office decor (rugs, paintings, lamps, etc.)	_____
electrical work (rewiring, new circuits, etc.)	_____
construction (adding walls, doors, etc.)	_____
professional association dues	_____
telephone (hardware and service fees)	_____
answering machine and voice mail service	_____
computer (CPU, monitor, and all other components)	_____
software	_____
modem	_____
printer	_____
fax machine	_____
cellular phone	_____
advertising (ads, flyers)	_____

Continues

Continued

other marketing costs
(announcements, promotional events, etc.) _____

postage _____

post office box _____

insurance _____

car (or change in car expenses) _____

education (seminars, workshops, books, tapes) _____

consulting fees and other contract work _____

other (itemize) _____

Figure 6-1: Checklist of Start-up Expenses

pay for each and every expense that crops up. It is a distraction that interferes with your effectiveness and can undermine your confidence. Have a plan for your first year so that you don't have to stop and look for money when you're on a roll.

Figure 6-1 is a checklist of start-up expenses to consider for your business. Use this to get going, then see if you need to add to it.

Recurring monthly expenses will include many of the items listed above (with the exception of one-time installation, registration, construction, furniture, and equipment purchases). Additional expenses to consider on a monthly basis include:

- ◆ personal salary
- ◆ employee salaries
- ◆ independent contractor fees
- ◆ payroll taxes
- ◆ employee benefits
- ◆ travel and auto expenses
- ◆ cleaning/maintenance
- ◆ cost of materials
- ◆ deliveries
- ◆ cost of supplies

- ◆ monthly service fees (on-line service, cellular phone)
- ◆ additional telecommunication service charges (call waiting, call forwarding, etc.)
- ◆ other

If you calculate your monthly expenses over a twelve-month period, you'll have a better sense of exactly what is involved in running the business. It is usually more than you think. (See the appendix for a sample "Pro Forma Cash Flow Statement.")

Seeking Financial Help

You should plan to finance as much of the start-up cost of your business as possible yourself. Not only will prospective lenders and investors expect you to, but it builds credibility in your venture. After all, if you're not willing to put your own money into it, why should anyone else?

Your savings, investment income, or retirement funds are possible sources. So are your credit cards. But your safest strategy, before drawing on savings or investments, is to first consult with your accountant.

Types of Financing

There are two kinds of financing: debt and equity. Whether you select one form or the other is more than a matter of money. Control is an even greater concern. With debt financing, you owe money but you control the business. With equity financing, you give up some of that control. Can you give up some control? How well do you listen to other people?

Debt Financing

When you borrow money from someone, you're into debt financing. You will repay the debt with interest. The interest rate varies depending on loan duration, the state of the economy, and the source of the loan. Banks, credit companies and the Small Business Administration are sources of debt financing. If you're lucky, so are friends and family.

The interest rate and terms of payment are sometimes negotiable. You may want to stretch a large loan over a longer period of time than you would a small loan for a short-term capital need.

Questions About Financing Your Business

When you go for financing, be able to answer these key questions about yourself and your business:

1. How much money do you need?

2. How much money will *you* contribute? What is your investment in this business?

3. How much collateral can you offer?

4. What sort of person are you? What is your credit history? Business track record?

5. Is this business a good idea considering today's economic climate?

6. How will the money (from the loan, venture capital investment, etc.) be used?

7. What net income do you expect per year from this business?

8. Can you draw a salary? Is it adequate?

9. Can you reinvest money in the business for growth?

10. Do you need additional capital? Where will you go for it?

Figure 6-2: Questions About Financing Your Business

Equity Financing

Equity financing requires that you give up a percentage of control in your business. Investors are interested in the return on investment you can offer them. How much control will you have to give up? It depends on how risky your business appears to the investor, how much money you seek, and how much management control the investor wants.

Venture capital firms and wealthy individuals ("angels") who invest in new businesses are other sources of equity financing. Angels find tax advantages in these investments that are more beneficial than stocks and bonds or more traditional investments. Venture capitalists are most likely to be attracted to skillful entrepreneurs who can articulate their business plans. Venture capitalists want both the right product and the right person when they make their decision.

The amount of venture capital money available today has been estimated to be close to $35 billion. The amount of angel money available has been estimated to be five times greater than that. But for every 100 business plans venture capitalists see per week, they will probably meet with only 50 percent of the entrepreneurs seeking financing and will make only about five deals per year.

To prepare yourself to present your business plan, go a step beyond the written materials. Make that plan come alive. Rehearse your presentation. You'll get only one chance to make a first impression. Pay attention to the details. It's what separates the five selected from the 100 submitted.

Loans from Family and Friends

Accepting personal loans is a very personal decision, and so much depends on your past and present relationships. Loans from family and friends won't appear on your credit history, are available quickly, and have flexible scheduling. The advantages are numerous, but so are the complications. You have to live with the results.

Remember that whatever patterns your past relationship formed will be enhanced when you borrow money. The mere act of borrowing can be either a lifejacket or a noose. If your relative is stretched to the limit, but wants desperately to help you out, can you assume this responsibility? Can you be sure to pay the person back no matter what? If your friends are strongly opinionated, can they sit back and watch you run the company once they've put some cash into it? Think through the ramifications of this option as carefully as you think through the accounting aspects.

Home Equity Loans

A home equity credit line account can be your solution, but it's a risk you should assess very carefully. If you tie up this resource for your business, will you jeopardize your home and family if you need funds for a non-business emergency? Your accountant can help you analyze the pros and cons for your particular situation.

Bank Loans

To be considered for a bank loan, you need to have a business up and running successfully for at least three to five years. Bank loans for start-ups are worse than scarce—they're impossible. For an existing business that needs to borrow to grow, your chances of getting a loan are better; however, many commercial lenders are still reluctant to lend to small or new businesses that need small loans or long repayment schedules.

For existing businesses, two types of bank loans are available: term loans and lines of credit.

Term Loans

These loans are paid back in a variety of rates, terms, payment schedules, and payment methods. You can work with your bank to tailor the conditions to your company's business and financial condition. Term loans are appropriate for purchasing equipment and expanding your business. When you apply for a term loan, the bank will be interested in obtaining as much information about you as possible. Be prepared to show:

◆ business operating statements (3 to 5 years' worth)

◆ personal statements about you as a business owner

◆ income tax returns (not every bank requires these)

◆ life insurance to cover your debts in case you die

◆ buyout agreement if you have partners

◆ projections of the revenue you expect to generate from the equipment purchased with the money borrowed

◆ details about the purchase you intend to make (prices and descriptions)

Lines of Credit

These provide immediate access to cash and are best to fund needs such as accounts receivable and inventory. Short-term business lines of credit give you a high degree of flexibility in borrowing. The bank will be interested in knowing your current assets for repayment and collateral and will want to see your accounts receivable and accounts payable records.

Letters of Credit: Domestic and International

Your bank can help you buy goods on credit or enter into a contract requiring a bond or deposit through a Letter of Credit. An international letter of credit enables you to buy from foreign suppliers.

Federal, State, and Local Loan Funds

Governments at the federal and state levels have established special financial assistance programs for small businesses to make available financing that would not have been possible through traditional commercial lenders. When traditional business loans are not appropriate for you, determine if you qualify for other sources of funds: Small Business Administration (SBA) Loans and Economic Development Cooperative Financing.

SBA Loans

The SBA provides guaranteed, direct, or intermediate participation loans to small businesses to help them acquire equipment, facilities, and supplies. These loans can only be used to finance the start-up, operation, or expansion of a business. Funds for direct loans are very limited, available to certain borrowers, such as:

- ◆ Vietnam-era veterans and disabled veterans
- ◆ low-income business owners
- ◆ businesses located in areas of high unemployment
- ◆ handicapped business owners

Most assistance is provided through SBA guarantees of loans made by local banks. Some banks, designated as certified and preferred lenders, have special contacts with the SBA which speed up the administration process. These loans are difficult to obtain as a home-based business unless you have equipment to purchase; a service business would have difficulty qualifying.

How to Apply for SBA Loans

Your contact with the SBA should be through the district or regional office nearest you. (A listing of these offices can be found in the Appendix.) The application process is as follows:

1. First, try to get a loan from at least one bank. If you are turned down (for reasons other than repayment ability), ask if the bank would make the loan if it were guaranteed by the SBA.

2. The bank contacts the SBA to determine whether or not the loan meets SBA criteria. The bank makes the final decision and will make all the arrangements to secure the guarantee with the SBA.

3. If the bank refuses to make the SBA guaranteed loan, try another bank.

4. Closing costs (about 3 to 5 percent of the loan amount) must be paid by the borrower.

Types of SBA Loans

Two new loan programs were introduced recently and have been very popular with small business owners: the Green Line Revolving Line of Credit Program and LODOC (Low Documentation) Loan Program. A brief description of these and some of the other loan programs is presented in figure 6-3.

Contact the SBA office nearest you for the latest details on the full range of loan programs available and the terms of such loans. Your local Small Business Development Center (SBDC) may be able to guide you toward resources for the microloan program in your area. Programs like the microloan funds are designed to encourage economic development in the local community, so you will need to search close to home for a resource.

SBA Loan Programs Summary

Microloan Programs

- ◆ available through select microloan institutions around the country

- ◆ loans can be as small as a few hundred dollars or several thousand dollars (each lending institution controls its own program)

- ◆ SBA mandates that loans be made available to anyone within the specified lending area without a means test

- ◆ maximum payback period is six years

* Most of the following programs have a loan maturity of 25 years for real estate and equipment; 10 years for working capital:

Green Line Revolving Line of Credit Program

- ◆ provides up to five years of revolving credit

- ◆ makes it easier for small businesses to gain access to operating capital

LODOC (Low Documentation) Loan Program

- ◆ provides small loans up to $100,000

- ◆ makes it easier for small businesses to obtain loans too small to interest banks

Basic 7(a) Loans

- ◆ up to $150,000 for direct SBA loans; $750,000 for SBA share of loans made by approved participants

- ◆ other sources of financing, including personal assets, must be used first

Basic Guaranty Business Loans

- ◆ no limit to the loan amount, but the SBA cannot guarantee more than $750,000 to one business and affiliates

Basic Direct Business Loans

- ◆ made only by the SBA

- ◆ loan amounts up to $150,000

Small Guaranty Business Loans

- ◆ Commercial lenders (banks) and certified non-bank lenders can make these loans

- ◆ SBA's share of the loan cannot exceed $50,000

Continues

Continued

- ◆ interest rates are linked to the amount of the loan; lenders may charge higher rates on smaller loans

Rural Guaranty Business Loans

- ◆ small businesses operating in a designated rural area are eligible

- ◆ SBA cannot guarantee more than $750,000 to any one business

8(a) Certified Business Loans

- ◆ made by either SBA or banks

- ◆ you must be certified as an 8(a) company. These companies must be 51% owned by an individual who is "a socially or economically disadvantaged citizen."

- ◆ direct SBA loans up to $150,000; $750,000 limit on SBA guaranty share of loans made by approved participants.

Figure 6-3: SBA Loan Programs Summary

Export-Import Bank (EXIMBANK)

If the scope of your business is international, another option is available. EXIM-BANK is an independent government agency that provides export financing to large and small businesses and to potential exporters who have had difficulty obtaining working-capital loans from commercial lenders.

Credit Cards

Debra Lessin strongly believes in the credit card method of financing start-ups. "As a small home-based business owner today, your choices are very often (1) no cash, or (2) high-interest cash," she says. "When you have no cash, the credit card route will be your lifesaver." She admits that in an ideal world, low-interest loans would be a better alternative. "But the chances of a start-up home-based business securing a low-interest bank loan are slim," she feels.

To finance your business with credit cards requires some planning and ingenuity on your part. You're in the best position if you started accumulating cards while in a corporate job, used them frequently, paid them up quickly, raised your credit limits to the maximum, then paid up the balance to give you the most borrowing power.

Lessin recommends that you always shop around for the lowest interest rates. Alyssa Lebovic even suggests that you take advantage of all introductory "no annual fee" offers. "When the annual fee kicks in, cancel the card for another one," she said.

Debra Lessin offers an eleven-step guide (figure 6-4) to financing your business responsibly through credit cards.

Lessin's Lessons for Credit Card Financing

1. Apply for as many credit cards as you can when you have money.

2. Use them often.

3. Pay them off.

4. Get your credit limits raised.

5. Repeat Steps 2 to 4 until you reach each card limit.

6. Shop around for the cards with the lowest interest rates.

7. Apply for these cards, too.

8. Transfer your balance on the high-interest rate cards to the low-rate cards.

9. Pay only the minimum amount due on each card.

10. The minute your cash crunch eases, repeat Step 3.

11. Monitor changing interest rates and "no annual fee" offerings.

Figure 6-4: Lessin's Lessons for Credit Card Financing

How does Lessin think this flurry of activity will look on your next TRW report? Won't you appear to be spread too thin? Lessin replies, "Don't worry about credit checks showing that you have too many cards. You weren't going to get a bank loan anyway, remember? That's why you're using this approach."

Safeguards

If you are going to borrow money from any source, it will be important to have your financial records in the best possible shape. Although you may not plan to borrow money to start your business, you might need financial help to grow and strengthen it over time.

When you are going to borrow money, remember to

1. **Use an accountant.** Your financial statements should be professionally prepared.

2. **Prepare a business plan.** You will have to demonstrate that you have thought through not only the concept but also the implementation of your business.

3. **Keep your business records in excellent shape.** You'll have to show just about everything to gain credibility, including your bank account. Be sure your healthy performance is clearly visible.

4. **Prepare to present your case to a lender.** Make sure you have everything you need well in advance.

5. **Practice.** Before you meet with a lender that you strongly hope will help you out, practice on someone else—a friend or associate who knows the process well. Be sure you can answer every question with confidence and support documentation.

If you need to borrow money to get your business off the ground and handle your first-year expenses, you will need to write a business plan for most sources of financing, aside from the "friends and family borrowing plan" or the "credit card crunch" plan.

Beating the Business Plan Blues

If you are overwhelmed by the prospect of writing a business plan, take a course to help you through it.

◆ The National Association of Women Business Owners (NAWBO) offers a nationwide training program called EXCEL "Start Right" that can be a tremendous help. The course is 15 hours long, but if you take the course seriously, you can have your business plan completed in the five weeks it takes to complete the course.

◆ Local Small Business Development Centers (SBDCs) offer classes as well as personal consulting on business plan preparation.

◆ The Service Corps of Retired Executives (SCORE) runs workshops and privately counsels individuals.

Figure 6-5: Beating the Business Plan Blues

Marketing Strategies for Your Products and Services

- ◆ Marketing Strategy
- ◆ Marketing Musts
- ◆ On-line Marketing
- ◆ Sales Strategies
- ◆ Public Relations
- ◆ Advertising and Promotions
- ◆ Networking
- ◆ Commitment

Marketing Strategy

Your marketing strategy is the comprehensive approach your business will take to achieve your business objectives. Your marketing strategy integrates your marketing, sales, public relations, advertising, and promotions. Each component has its own special function and benefit; all aspects work together to enhance your image and impact.

Before you start paying for ad space, running events, printing up mass quantities of very expensive promotional materials, or hiring sales reps think about the big picture:

Who do you really want to appeal to?

What are you trying to sell?

Where is your market?

When are your potential customers likely to buy?

How can you reach them?

Each of these questions has a critical impact on the direction of your marketing strategy. Your answers to these questions will help you define an effective marketing plan. Keep a clear focus on what you are selling and who you are selling it to.

The components of your marketing strategy should all fit together well. These components include your range of services and products, your prices or rate structure, an advertising plan, public relations endeavors, promotional campaigns, and more. Think through your strategy and gather information about your market and your competition *before* you set your fee structure or book ad space.

If you provide a product, your packaging will be a crucial early consideration. If you are not a trained or talented designer, seek assistance for this. Packaging has a huge impact on the consumer's decision to buy.

If you provide a service, the "package" is you. Your company image should be defined before you begin any other marketing efforts. The image of a professional, such as an accountant, involves building a private practice that will be distinctly different from an advertising agency seeking clients in the fashion industry, for example. Your message should come across loud and clear. You are conservative. You are trendy. You are focused on the environment. You are flashy. You are cost-conscious. You are extravagant. Friendly. High-tech. You are going to look schizophrenic if you try to project too many images at the same time. Keep it simple for your market. Be consistent. Your marketing efforts, your sales pitch, public relations activities, advertising, and promotional campaigns should be supportive of one another and of your image.

Your business goals, as defined in chapter 3, should guide the direction of your marketing strategy. In order to define the elements of this strategy, try to conceptualize your new business in great detail.

Marketing is one area in which assistance is offered through a wide variety of sources. At its best, it is a specialized field where you can quickly learn a lot by listening to experts. Your local Small Business Development Center (SBDC) offers workshops on marketing and publications and reference materials at little or no cost to you. It will have consultants on staff or readily available to help you out. Self-help business books are also available in abundance on every aspect of your marketing plan. The reference section and bibliography of this book list several current sources, including some best-sellers, that are great to get you started or to rejuvenate an existing business. The "guerrilla books" are among the best for simple and affordable solutions. My purpose in this chapter is to outline the basics. From this point, determine where you need the most help, then check the reference section for specifics.

There are some marketing experts who vow that marketing a home-based business is distinctly different from marketing a business with a formal outside office. Other experts say there is absolutely no difference in strategy; your strategy is based on your target market segment and niche. Not to mention your budget. From my experience working with home-based businesses, I have seen more similarities than differences. However, the differences are important. Here are some points to keep in mind when marketing a home-based business.

1. Do not highlight location in any promotional materials. Many corporate executives are still not ready to accord home-based business the same standing as traditional businesses. This is changing rapidly, but I believe it is still too soon to put an obviously residential neighborhood address (Cozy Court, Absolutely Adorable Avenue, etc.) on a letterhead that will cross a corporate executive's desk.

2. Recognize that the quality of your materials must be better-than-average. Design the best you can afford and think of how to make it look even better. Then do whatever you can to achieve this look.

3. Never let your public relations efforts slip. Without recognition in the media, a home-based business can get lost in the shuffle. There's no internal corporate support network to recognize your outstanding performance.

4. Make networking a high priority. Of course that's true for any business, but a home-based business could perish without it.

As you define your marketing strategy, you will follow these steps in detail:

◆ Define your customer target.

◆ Define your source of business.

◆ Define, refine, and redefine your sales pitch.

◆ Create the materials needed to implement your marketing plans: brochures, articles, business cards, promotional materials.

◆ Create the materials to implement your public relations plans: press releases, articles, news features.

◆ Create an advertising campaign for print, radio, and television. Establish your budget.

◆ When that budget explodes, go back to the public relations step again—most of us swear by that approach anyway, much to the dismay of advertising sales staffs.

Some of the most common ingredients of home-based business marketing strategies are:

◆ Innovative logo, letterhead, company brochure—a good fit among all of these is essential

◆ Personal sales calls—a good way to find out for yourself what the customer thinks

◆ Newsletters—you can look like a big company even if you aren't by the use of a creative newsletter

◆ Networking—to stay connected professionally and to build prospects and referrals

◆ Public relations work—giving speeches, running workshops and seminars, gaining exposure in the trade press, being featured in an article, volunteering in a community activity

◆ Trade show exhibits—renting a table to display your product can be a good way to attract attention quickly. Sharing a table with another small business could reduce your costs.

Marketing Musts

The following four activities help you organize your efforts in the most effective direction.

Carve Out Your Product and Service Offerings

This will help you define your market niche. What will *you* offer that is distinctly different (better, less expensive, faster, higher quality, etc.) from *your competitors*? Why should anyone buy from you? What market share can you seek?

Define Your Customers

What *type* of individuals and/or businesses do you plan to serve? Start by answering in general terms (professionals, service companies, manufacturers, retailers, etc.); then try to be very specific. Spell out the demographics—age, sex, income, and so on. When you clearly define the population you hope to sell to, you'll have a better view of what services they require. Where do they spend their free time? What activities are they involved in? This information leads you to details about what they read (therefore, where you'll want publicity and advertising coverage), where they hang out (for promotions and appearances), what they watch and listen to (if television and radio spots are on your mind). Then *go out and ask them what they want—don't try to guess.* Find out what they really *need.* If your market is local (and where *is* local, anyway?), your small local newspapers offer affordable ad packages; chambers of commerce and professional organizations have newsletters that offer insert opportunities. But if you don't know *exactly where your market is*, you can't determine what your market reads.

Create Your Pitch

Define precisely what "your product/service attributes" mean so that your product or service comes alive for your prospective clients. Make it *so* important that they will no longer want to live or work without it. Appeal to their individual needs.

Set Prices for Profits

The goal of your business is to make a profit. Many home-based businesses fail to make a profit because they don't price properly. Know what your competition charges, and determine if you should be less than, equal to, or higher priced. Be sure for product pricing that you have covered your materials, labor, and overhead costs. Don't forget shipping, handling, or storage in the total price. Service, like consulting, can be difficult to pinpoint. Some products and services will fall into an "hourly" rate structure; others are better suited to a "service fee." If you provide a service, you may even be "on-call" for a monthly service fee. Remember that small businesses often do not have big budgets, so if this is your market, your pricing decisions will have to take into account what your market will bear. Learn what your competition charges.

On-line Marketing

The *Harvard Business Review* created the term "marketspace" to describe today's phenomenon of marketing in cyberspace. The greatest advantage of this form of marketing is that it offers a home-based business the same ability as a huge corporation to present a pitch. The costs are as low as about $9.00 for monthly service, with hourly rates as low as $3.50. Compare that to a business sales trip and phone calls, and you can see that the benefits to small business are great.

In chapter 5, we reviewed some options for on-line services and linking up to the World Wide Web. The move to explore marketing possibilities on the Web is evolving rapidly, and conditions change daily. Be sure you select a service that you can work with, i.e., one you can learn to use. Many businesses have decided to bypass services like America Online and Prodigy and start right up on the Web.

To conduct electronic commerce from the convenience of your home-based computer is quite an appealing prospect. You will quickly find that advertising is not permitted in the bulletin boards of most special interest ("discussion") groups of the on-line services. Classified ads are permitted, but these won't appear in the interest group area.

On-line marketing creates concerns that are unique to this form. Consider the following:

◆ Learn the culture of the Internet and absorb as much information as possible about the communication patterns of different groups.

◆ You should not assume that advertising will be welcomed by the group or groups you are addressing. Even if it seems that this group represents your target market, the group norms may dictate that selling is off-limits.

◆ Learn what your target groups consider acceptable. Each group is different.

◆ A soft-sell through provision of free advice or information may get by.

◆ Do not send unsolicited E-mail to groups that don't like this method. My first attempts to collect data for this book were quickly suppressed—and not very delicately—on Prodigy by an overzealous custodian of correctness. (I've since switched to America Online.) Watch out or you'll get your hand slapped, too.

◆ Always make your purpose clear if you are gathering market research data on-line. Get permission.

◆ Be prepared to handle a possible high volume of responses. If you have approached a group that accepts this form of marketing, your response could be terrific.

◆ Be careful about security. You don't want someone else using all your data or new customers.

The best way for you to learn what will work for you will be to try different approaches. Track your results as you would any marketing technique. Measure whether or not this form of marketing gets results for you. Find out before you depend too heavily on this strategy.

In summary, remember to:

1. Sell softly.

2. Broadcast to the best groups for your goals.

3. Entice by offering a sample of your specialty.

4. Set up a signature. Pass out an electronic business card.

5. Network via the network. All networking rules apply (e.g., don't monopolize the conversation).

Sales Strategies

When your business is new, you will be the most influential salesperson for your company, whether or not you enjoy selling. Your pitch is from the heart, and sincerity and honesty may open doors for you in the beginning. You are responsible for the success of your business, so no one could be more committed to selling than you. You know all there is to know about what you're selling, so you can counter any objections spontaneously.

As the owner of the business, you can inspire confidence in your customers. This confidence is contagious. You can also negotiate on the spot. Deals that no one else could authorize can come from you. The personal touch is also an important distinction between you and bigger businesses. It is your advantage over your larger competitors.

Experts agree that the best tactics for selling are subtle.

Learn to Use the Phone Effectively

Remember to monitor your tone and volume carefully, since this is all you have. On the telephone, you have no body language or great wardrobe to bail you out. Your voice stands alone.

Identify the Key Decision Maker

Find out who the decision makers are for your product or service and get to those individuals. Don't waste time with people who can't make decisions. Have a brief pitch (about 25 words) to open a conversation and identify the reason for your call. Get an appointment for a personal meeting.

Follow Calls with a Brief Letter

A cover letter to introduce yourself and a one-page attachment to summarize your pitch may help to set the stage before a meeting. If you can't reach a particular contact by phone, a letter (faxed or mailed) may open the communication channels for you. You can then honestly say, "Ms. Smith is expecting my call . . ." when a secretarial screen attempts to shut you out.

Focus on Your Customer

Concentrating on your customers and learning how you can meet their needs, or solve specific problems, will make your approach to sales most effective. Listen. Ask open-ended questions to elicit maximum information.

Highlight the Benefits

Present your product or service in terms of the customer's needs rather than as a recitation of a list of your product's features.

Close the Sale as Soon as Possible

Do this without being pushy, that is. Learn to sense the proper time to ask for the sale so that you don't overtalk.

Ask for Referrals

Referrals from satisfied customers can be a great source of sales prospects and future clients.

If you have never sold for a business before, don't be discouraged. You've had practice selling throughout your life, and you've done it without thinking. If you've ever tried to convince anyone about anything, you've had a dose of sales.

Learn fundamental sales techniques *fast*. Pick up whatever information you can from books and tapes. Listening to tapes in your car can be a good use of your time and can be especially helpful when you are driving to meet potential customers.

Even if you plan to hire sales representatives as the business grows, you'll need to understand the process of selling your product or service in order to refine your pitch and support materials. If your approach doesn't work, you have to readjust quickly. You won't know until you've tried it.

Public Relations

Activities that show your strengths and the terrific qualities of your business in a newsworthy way can be of more value in the long run than the most expensive advertising campaign. Public relations campaigns strive to build credibility in the marketplace through routes that are more discreet.

Seek opportunities for press coverage of your work and your accomplishments whenever you can. The impact of public relations is cumulative. You won't see immediate results in most cases, so consistency is critical. A simple press release, preferably one-page, accompanied by a photo, can gain more visibility for you than an advertisement if the newspapers pick it up.

Press releases should be interesting, "newsworthy," concise, and sent to the right person. Watch the newspapers carefully to determine who is the correct contact for your press release. The "Business Editor" generally receives huge numbers of releases. If a specific reporter tends to cover stories about your industry or interests, try addressing the release to that individual instead.

The media brings you into the broader public view than your advertising can. It is your way to reach larger numbers in less time. Use it wisely.

Send your press releases to:

1. Weekly newspapers—reporters are always looking for great new stories.

2. Daily newspapers—usually want only a local twist, so stay close to home unless it's a national story.

3. Wire services—seek up-to-the-second news items, so move quickly if you have a hot item to report.

4. Magazines—offer a chance to look like an expert, but you will need longer lead time. Plan ahead.

5. Radio—attracts the attention of both the mobile and the sedentary. A guest spot can boost you into a whole new spectrum.

6. Television—the most important medium to be prepared for. Take the time to learn how to present yourself on television to make effective use of the incredible power of this medium. With television, you need to be concise and controlled, speaking in soundbites to be sure your point gets across the way you want it to and isn't edited out.

You can prepare your own press kit or hire a marketing consultant to help you out. Your press kit should build your credibility as an expert in your field or profession. It should include a biography (short and directed to events that are significant today), a photo (headshot, 8×10 or 5×7 black-and-white), your brochure, and copies of articles that have quoted or featured you.

The press kit doesn't accompany every press release. It is used to introduce yourself as a resource, as an "expert" available when members of the media need a resource for quotes, opinions, inside information, validation, and more.

Advertising and Promotions

Advertising and promotions are the most potentially expensive investments of your marketing strategy. Because of the high costs involved, the efforts should be researched thoroughly before you begin. This is not an area for amateurs. If you hire no other consultants, and you know you need to advertise your business, hire someone with advertising expertise. The standards today are very high, even in the smallest local papers. Graphics, photos, layouts, text, and design have to be completely professional for a positive impact.

If you can pinpoint your target market in the finest detail, you can specify precisely where your ad campaign should be located. Size, timing, duration, and frequency all come into play. Don't advertise by trial and error. Get guidance from an expert.

Networking

Networking can mean the difference between isolation and involvement for anyone, but for home-based businesses it takes on a particularly significant role. It replaces the water-cooler and coffee-pot contact that occurs daily in every corporate office. Networking is by definition a supportive system of sharing information and services among individuals and groups having a common interest. Networking will keep you in contact with the outside world, help you avoid isolation and stagnation, and build your business contacts for current and future plans.

Networking is a two-way street, an *exchange* of information. Real networking requires that you do *more* than reach out to give and receive business cards. *Give* a little information and *get* a sincere grasp of what one another's skills are. Then you've *really* reached out.

A few basic networking rules to remember include:

1. **Work the room.** Don't linger too long in one conversation. About 5 to 10 minutes per contact is enough.

2. **Ditch the dogs.** Sorry, it sounds nasty, but your time is limited. Don't be cruel, but don't be caught with a bore (see "not-networking" below).

3. **Keep the cards.** Write a key point about the person whose card you've taken on the back of the business card so you'll remember later. Don't just exchange business cards.

4. **Keep the contacts alive.** Pick up a hint of how you and others can honestly work together and offer one another leads. After you've met someone new, pick up the phone to call to keep the contact alive. Send a brief note. Follow up on the contacts you've made, even if these contacts are businesses or individuals who can't immediately help you. Someday they might.

5. **Beware of not-networking.** Not-networking occurs when someone who approaches you about business contacts wants to do all the talking *and* all the taking. Not-networking is one-way in the wrong direction. So beware if any conversation has gone too far before the speaker says, "Tell me something about *you*. . . ." If you are speaking with someone who hasn't asked about your business or reason for living, this individual is saying, "Give me your time to hear about *me*." Give me a lead. Give me a referral. Give me your business. Give *me* a break!

You will need to become involved in several levels of networks to provide contacts for yourself within the business community at large, your peer group of professionals, your local community, and the world in which you live.

Involvement in some organization at each of these levels of networks will provide public relations opportunities that will not develop from within your own home. Following are a few ideas to get you started in each of these four areas. Chapter 14 and the appendix provide details about how to contact specific resources to make connections in organizations and associations that can help you.

The Business Community

Small-Business Organizations

Small-business organizations offer the potential for small business owners to pull together for a bigger impact. The impact can be political, as it is in organizations whose mission is to lobby, or it can be economic, as in those organizations that emphasize member benefits and discounts. In larger numbers there is certainly more influence. As a member of these groups, you may qualify for corporate rates on products and services, special discounts, and/or group rate health insurance. Examples include the National Association for the Self-Employed (NASE), National Small Business United (NSBU), and a host of local home-based business support groups.

For Business Owners—Various

It is a comfort to know that other business owners share your concerns and interests. The organizations mentioned above are very large national groups. Subsets of the business community may find what they need in other organizations, and often it's a good idea to join more than one if time and finances permit. The National Association of Women Business Owners (NAWBO), for example, is designed for women business owners of any size firm. NAWBO has statewide chapters that independently run monthly meetings and events as well as a strong nationwide offering of conferences and workshops. New corporate discount packages are made available fairly often as this group draws the attention of major corporate sponsors.

Industry Organizations

These groups often combine large corporations and small businesses, offering the home-based business owner an opportunity to meet with representatives from big businesses. If your home-based business does not keep you in contact with a wide range of businesses on a regular basis, seek out the organizations near you that will. In New Jersey we have a statewide Chamber of Commerce and a regional Commerce and Industry Association, for example.

Your Peer Group of Professionals

Professional Associations

Professional associations are your link with other business leaders or owners, prospective customers/clients, sales leads, and sources for general business information. Membership fees vary, and benefits of membership include a wide range of products/services, such as membership directories, newsletters and other publications, discounts, group rates for programs, educational opportunities, and more. Membership in these groups serves a different purpose for you. These groups are your resource for new information in your profession, mentors, support resources when your business grows and you need to hire help, virtually or actually. You may find it difficult to sell here, especially if you're among a group all selling the same thing. But you will absolutely need these contacts. And if you achieve a leadership position, you can also achieve public recognition. Not bad for public relations purposes.

Trade Associations

For almost anything you do, there's a group you can join. You'll learn the secret handshake for your peer group with the same credentials as yours, just as in professional associations. Membership rates and offerings vary. Monthly and annual meetings can help to keep you current in your own field and help you find the best suppliers, vendors, and other contacts for your work. But the same word of caution applies here as above—you may not be closing sales deals within a group of your peers, but you need these contacts to thrive. As a leader, your opportunity for public recognition in your field will help you grow your business.

The Community

Civic Organizations

A home-based business gives you the best opportunity to become active in local community and civic groups. As a commuter to a different city, it is always more difficult to find time for local interests. Your local Chamber of Commerce is a good start. Local chambers will promote their own members' products and services over those of anyone else in the community. They will often publish their own directory and run their own schedule of business functions. If the mission of the group doesn't track with your objectives, keep the time you spend to a minimum but don't be a stranger. Let your specialty be well known and define your area of expertise so that referrals will be passed your way. Lead a workshop. Be a speaker at a meeting.

Volunteer Activities

The local hospital, schools, libraries, and colleges have an endless list of tasks for their volunteers, their auxiliary groups. Fundraising activities are usually a top priority. Volunteer to help with a task that offers you an opportunity to demonstrate your skill and talent. In this way, you'll not only help the organization, but also promote your talent through demonstration of your abilities.

Your World

National Focus

Watch for events and opportunities that can bring you in contact with a wide range of people around the country, even if your business is geared to your local community.

You can do a better job of serving *any* market you select if you are in touch with the outside world. In 1995, for example, about 2,000 representatives from all over the country met in Washington, D.C., for the 1995 White House Conference on Small Business. I was elected to represent New Jersey along with about 30 other delegates. The conference was characterized by diversity, in the nature of the businesses represented and in the scope of their concerns. Our mission was to select 60 top-priority recommendations from hundreds of issues identified at state and regional conferences throughout the year. Small-business owners agreed to send Congress and President Clinton an exceptionally wide-ranging list of policy recommendations. The final list included day-to-day survival issues as well as hopes for the future. Regulatory relief, lower taxes, and improved financing scored high on the final "wish list," but were not to be outranked by the very practical concern of the meals-and-entertainment tax deduction.

In this process, delegates were able to work to change legislation and build business contacts for the future at the same time. Meetings started as early as 6:00 A.M. and as late as midnight. Small group caucuses and coalitions met around the clock in preparation for the formal work sessions the following day. NAWBO and other nation-wide organizations met separately and together to identify their most important agenda items and to rally support. NAWBO's large representation at this conference gave women business owners a stronger voice than ever.

International Focus

As soon as you realize your business has potential beyond the borders of the United States, start making connections in the global community. Use the contacts of corporations that have already opened doors to gain introductions and entry into this rapidly growing area for opportunity. Seek the international organizations that will give you both support and recognition.

Commitment

Your degree of involvement in any organization should reflect the importance of this organization or association to your business success—unless, of course, you are joining for purely social reasons. The best use of your time, however, will be to find and focus on a few organizations that offer both business and personal satisfaction. Why waste your time? In a position of leadership in any type of organization you will give the most time but you will gain the best contacts. You will get to know the most people. You will have the most opportunity for media exposure.

If you know that one particular organization is a great source of direct leads for your business, work your way into an active role in the leadership of the group. Start by participating on a committee to get a sense of the group and the internal dynamics. Determine how you can volunteer your time in a way that also provides you with an opportunity to showcase your skills. Your talents will be most visible to the group if you share them and help the association accomplish its goals. If you are only a name on a mailing list, you are less likely to be approached personally.

Chapter 14 and the appendix provide details about how to contact specific resources to make connections in these organizations and associations.

For many small-business owners, survival has come through four steps:

Use One Another

When you need a service, check out your network of sources and resources first. If you need advice, contact them. When you need a service, check out your network. When you need a product, buy from your network.

Partner with One Another

Partnering means becoming more involved in your clients' businesses and becoming partners with them. It involves saying "What can I do for you?"

Seed Prospects for Your Future

Get your name out now for contacts you can work with later.

Throw a Lifejacket

Help out other small businesses whenever you can. When you take a step forward, bring someone along with you:

- ◆ offer a referral
- ◆ act as a mentor
- ◆ extend encouragement
- ◆ provide a lunch for someone on a tight budget

We represent more than the secret to one another's survival. We are the secret to one another's *success.*

Expanding Your Potential and Building Your Image

- ◆ The Reality of Virtual Corporations
- ◆ Simple Joint Ventures
- ◆ Virtual Staff
- ◆ Image

The Reality of Virtual Corporations

One of the hottest new trends in entrepreneurial growth is the virtual corporation, offering a great way for any small business to expand into larger markets. In a virtual corporation, which is by definition a temporary network, different businesses can pool the best of their individual resources to take advantage of a specific market opportunity. All parties contribute what they are best at—their core competencies or key capabilities. The enterprise disbands when the market need disappears.

The concept of a virtual corporation has heightened appeal because it emphasizes speed of implementation and a dynamic response to a target market segment need. For start-up companies, a virtual corporation offers an opportunity to seek business beyond the scope of their own limited resources. On the other hand, small businesses will also have the most to lose if the endeavor fails.

"It is important to protect your own interests in any type of joint enterprise," cautions Fred Nicoll, a litigation attorney with offices in Paramus, New Jersey, and New York City. These kinds of business arrangements are not really new. In the nineteenth century they were known as *joint ventures*. "Whether you describe the business opportunity as a joint venture, strategic alliance, or virtual corporation, you should know what the potential problems are so that you will be prepared, not surprised."

Nicoll has had firsthand experience dealing with joint efforts that have gone awry. He has represented partners in enterprises that went from honeymoon to divorce in spite of their initial bliss and enthusiasm. Nicoll advises that a framework be established from the onset of formation of the virtual corporation, considering the following questions:

What is its purpose?

How will you share in the profits and losses?

What are the interests of each of the participants/partners?

How long will this enterprise last?

In defining a general framework, you must be aware of the special considerations that apply depending whether the firms involved are in the established or start-up phase. And even though there is no legal requirement for a written agreement in a virtual corporation, Nicoll strongly recommends that the parties involved put their ideas on paper. "The legal system will treat this entity in accordance with the actions and intent of the parties whether or not there is written documentation," said Nicoll. An agreement written in advance can offer clarification and protection for all involved, serving as an aid rather than as an impediment.

Nicoll offers an example of two friends, businessmen who became successful working for different large companies throughout their careers and eventually worked together in the same sales consulting firm. One left to develop a new product and start his own business, devoting about a year to development (i.e., no product, no sales). The second left, and after some discussion, it seemed a natural fit for the two to become partners in the new venture: one had a product to offer, and the other had sales and marketing expertise. They were instantly successful and made a great profit in their first year of operation. They worked from a verbal agreement.

For reasons of "personality," the founder said his partner wasn't carrying his weight and bringing in the sales he promised. According to Nicoll, "Perhaps the real problem was that the first guy decided he could keep all the profit for himself and not share it." After much wasted time, they decided to dissolve the partnership. A long process of determining who gets what followed.

They used arbitration, which was the fastest and least expensive option available, but the time and cost were still extremely high. "Worst of all," said Nicoll, "the resolution was something neither was happy with, but after arbitration no one had the ability to change it." If partners don't determine how to allocate business assets and liabilities, state law will gladly do it for them upon dissolution of the business.

"A well-drafted agreement is no guarantee of success, nor does the absence of an agreement ensure failure, but in case of trouble or disagreement the parties will wish they had one," said Nicoll.

If a virtual corporation is undertaken by established businesses, Nicoll recommends the followings steps be taken to clarify the venture from the start so as to avoid problems later:

1. Define the new enterprise.

    ◆ What is your mission? Specify what you're trying to accomplish.

    ◆ How long will it last?

2. Define the role of each participant.

    ◆ How will you decide who will make the decisions for the virtual corporation?

    ◆ Will parties have an equal say? Control and management of the virtual corporation will need to be spelled out as if the business were incorporated.

    ◆ How will you manage the overall operation? A management committee can oversee operations as well as act as the decision-making body.

3. Define the contributions of each party.

    ◆ Contributions may be financial (e.g., cash or capital, use of buildings or equipment), time and effort, personnel/staff, other.

4. Define how you will divide profits and losses.

   ◆ Will there be equal distribution or will you share in proportion to your investment?

   ◆ Don't wait until you're making money to discuss money. Profit and loss can be easily misunderstood.

5. Examine other requirements of this business.

   ◆ Are there new or additional licensing requirements, copyrights, trademarks?

6. Define how the business will be dissolved.

   ◆ Distribution of assets is only part of your concern. "Unscrambling the omelet" can involve many aspects of the business.

   ◆ Good will, for example, counts too.

For start-up businesses, Nicoll advises that these steps be taken with additional caution. "When you consider the fragility of start-ups in general, you want to protect the individual," he said. "It is even more important to know what the potential risks are, because there is little if any buffer to absorb a loss."

Business Week once described the virtual corporation as the business organization of the future. Experts predicted an explosion of virtual corporations in the next decade. Yet it appears that only a handful of small businesses have engaged in enterprises that really resemble a virtual corporation. As more businesses realize that a fast response to market demands need not preclude a responsible approach to business alliances, there may be a wider use of the virtual corporation. As always, the potential for business opportunity is limited only by imagination.

Simple Joint Ventures

If you are creative and ideas or designs are your specialty, manufacturing and distribution of your design can be handled by one or more companies under a wide variety of arrangements. If you are not in a financial position to invest up-front, take this process one step at a time. You will need to find someone who considers your design interesting enough to want to make it a reality. At that point, an agreement can be formulated, specifying each participant's role in design, manufacture, sales, and distribution of the product. You may ultimately form a partnership, joint venture, or virtual corporation. But all roles and responsibilities—including how you share profits and expenses—must be in writing for everyone's protection.

Virtual Staff

Sole proprietors and other small business owners operating from their own home offices, locally or long distance, join forces to meet specific project goals. Without the hassle of a large office and without the daily headaches of supervising a staff, you can have the advantages of extra power.

Image

After working for a while in a small business, we recognize that many corporate people still believe that bigger is better. Slowly small businesses are chipping away at this misconception. After all, we employ more than 54 percent of the nation's workforce, and many of us have been in business for over a decade. Yet we have to work against stereotypes for now. We face a marketing challenge: How to look big when you're not.

Has *anyone* benefited more from advances in technology than home businesses? Technology is our strongest ally in the campaign to build corporate credibility in a world dominated by takeovers. Support services also help create strength in our weak areas. Using the best image-building packages—from office suites to guerrilla marketing tactics—we defy the rules and *act* as big as we choose.

Experience has taught many of us that there are a few rules you must follow to strengthen your company image, build credibility, and offer the professionalism of a big firm:

1. Go for the best in telecommunications services. That means no home telephone lines for business, no busy signals, no tacky answering equipment, and no unplugged fax machines.

2. Get the best business cards, stationery, and handouts that are appropriate for your company. Have them professionally designed and use quality paper. Don't cut corners here.

3. Buy the best basic equipment you can afford, specific to your needs of course.

4. Get on-line. Be able to E-mail your tech-conscious clients and work with them at their level.

5. Don't use your home address. Use a P.O. Box if necessary.

6. Don't schedule professional meetings in your home. Book a conference room, executive suite, or shared office. Schedule a meeting over
   a meal in a restaurant if necessary.

7. No family background noises please!

8. Practice your telephone voice. Smile with your voice. Express enthusiasm. Sound convincing.

Honesty may be the best policy, but when you're trying to get your business off
the ground, these tips help.

Understanding Legal Logistics

- ◆ When You Need an Attorney
- ◆ Selecting Your Business Structure
- ◆ Sole Proprietorships
- ◆ Partnerships
- ◆ Limited Liability Partnerships (LLP)/Limited Liability Companies (LLC)
- ◆ Corporations
- ◆ Protecting Your Intellectual Property
- ◆ Litigation

When You Need an Attorney

What are the legal considerations of starting a new business? Should you operate as a sole proprietor, seek a compatible partner, or incorporate? Selection of the legal form of organization a business should take is one of the many critical decisions that make or break a new venture.

When should you involve an attorney in your business? An attorney can help you decide what business structure is most appropriate for you. Don't wait until you run into major problems to select your lawyer. Louise Reich, a Hackensack, New Jersey, attorney who works with many small business start-ups, suggests that many of your early business activities can benefit from legal counsel. Your relationships with landlords, vendors, distributors, employees, customers, and clients may in some cases benefit by written formalization.

Reich offers two guidelines to help you decide whether or not to seek legal counsel. "First, determine how familiar you are with the activity or situation," Reich advises. "Second, determine what level of risk you can tolerate." "If you have a track record with the relationship or situation," she explains, "then there may not be many unanticipated problems." But if the circumstances or parties are new, she advises that it is probably a good idea to contact your attorney. To summarize, call your attorney:

- ◆ to identify and set up the best business structure when you decide to start your business

- ◆ to see if your business structure and business relationships should change when your business changes

- ◆ to protect yourself if you are about to sign anything significant

- ◆ to protect your intellectual property rights if you have invented, designed, created, or written something new

- ◆ to have the business and financial records reviewed if you want to buy or sell a company

- ◆ to see if you can avoid suing or being sued

Selecting Your Business Structure

Each form of legal organization has advantages and disadvantages. It is important to think through the options carefully. Many people make their decision about business form without weighing the consequences. Often sole proprietors neglect to incorporate because they view it as an expensive and cumbersome process. Business partnerships sometimes arise from the convenience of social friendships. Some individuals may incorporate unnecessarily, when in reality they are independent professionals. Liability exposure, management control, initial financial investments, as well as the tax implications of one structure compared to another, are certainly important to consider.

The major considerations of each form of business structure are discussed below. Figure 9-2 summarizes the advantages and disadvantages of each structure in chart format for easy reference. (See chapter 10 for a review of this material from an accounting and tax perspective.)

Reich's Reality Check

Factors to Consider in Choosing a Business Structure

1. Participation and Control

    Who will operate the business on a daily basis?
    Who will manage the business?
    Who will make broad decisions and/or long term plans?

2. Financing and Start-up

    What resources do you need to start the business: money, expertise, contributions-in-kind?
    Where will these resources come from: bank, personal resources, friends and family, employees?

3. Longevity of Enterprise

    How long do you expect the business to continue?
    How quickly must dissolution be completed?

4. Taxation

    Form of business chosen will determine how business is taxed and how profits and losses are treated.

5. Liability/Exposure

    How great is your potential exposure?
    How important is it to limit your liability?
    What level of personal risk can you tolerate?

6. Work Style/Operation of Enterprise

    Are you willing/able to share decision making?
    Can you delegate authority?
    Are you good at record keeping?
    What is your attitude toward paperwork?

Figure 9-1: Reich's Reality Check: Factors to Consider in Choosing a Business Structure

Sole Proprietorships

A sole proprietorship, with its simple legal structure, informal management, minimal paperwork and record keeping, offers an immediate appeal for the start-up professional. The sole proprietor must file a trade name with the county clerk. The business does not have a separate tax status, so business income and expenses are reflected on the personal tax return. "But the sole proprietor is not a separate legal entity, and you are personally liable for all debts, accidents, and actions related to the business," cautions Frederick A. Nicoll, a Paramus, New Jersey, and New York City–based litigation attorney.

Sole proprietorships offer the advantage of ease of formation, because all you need to do is file with the county clerk to get started. Duration of the sole proprietorship is as long as you want. And there is no legal limit on the type or size of business you can operate. You can maintain the structure of sole proprietorship even when you hire employees. However, you must be active as proprietor in order for the business to continue to exist.

Filing Requirements:

1. Certificate of assumed name—obtain from the county clerk's office

2. Local licenses and permits

3. Professional licenses

4. Sales tax permits—if you are selling a product (see chapter 10 for details)

5. Federal Employer Identification Number (EIN)—if you hire people, you'll need to fill out an SS4 (see chapter 10)

6. Circular E—government guidelines on all payroll taxes (see chapter 10)

7. State REG-1—to register business with division of taxation; you will be assigned a state tax identification number

8. Employee taxes and insurance, including state unemployment compensation, workers' compensation, and federal and state tax withholding

The Five Ways to Set Up Your Business: Their Pros and Cons

	Sole Proprietor	**General Partnership**
Why choose one form of business over another?	This is the most basic form of doing business. As one tax analyst puts it, "You keep all the profits and accept the entire risk of loss. It is capitalism at its most basic." Best for very small businesses and in early start-up phases when you intend to grow large.	You create this structure by an agreement which can be oral but which should be in writing (often with the aid of lawyers to avoid unnecessary troubles). The agreement should, among other things, set forth the respective ownership interests of the partners, the extent of each partner's investment in the business and other important matters. The number of general partnerships has declined as more businesses form LLCs and LLPs.
How complicated is it to create and operate?	You need take no formal action, merely start doing business. However, your municipality or state might require various licenses, depending on the nature of the business, and where it's being operated.	Because so many forms must be plugged into the agreement — including the rights and obligations of each partner, what happens if a partner dies, and so forth —a partnership can be more complicated than it might initially appear. With so much to consider, it's a good idea to have a lawyer advise you on the issues and to prepare and negotiate the agreement. In terms of running the business, note that partners can have differing views of what it should be or the feeling that one person is doing more work than the others
What tax issues should I consider?	You report business profits or losses on an individual tax return. On Schedule C you list business income and take deductions for expenses. The net profit is then taxed at personal income tax rates —federally from 15 to 39.6 percent. If you lose money, you cannot deduct losses but can carry them forward to the next tax year. Should you make a profit that next year, you deduct the previous year's (or years') losses from profit (as long as it doesn't reduce your net business income to less than zero).	Although it is not taxed as a single entity, total profits and losses are tallied for the business. Each partner then files an individual tax return (using Schedule K-1) that includes the amount of his respective tax liability and is taxed accordingly. Setting up retirement plans becomes complicated because all partners must agree on the type of plan or no plan might be possible.

C Corporation

By incorporating your business, you create an entity that is separate and distinct from you as an individual. Special laws and taxes apply to any corporation. A C corporation (the standard type) may not be the best structure for a small business, especially one in start-up phase. The formalities are many, and the tax consequences may leave less money in your pocket. Moreover, liability protection can also be found in a limited liability company or a subchapter-S corporation. However, if your business is growing large and you want to raise money through the sale of stock, a C corporation may be the way to go.

To incorporate, you must file articles of incorporation, create corporate by-laws, and fulfill other state requirements. Stock must be issued, even if you're the sole shareholder. If you commingle corporate and personal assets or otherwise fail to conduct the corporation as a separate and distinct entity, you may lose your right to limited liability (a primary reason for forming a corporation).

The business reports income on a corporate tax return, separate from shareholders' returns. Also, regardless of profitability, many states have minimum taxes that are owed by corporations. Shareholders will be taxed for dividends received, and of course any salaries from the corporation will be taxed at individual rates. Corporate tax returns are more complicated than individual ones, which generally means higher fees paid to a tax professional. On the other hand, corporations are usually taxed at a slightly lower rate than individuals—34 percent maximum versus 39.6 percent.

Subchapter-S Corp.

To combine corporate liability protection with the tax aspects of a partnership, consider this popular structure. There are, however, restrictions as to who may participate, which can be problematic when raising capital. For example, in addition to the limited number of shareholders, a foreign national may not hold subchapter-S stock.

Creating a subchapter-S corporation is about as complicated as forming a C corporation (see left).

Shareholders are taxed as if they were in a partnership and file individual rather than corporate tax returns.

Limited Liability

This relatively new business structure is currently permitted in 35 states, including Florida, Texas, and New Jersey, but not (as of July 1994) New York, California, or Ohio. A limited liability company (LLC) has the limited liability of a corporation, but the flexibility and tax status of a partnership. That makes it an up-and-comer in business circles. A structure in a few states, such as Utah and Delaware, is the limited liability partnership (LLP). Within a year or two, all states will permit LLCs and most will permit LLPs.

A filing must be made with the appropriate state authorities. Usually this consists of the articles of organization and the operating agreement. It is important to pay meticulous attention to detail when creating this structure, so you should retain an attorney who understands your state's specific laws.

In fact, tax liability is the same as in a partnership. The IRS has, for the most part, accepted the LLC, but be sure to ask if the law in your state has been approved. You report profits and losses on a personal, rather than corporate tax return.

Continues

Continued from page 145

	Sole Proprietor	**General Partnership**
Would my assets be at risk if I'm found liable for a problem?	You are personally liable for every business debt as if you had incurred such liabilities as personal expenses. That means all of your personal and business assets are at risk.	Each partner is personally responsible for all of the business liabilities of the partnership and even for the individual liabilities incurred by partners during the course of partnership activities. Each partner's personal assets are potentially at risk. If a bill isn't paid, you can be made to pay the entire amount if your partners are unable to pay their respective shares.
How easy is it to raise money?	Most banks and other lending entities will require personal collateral (home equity or other valuables). Too often, capital is generated only from your personal resources — by borrowing on credit cards or from family.	Partners contribute time, money or property to receive equity interest. These contributions must be tracked and will have ramifications for each partner. Borrowing from banks or other lending sources is as problematic as for sole proprietors; personal collateral is often necessary.
What happens to my business if I sell, become disabled or die?	You have no separately existing business entity. Thus, if you die or become incapacitated, your business goes with you. Selling is a bit more feasible — but only if you have an established service business or a readily assumed product-based business. All this makes estate planning vital for sole proprietors.	Partners can provide for the contingency of another's death, incapacity or desire to sell his equity in the partnership agreement or in a buy/sell agreement. For example, a buy/sell agreement can say that upon death, the dead partner's heirs will receive the proceeds of a life insurance policy taken out for that purpose, and, in return, lose all rights, title, and interest in the partnership business.

C Corporation	Subchapter-S Corp.	Limited Liability
Limited liability for shareholders is a vital benefit. Under normal circumstances, a corporate owner's liability is limited to funds invested in purchasing stock. Stockholders cannot be held personally liable for corporate actions, and creditors are limited to corporate assets when seeking to collect money owed.	As with a C corporation, there is no stockholder liability beyond the assets of the corporation.	As the name implies, liability is limited to the assets of the LLC.
Corporations have a method of raising money not available to other types of business structures — selling stock to the public. Furthermore, with a standard C corporation, there are no limits as to who can own stock or to the number of shareholders, thereby maximizing the potential access to capital.	A subchapter-S corporation can have up to 35 stockholders. That enhances its ability to raise working capital. However, if you wish to offer shares to investors at large, you will have to form a standard C corporation.	The problem of securing capital is the same as that of a general partnership, which means your revenue options are limited because you cannot raise money through shareholders.
Once formed, a corporation continues in existence until formally shut down. Thus, if a key player in the corporation dies, formal action by the corporation is not required; ownership will pass to the heirs. Also, under most circumstances, stockholders can sell their stock whenever and to whomever they please.	A subchapter-S corporation offers the same flexibility as a C corporation (see left).	You will have to engage in succession planning, as you do in a general partnership (see left).

Figure 9-2: "The Five Ways to Set Up Your Business: Their Pros and Cons,"
reprinted with permission from **Home Office Computing** *magazine.*

Partnerships

Partnerships offer an excellent way to pool both assets and talent. Reporting and accounting are relatively uncomplicated, and individual partners pay taxes on net earnings. "But what happens when the partners are incompatible?" asks Nicoll. "The entire business is at risk." An individual partner's actions can create liability for the partnership and, consequently, liability for other partners. It is important to pick a partner wisely, and according to Nicoll, "even the best partnership should have a written partnership agreement to spell out areas of concern." Good friends and good business don't necessarily mix. Enthusiastic sharing of dreams about an idea will not carry you past the initial days of development. After that, dedicated efforts, compatible skills, knowledge, and resources provide for a long-term business partnership.

According to Reich, working through the details of a partnership agreement can help you uncover potential problem areas and resolve details about how the business will operate. "Management responsibilities must be defined," said Reich, "but style may be informal. Day-to-day operation may be shared equally or unequally and may be allocated formally or divided informally." Louise Reich's guidelines for a partnership agreement are shown in figure 9-3.

Filing Requirements:

1. Certificate of assumed name—obtain from the county clerk's office

2. Local licenses and permits

3. Professional licenses

4. Sales tax permits—if you are selling a product (see chapter 10)

5. Federal Employer Identification Number (EIN)—if you hire people, you'll need to fill out an SS-4 (see chapter 10)

6. Circular E—Government guidelines on all payroll taxes (see chapter 10)

7. State REG-1 (to register business with division of taxation; you will be assigned a state tax identification number)

8. Employee taxes and insurance, including state unemployment compensation, workers' compensation, and federal and state tax withholding

9. Federal and state partnership informational returns

Reich's Recommendations for Partnership Agreements

Your partnership agreement should address these issues, providing as much detail as possible:

1. Description of partners (names and addresses)

2. Name of enterprise

3. Location of business (including local and out-of-state addresses)

4. Date of commencement of partnership and period of existence if known

5. Identification of enterprise as new or existing business (and relationship to old business if this is a change of form or a change of management of an existing business)

6. Description of nature of business (especially if more than one activity will be carried out and/or each partner has a different responsibility)

7. Description of capital contributions (including cash, property, or services; the percentage of capital attributed to each partner; and loans)

8. Description of distribution and/or salary arrangements (define salaries; percentage of profit/loss; time and method of distribution)

9. Time devoted to business (full-time and/or part-time work; conflicts of interest; vacation time)

10. Management and control (Is there to be an "executive partner" or do all have equal voices? What actions require partner consensus?)

11. Accounting and banking (including check-signing arrangements, access to partnership funds, bookkeeping and responsibilities)

12. What method will be used to make decisions/settle disputes? (majority vote, arbitration provision)

13. Admission of new partners (how and under what terms?)

14. Termination of partnership on resignation, death, disability, or expulsion

15. Procedures on dissolution (Which partner will wind up with the enterprise? How should remaining assets be distributed?)

Figure 9-3: Reich's Recommendations for Partnership Agreements

Limited Liability Partnerships (LLP)/ Limited Liability Companies (LLC)

The Limited Liability Company can be considered in addition to the alternatives of the S Corporation, the limited partnership, or the general partnership. The limited liability company is a separate legal entity and has the limited liability of a corporation with the flexibility and tax status of a partnership. It is a relatively new business structure, and almost all states permit it. Most states also permit limited liability partnerships.

In most states, ownership of LLPs and LLCs must entail two or more partners or "members" (however, New York permits one-member LLCs). Limited liability companies must have an article of organization, an operating agreement, and a member control agreement. The profits, losses, and distribution of cash or other assets of an LLC are allocated among the members in the manner described in the operating agreement. Usually there will be a general partner (or managing partner) and one or more limited partners. Members have no personal liability under the corporation's protection. Rights of the owners are determined by their relative contribution to the business (prorated according to their investment). Unlike a sole proprietorship, which just stops when you decide to end the business, this type of partnership or company must be terminated through liquidation, merger, or something similar. Limited Liability Companies/Partnerships also must have a limited life, usually less than 30 years. Often this type of business structure is selected when the partnership has been put together for a certain purpose. The agreement must be structured carefully to ensure partnership tax treatment.

Filing Requirements:

1. Complete a certificate of formation and file it with the Secretary of State in your state. This includes:

    name of the limited liability company

    name and address of the registered agent

    address of the registered office

    latest date of dissolution

    other pertinent matters the members choose to include

    statement to verify the number of members of the LLP/LLC

2. Create an operating agreement. This contains details related to membership, including:

    relative rights, powers, and duties (e.g., voting)

    identification of LLP/LLC head (e.g., manager in charge)

    provision for classes or groups of managers having relative rights, powers, and duties

Corporations

A corporation is a legally separate entity offering some degree of legal protection for the stockholders. Corporations can be one person and have only one stockholder. Generally the title to corporate property is held by the corporation. Management is centralized—there is either a board of directors or an individual who makes the decisions for the corporation. There is no partnership agreement. The designation "Professional Corporation" can be used for doctors, lawyers, accountants, and other businesses with a professional association. Corporations offer continuity of operations, since the corporation can exist as long as there are stockholders. Ownership is easily transferable through the sale of stock. Liability is limited to corporate assets. You are not personally liable for all business debts and you don't pay taxes on the net earnings. But incorporation requires extensive record-keeping, articles of incorporation, by-laws, initial tax and filing fees, and shareholder meetings. The board of directors holds legal, formal control. The corporation pays taxes, and the shareholders pay personal income tax on dividends (therefore, double tax). "Incorporation isn't for everyone; but make the decision based on a logical analysis of the nature of the work you do and the direction your company will take," said Nicoll. "As your business grows and develops over time, you may need to reconsider your initial organizational decision."

If you choose incorporation, your financial advisor should counsel you about the advantages and disadvantages of S Corporations or Limited Liability Companies, categories created expressly for smaller business. One may be right for you. Be sure to contact your accountant about the designation of the type of corporation that is best for you as soon as possible. You must select S Corporation status within seventy-five days of forming your corporation.

To formalize a corporation you must:

1. Draw up Articles of Incorporation or a charter.

2. Obtain name clearance from the state. (Most states will help you out with this. The state has some discretionary control over business names and may issue a duplicate name if two businesses are vastly different in function or in location.)

3. Register the corporation with your state (and any state where you do business).

4. Get a federal and state taxpayer identification number.

C Corporations

This is the oldest form of standard corporation. It offers flexibility of tax year (e.g., you can pick your year end and tie into business cycles if you choose). Medical reimbursement plans are permitted, and owners' group term insurance and group health insurance are deductible.

S Corporations

S Corporations are probably the best option for small businesses that choose to incorporate. This business structure is permitted even if your sales reach $100 million. However, there are certain limitations to the S Corporation.

1. You are limited to 35 or fewer shareholders. A husband and wife will be considered a single stockholder.

2. Corporations, partnerships, and certain types of trusts may not hold stock; non-U.S. citizens may not hold stock.

3. There can be only one class of stock issued and outstanding. Differences in voting rights do not mean shares of stock are different classes.

4. There is no flexibility in your tax year; S Corporations must use a calendar year unless it can be proved that connection to your business cycle warrants the need for a change.

Protecting Your Intellectual Property

Your designs, products, inventions, and ideas can be protected under United States and international intellectual property laws. Intellectual property laws cover trademarks, patents, and copyrights. Intellectual property is a highly specialized area of the law and it is best to speak with an expert who can go over the unique details of your own design.

Patent

A patent secures an inventor's exclusive right to make, use, or sell an invention for a term of years. Your design for a new product may not be an invention in a technical sense, but the idea is certainly your intellectual property. According to Paramus, New Jersey, attorney Frederick Nicoll, you may be able to obtain trademark protection (or trade dress, a subset of trademark) for your unique designs.

Trademark

A trademark, by definition, points distinctly to the origin or ownership of merchandise to which it is applied; it is legally reserved to the exclusive use of the owner as maker or seller. A number of commercial products work under trademark protection today. "If you have some distinctive logo or insignia," Nicoll said, " you can protect this specifically."

When you have applied for a trademark, the designation "TM" may be displayed adjacent to your mark when it is used. The designation "TM" gives others notice that you are claiming exclusive rights in the mark. The symbol ® should only be used when a mark is registered in U.S. Patent and Trademark Office. Separate applications must be filed, country by country, for international use of the mark.

Copyright

Anyone who gives an idea original expression in a physical from (e.g., on paper, in clay, on a computer disk, on film) has federal copyright protection. You have a copyright in anything you write, even if it is not registered with the copyright office. You may put a notice on it. Notice consists of the copyright symbol "C" in a circle © followed by the year the work was made for distribution, and the name or identifying symbol of the copyright holder. In most cases, others may not copy, adapt, distribute, or publicly perform or display your work without your permission.

Confidentiality Agreements

A simple confidentiality agreement, according to Nicoll, can also work for you. The confidentiality agreement is a statement you would present to any company before you disclose the design or the unique characteristics of your idea. The confidentiality agreement would apply whether or not you proceed in negotiations; that is, the company agrees not to disclose or make any use of your design whether or not they decide to go forward.

Design ideas have been protected by large (and not-so-large) businesses, so you'll be in good company. Flip through any issue of *Vogue* or *Bazaar* for a quick study of how successful designers exaggerate their ownership of ideas. Take handbags, for example. Initials, colors, logos, and monograms are built right into the design, making it even more difficult to copy. Dooney & Bourke didn't invent the handbag, but they *did* design The All-Weather Leather Collection and protect it with the symbol for "registered trademark": ™. Coach bags have a characteristic leather name tag attached to a gold chain, while Capezio bags sport a gold nameplate on the front. Louis Vuitton bags and suitcases are completely initialized. Their products are definitely theirs. Your product can definitively be yours.

Litigation

Contrary to public perception, responsible attorneys recognize the potential benefits of dispute prevention and resolution rather than rollerblading into court. Fred Nicoll has demonstrated that negotiating instead of litigating can often achieve a more satisfactory result.

The decision to go to court has a huge impact on a small-business owner or self-employed individual. Litigation is not only expensive but tremendously time-consuming and energy draining as well.

Partners and members of corporations need to seek agreement on issues of importance to the company. The cost and distraction of a dispute among shareholders can cripple a business and is often fatal. "It is almost invariably better to work the problem out yourself rather than to have the court do it for, by then, there may not be much left," said Nicoll. The same holds true for issues of confidentiality, copyrights, and other intellectual property concerns.

Preventing problems in advance can save you time and expense later on. Litigation can be a long and expensive undertaking, robbing small-business owners of money and stealing irreplaceable time and effort from a growing business. Nicoll offers the following advice to help you avoid potential problems.

Lessons in Litigating Less

Clearly define what is important—critical—to you. If you know what points you cannot live without, you'll know your base position.

Do not give ultimatums. If you convince yourself "I'll never do that" before you begin to negotiate, you may want to eat your hat later on.

Listen. And listen actively. Active listening involves allowing one party to finish speaking without interruption and only then questioning any areas of concern.

Do not attack. Assume that the other party has as much at stake in this as you do. The other party always does. But if "gotcha" is your game, you will both end up losers.

Be receptive to alternative solutions. More often than not, the best negotiated settlement involves terms that neither party had specifically demanded at the start. Rather, the best agreements evolve when both parties create a new plan together.

Figure 9-4: Lessons in Litigating Less (adapted from Frederick A. Nicoll)

Accounting Considerations and Concerns

- ◆ Potential Tax Advantages: The Home Office Deduction
- ◆ Your Business Record-keeping Needs
- ◆ Sole Proprietorship, Partnerships, and Corporate Tax Structures
- ◆ Federal and State Identification Numbers
- ◆ Sales Tax
- ◆ Payroll Taxes
- ◆ Federal and State Tax Filings
- ◆ Employees
- ◆ Independent Contractors
- ◆ Self-employment Tax
- ◆ Payroll Services
- ◆ Hiring Family Members
- ◆ When to Call an Accountant
- ◆ Estimated Taxes
- ◆ Pension Planning
- ◆ Cash Flow
- ◆ Profit and Loss
- ◆ Surviving an Audit

Potential Tax Advantages: The Home Office Deduction

The home office deduction refers to taking a percentage of your total home expenses as a deduction on your federal income tax. If you are entitled to a home office tax deduction, you should identify what portion of your home (in square footage) is allocated to business use. This portion determines the percentage you are permitted to deduct.

Expenses pertaining to the whole house (not including any specific non-business-related rooms) for which you can deduct a portion include:

◆ mortgage interest

◆ property taxes

◆ homeowner's insurance cost

◆ household utility bills

◆ plumbing and other general repairs and maintenance

◆ exterior painting

◆ roofing

◆ landscaping

◆ central air conditioning

◆ 100 percent of repair costs to the home office itself

Even if you didn't qualify for a formal home office deduction, you can deduct *everything within your home office.* This includes

◆ business auto expenses

◆ furniture

◆ wall hangings

◆ window treatments

◆ carpets

◆ shelving

◆ computer equipment

◆ telephones, special phone lines, and all long-distance business calls

- cellular phone, if used for business—or at least the business calls you make

- subscriptions to professional publications and journals

- fax machines

- supplies

and anything else you need to run your business, such as

- employee wages

- business gifts

- business travel, meals, and entertainment costs

The eligibility for claiming a home office tax deduction was narrowed by the January 1993 Supreme Court decision *Commissioner of the IRS* v. *Nader Soliman*. This decision caught many home-based business owners by surprise. Soliman was an anesthesiologist who was denied a home office tax deduction because he saw patients at four hospitals. None of the hospitals provided an office for him, so he arranged appointments, kept records, contacted patients, and handled his billing from his home. The Supreme Court decided that because he did not see patients in his home, he did not qualify for a home office deduction.

The ramifications of this decision for small business owners resulted in aggressive action by several national organizations to put pressure on legislators to overturn the Supreme Court's ruling. The National Association for the Self-Employed and the National Association of Women Business Owners led the effort all the way to the 1995 White House Conference on Small Business. Protection of the home office tax deduction made the list of top 60 Final Recommendations which emerged from this conference.

The Home Office Deduction Act clarifies the definition of principal place of business as follows:

> **A home office shall in any case qualify as the principal place of business if**
>
> **(a) the office is the location where the taxpayer's essential administrative or management activities are conducted on a regular and systematic (not incidental) basis by the taxpayer, and**
>
> **(b) the office is necessary because the taxpayer has no other location for the performance of the administrative or management activities of the business.**

Finally, the IRS requires that you identify a separate room for business use in order to qualify for a home office deduction (so a portion of your basement, while isolated and quiet, will work for you but not for the IRS, unless it's formally partitioned as a separate room). However, if you wanted to take an aggressive position and demonstrate your use of a home office (in spite of the fact that it might not be *quite* up to their standard), you could try a comparison of last year's utility bills to this year's. The increase in wattage for business equipment usage is usually readily apparent.

Also remember that a home office deduction is only allowed to bring your self-employment income down to "zero." If your deduction exceeds that, you're allowed to *carry the excess deduction forward* to a future year. If you are operating in a corporate form (see later discussion), this limitation does not apply and you would literally pay yourself rent and record it as rental income, offset by proportionate costs associated with that portion of your house including depreciation.

Consider putting the home office deduction on your Schedule C if you are a sole proprietor. This reduces your income level, and subsequently reduces your self-employment tax. In addition to qualifying for a deduction of a percentage of your mortgage, interest, and real estate taxes, there are other advantages. By qualifying as a home office, all miles *from your home to your clients/customers, distributors, prospects, etc.—* are now business miles.

If a tax deduction for your business is one of your most important considerations in deciding on a home base, be careful. *Your office might not qualify as a business deduction on your taxes.* Almost any office space *outside* the home rented by a business qualifies for a business expense tax deduction. The same liberal standard does *not* apply to home-based business today. For certain kinds of businesses, you may have difficulty justifying the deduction on your taxes. This may change soon, as momentum builds to make home office deductions more accessible. Why should the IRS care where the office is located if the business has an office used exclusively for the business, and generates income sufficient to claim an office deduction? Well, the IRS cares. The IRS has repeatedly sought to limit home office deductions. Current tax laws require that the home office must itself generate revenue.

Your Business Record-keeping Needs

Your record-keeping system, according to Alyssa Lebovic of Keller and Lebovic, CPAs, should not be set up for the amusement of your accountant but rather to enable you to keep track of how your business is doing. You will want to develop a system that will give you information you can use to manage the business, so it will be important to establish a framework that fits the style and size of your business.

Your accountant can help you identify what your specific record-keeping needs are. Whether you select a manual or computerized system for tracking will depend to some degree on your volume of information, your other computer needs, and the type of data you need to keep. Some examples include:

Unnecessary Minutiae

If you use your automobile for business on a regular basis, it may not be necessary to keep every $.35 parkway toll receipt, as long as you keep a business diary documenting where you traveled to and how many miles you covered. You will also be wasting time if you keep every coffee and bagel receipt for yourself. And while it may save you time in the long run to summarize your business expenses once a week, as if you were submitting an expense to a "boss," the truth is that many small business owners skip the weekly summary step. These expenses do add up over a year's time so at least jot them down in your diary.

Being Meticulous

In your business diary, in addition to mileage, document the names, titles, company, and purpose of every business meeting. Log where you went for lunch, and keep the receipts. Keep a log of all your out-of-pocket expenses, like printing, postage, and office supplies, and keep receipts. Summarize monthly so you know where you stand.

Mandatory Receipts

If that business lunch was over $25, you *must* have a receipt. If less than $25, you don't need to show a receipt in order to claim the deduction (but it doesn't hurt to have it). Keep receipts for all other business purchases—for equipment, supplies, subscriptions, stationery, postage, advertising, shipping, and handling. And keep everything related to *employees*.

Sole Proprietorships, Partnerships, and Corporate Tax Structures

When you decided what your formal business structure should be, tax accountability was one consideration. The most important tax considerations are discussed below.

Sole Proprietorship

Advantages

The tax advantage is that you are taxed only once as an individual and the record-keeping and tax filings are much simpler. You do, however, pay self-employment tax. If you operate a capital intensive business, you've paid tax on the whole profit even though you may not have taken the money out of the business. All you can claim is the depreciation. You may write off up to $17,500 of capital equipment each year (but not if this brings you below zero). The excess deduction would be carried forward again. Business deductions and income are recorded on your 1040, whether you file jointly or singly, using Schedule C. Net profit is taxed at personal income tax rates.

Disadvantages

As discussed in chapter 9, you have unlimited liability—your personal assets become your business assets. "Commingling of personal and business assets and liabilities can become an accounting nightmare," according to Harry Zarrow of the CPA firm of Zarrow, Zarrow, and Klein.

Partnerships

Advantages

A major advantage is flexibility of ownership. Ownership can be handled creatively as to distribution of profits. This is an excellent vehicle when you have an investor partner and a working partner. Partners, like sole proprietors, are taxed at the individual level so again, there is no double taxation. Total profit and loss are calculated for the business, then each partner files a Schedule K-1 showing his share of the income (or loss) to report on the individual tax return, using a Schedule E and again paying SE tax. "The partnership," according to Harry Zarrow, "is a conduit to pass through profit to the partners."

Disadvantages

You still have unlimited liability, and from an accounting standpoint, partnerships are more complicated than sole proprietorships. "You are required by the IRS to use an accounting system that clearly shows income separately through a:

- ◆ separate checkbook, and/or
- ◆ journal for cash receipts and cash disbursements
- ◆ a separate tax return (Form 1065) in addition to your personal 1040

Your record-keeping system can be manual or mechanized. If you would like information about using a computer system, have your accountant help guide you to identify a system that will meet your business needs. There are some simple, relatively inexpensive record-keeping systems like Quicken (retails for about $80). Quicken provides a system of showing deposits and income, and receipts and disbursements, meeting all tax filing requirements.

Limited Liability Partnerships and Corporations

Advantages

Again, there is no double tax and you are no longer personally liable. Only the actual assets of the company are at risk. Losses are limited to the basis of each partner; that is, you cannot take a loss greater than what you have invested in the business—your basis. This is also true of partnerships, although personally guaranteeing a loan also counts toward deductibility. Limited liability entities have not as yet been approved in all 50 states.

C Corporations

C Corporations must report business income on a corporate tax return, separate from the shareholders' returns. However, there is double taxation. The corporation is taxed at the corporate level, and then shareholders are taxed for the dividends they receive, and any money paid as salary is taxed at individual rates. Double taxation is often avoided by salarying out all current year earnings. However, sometimes this is not feasible, as when you need to leave funds in for operating capital or future expansion. You must also be aware of unreasonable compensation rules. The tax law's unreasonable compensation provisions prevent attempts to pay stockholders high salaries from pre-tax dollars instead of dividends. Dividends must be paid from after-tax corporate dollars. The corporation may be liable for a minimum state tax, depending on where you are located, regardless of your profit. The net effect is that you are taxed twice— once as a corporation, again as an individual. The good news is that the corporate tax rate is slightly lower than the individual rate. However, corporate and partnership tax returns are more complicated than individual ones so accounting fees can be expected to be higher.

The greatest advantage of a corporation is that your personal assets are protected from the legal liabilities of the company. Be aware, however, that in a service business, basically you are the business. In a lawsuit, you could still be named personally in addition to the corporation.

S Corporations

Usually the best thing to do for small businesses that select incorporation as their business structure is to form an S Corporation.

Advantages

Unlike a C Corporation, you are taxed only once. All taxable income, losses, deductions, and credits are passed through to the corporation's stockholders with proper basis.

Disadvantages

As with sole proprietorships and partnerships, taxable income of S Corporations is taxed to stockholders even if the income is not actually distributed to them. If corporate cash flow is inconsistent, S Corporation status may not be the best choice. In addition, certain items that are tax deductible for a C Corporation (like the cost of some fringe benefits, such as health insurance for the owners) are not deductible for S Corporations, although these restrictions are being reconsidered by the IRS. Furthermore, there are many restrictions regarding ownership and distributions to owners. You will also be required to use a calendar year-end.

Note: You must file a Form 2553 with the IRS and similar forms with your state to receive the benefits of S Corporation status within the first 75 days of your corporate year—no exceptions—or else wait until the following year.

S Corporation status must also be approved by all stockholders. Your accountant can advise you of additional benefits such as advantages for state franchise taxes, unreasonable compensation restrictions, and other considerations unique to your situation.

You should always discuss the type of entity to choose with your accountant.

Federal and State Identification Numbers

The federal identification numbers you will need depend on the business structure you have chosen and the way you run the business.

Incorporation and Partnerships

You must get a federal identification number right away. To get the nine digit number, called an EIN, you must first complete Form SS-4. You can obtain an SS-4 by calling the IRS's forms distribution center's toll-free number—(800) 829-3676. You can also pick up the form at one of ten home service center sites operated nationwide by the IRS. Follow the instructions on the SS-4. The fastest way to file for your EIN is to submit the information from the form over the phone (using the IRS Tele-tin program). You will be assigned your EIN right away. The IRS requires that you fax or send the SS-4 paperwork within five days as a follow-up. You can obtain your EIN by filing an SS-4 as soon as you start the business. Use your EIN to open your business checking account instead of using your social security number.

Sole Proprietors—Not Incorporated

You can use your social security number to identify your business until you hire employees or charge sales tax. You will need a federal employer ID number (i.e., the EIN) if you have to pay employees or if you remit sales tax.

Until you have a federal EIN, you may open a bank account with your social security number.

State Identification Numbers are assigned after your federal identification number. The Appendix lists state resources to obtain this information.

Sales Tax

As a general guideline, products are subject to sales tax. Services usually are not. But don't take this simple rule-of-thumb as the last word. Check locally for your state rules.

1. Call your local sales tax department. This office is usually located in your state capital, but in some larger states there are local satellite offices. Check the Appendix of this book to get you started.

2. Describe what you're thinking of selling or doing. Find out under what circumstances you will need to collect taxes.

3. Keep your records separated for taxable and nontaxable items.

4. In general, you do not need to collect sales tax on out-of-state sales. However, sometimes neighboring states have cross-state agreements. "Check with the states you will interact with to see if there are any 'cross-state sales agreements' for commercially interrelated locations," Alyssa Lebovic recommends.

5. If you are not sure when you will incur your first sales tax, do not enter a date on the SS-4 form. The minute the IRS spots a date, you are accountable for all the related paperwork, whether or not you *actually sold anything.*

Payroll Taxes

There's no getting around it: When you hire employees your paperwork and tax filings become more complicated. You cannot wait until the end of the year to review your records. You will need to file forms and pay taxes quarterly.

"Many businesses go under for non-payment of payroll taxes," said Alyssa Lebovic. "If you are collecting payroll taxes or sales taxes you have a fiduciary responsibility to remit them," she said, "and you cannot hide behind the protection of a corporation." Lebovic recommends several steps to take the pain out of your payroll tax payments. These steps are listed in figure 10-1.

Taking the Pain Out of Payroll Taxes

1. Put aside the money for payroll and sales taxes away right away. Cover the **gross amount**.

2. If you are not sure when you will have a payroll, do not enter a date on the SS-4. The date you record as the date of payroll will trigger all the IRS paperwork requirements related to employees.

3. Don't ever be late in paying payroll (or sales) taxes. The penalties are very high. If you don't have the funds, at least file the quarterly forms on time. This way you can avoid the separate penalty for late filing.

4. If you don't have the funds to cover your payroll in a given time period, don't write your check. You'll still be liable for the payroll taxes on a quarterly basis, even if you didn't **cash** your check.

5. Write your payroll checks on the first day of the new month rather than the last day of the month. This extends the date when your remittance of payroll taxes is due.

6. If you use a payroll service, tell them not to cut your check if you are running short.

7. Your salary doesn't have to be consistent as far as the IRS is concerned. The IRS understands that business owners will vary their salary as cash flow allows.

8. If you don't need money from the business to live on, wait until December to write your check. Call it a bonus, if you will. It is not unusual for business owners to leave money in the business until December. Besides avoiding quarterly payroll taxes on their salary, this enables business owners to decide the amount of salary after determining the overall state of the business.

Figure 10-1: Taking the Pain Out of Payroll Taxes

Federal and State Tax Filings

Quarterly tax forms must be filed to remit social security, federal withholding, state withholding, and state unemployment taxes. When you have employees other than owners, you also need workers' compensation/disability, paid either through the state or private agency, depending on what state your business is located in.

You have to file forms quarterly but you may have to remit funds monthly or more frequently, depending on your payroll schedule. Usually you have to remit what you've withheld on the fifteenth day of the following month. *Penalties and interest at the federal and state level are **very** high if you don't file and pay on time.*

Employees

When you hire even one employee, you are responsible for:

 ◆ obtaining federal and state identification numbers

 ◆ withholding income taxes on employees' wages every time you pay them

 ◆ withholding the employees' portions of Social Security (FICA) and Medicare taxes from their pay, and contributing your share of FICA and Medicare as the employer

 ◆ withholding a portion of the state unemployment tax (in certain states)

 ◆ possibly responsible for paying federal unemployment (FUTA) tax

 ◆ securing workers' compensation

 ◆ paying unemployment and possibly disability insurance to your state

Deposit these taxes on a specific schedule, because there are serious consequences and high penalties if these taxes are not withheld or deposited on behalf of your employees.

From the IRS point of view, not all individuals are created equal. Some people should be viewed as employees, and some may qualify as independent contractors. Basically, if you set the work hours, provide tools, tell your workers what to do and how to do it, and can fire them, they are probably "employees" according to the IRS. The key areas that determine differences in classification are control over work schedule, method of compensation, number of clients, and chance for profit and loss.

Independent Contractors

Independent contractors, like you, actually run their own businesses and have other clients besides you, according to the IRS. Independent contractors can set their own

20 FACTORS

What makes a worker an employee? According to the IRS's 20-factor test, employees:

1. Comply with the employer's instructions about the work.
2. Receive training from or at the direction of the employer.
3. Provide services that are integral to the employer's business.
4. Provide services that must be rendered personally.
5. Hire, supervise, and pay workers for the employer.
6. Have an ongoing relationship with the employer.
7. Follow set hours of work.
8. Work full time for the employer.
9. Do their work on the employer's premises.
10. Do their work in a sequence set by the employer.
11. Submit regular reports to the employer.
12. Receive payments of regular amounts at set intervals.
13. Receive payments for business and/or traveling expenses.
14. Rely on the employer to provide tools and materials.
15. Lack a major investment in resources for providing services.
16. Cannot make a profit or loss from their services.
17. Work for one employer at a time.
18. Do not offer their services to the general public.
19. Can be fired by the employer.
20. May quit work at any time without incurring a liability.

Source: Approaches for Improving Independent Contractor Compliance, General Accounting Office, Washington, DC

Figure 10-2: 20 Factors:

hours and procedures for work, and do not report to you on a regular basis. The IRS has a list of 20 factors to distinguish between an employee and an independent contractor. Use this list to identify your status, too.

Figure 10-2 outlines the IRS factors that determine the difference between an employee and an independent contractor.

The IRS is not your only source of concern. Minimum wages, overtime pay, Employee Retirement Income Security Act (ERISA) benefits, unemployment, and workers' compensation benefits all hang on whether a worker is an employee or an independent contractor. So a whole host of other agencies will be ready and willing to slap a penalty on you if you don't pay on time, including the U.S. Department of Labor and your state tax authority.

Finally, if you make payments totaling $600 or more in any year to an unincorporated independent contractor or landlord, you need to file a Form 1099-MISC, "Miscellaneous Income" with the IRS at the end of the year. If you have work as an independent contractor, get this from the business hiring you as an independent contractor. You are then responsible for paying your own income tax and self-employment tax.

Self-employment Tax

Self-employment tax is the self-employed individual's equivalent of payment to cover the cost of Social Security and Medicare benefits. It is highest if you're not incorporated. "As a self-employed individual," Lebovic explains, "you are both the employer and employee." This means you are responsible for collecting your own Social Security tax and for paying it in a lump sum along with your income tax. "This kills many home-based business owners in their first year." If you have started a business or become a consultant after a period of unemployment, remember there has been no withholding tax on your unemployment checks, but this payment *is* subject to tax. Put aside some money throughout the year whenever possible to ease the pain of payment at the end of the year.

Payroll Services

Payroll services handle not only your employee paychecks and withholding, but also the associated record-keeping and filings. Most payroll services cut the payroll checks and file the government forms as part of their basic services. For an additional fee, they will also make the appropriate deposits for you (to avoid potential late penalties).

Alyssa Lebovic suggests that three employees is the point at which most small businesses should consider using a payroll service. However, Lebovic adds, "Many firms with only one or two employees will use a payroll service. It frees up your time and ensures that everything is done on time."

In general, Lebovic also recommends using a small payroll service that specializes in small business, rather than the small-business division of a large corporation.

Payroll service fees are based on the frequency of the payroll. If you switch to a bi-weekly payroll you will save money. Payroll services can also save money for you on accounting fees.

As your business grows, you can save money by not having a payroll service handle your deposits for you. You do not need to remit payroll taxes until the fifteenth day of the following month, regardless of when you cut the paychecks. You can save money and earn interest by not writing the check for payroll taxes until it's due.

Sample Calendar of First Quarter Filing Dates

January	**15**	Last installment of estimated tax with Form 1040-ES due	(Individual)
	31	Form W-2 to be distributed	(Employer)
		Form 1099 to be distributed	(Business)
		Form 941, Quarterly Return for Withheld Income and Social Security Taxes	File and pay quarterly deposit (Employer)
(Employer)		Form 940, Annual Return of Federal Unemployment Taxes	File
		State Quarterly Payroll Tax Returns	
February	**10**	Deferred due date for Forms 940 and 941 if deposits were made on time	(Employer)
	28	File previous year's Forms 1099 with the IRS	(Business)
		File previous year's Forms W-2 with the Social Security Administration	(Employer)
March	**15**	Calendar year corporations file Form 1120(A) tax return and pay	
		S Corporations file Form 1120S	
		File Form 7004 for a six-month extension	
		Elect S Corporation status for current tax year. Calendar-year corporations must file Form 2553	

Figure 10-3: Sample Calendar of First Quarter Filing Dates

Hiring Family Members

The first time the whole family joins in to help you with a special project in your home-based business, they probably won't mind pitching in. More often than not, the owner is the only one who draws a salary or pay out of the business, and the spouse, children, and other relatives are thanked but not compensated financially. Sometimes, however, it pays to pay. Consider the following tax advantages and other benefits:

- ◆ Children (over 14 years old) who are employed by your business will be in a 15 percent tax bracket, compared to your 28–39.6 percent federal income tax bracket (unincorporated). Unincorporated business owners' children under 18 years old do not have to pay FICA. You can claim a deduction for the full amount of their pay. And you have reduced the amount of your business earnings subject to self-employment tax.

- ◆ Social Security benefits can be higher if both spouses have a significant history of earnings.

- ◆ Retirement plan coverage for the owner's spouse can be more favorable, especially if you are contributing the maximum allowed.

- ◆ Tax deduction for health care coverage for self-employed individuals now is limited to only about 30 percent. But the business can pay for family health coverage for an employed spouse, and then the whole cost can be deductible (if the owner waives coverage).

When to Call an Accountant

The best time to call your accountant is *before* you make most of your major business decisions, like determining your business structure, purchasing a major piece of equipment, or entering into a lease. Very often you can reduce your taxes by planning and timing your actions to your best advantage. Your accountant can advise you about all your options and recommend the best direction.

"You should be paying your accountant for advising—not adding," says Lebovic. It is far less expensive to pay someone to keep your books—a professional bookkeeper, for example—than to hire your accountant for this service. Don't pay your accountant for bookkeeping services. Further reduce your costs by preparing for your meetings with your accountant. The more complete your records are when you meet, the lower your fees will be. You'll be taking up less of your accountant's time.

Talk to your accountant before the end of the year to do a projection. "This is your chance to make eleventh hour decisions," adds Lebovic. "Your fourth quarter estimate is critical as an adjustment opportunity for your end-of-year actuals." You may decide to step up or slow down collections, spend more money or wait to spend, make equipment purchases now or wait until the new year.

Lebovic's Ten Commandments
of Home-Based Business Accounting

1. Open a separate checking account for your business. Don't use your personal checking account for business expenses and don't pay personal expenses from your business account—just write a check to yourself.

2. If you are paid under your name and not a business trade name, establish a separate *personal* checking account under your name.

    a) Business checking account fees are usually higher than personal checking fees.

    b) The separate account will help you keep better business records.

    c) The account legitimizes your business for checks which the IRS could question; e.g., *Were those shelves you bought for personal or business use?*

3. Credit cards should be separated. You don't necessarily need to obtain new business credit cards, but you should be sure that certain credit cards are used for business only. These finance charges are then *clearly* deductible.

4. It is okay to carry balances on a business credit card because those finance charges are deductible (if you adhere to #3).

5. It helps to have your business and personal bank accounts in the same bank. You should keep a small balance in your business account and transfer funds from your personal account when needed.

6. Introduce yourself to your banker—before you need to. Don't wait until you need a loan. Your banker can also be an invaluable help to

    a) clear your checks quickly

    b) provide referrals

    c) help solve problems

7. Keep excellent records of all

    a) cash receipts

    b) cash disbursements

    c) business activities and trips

8. Summarize monthly.

9. Never be late with payroll taxes, sales taxes, or the associated filings.

10. Call your accountant *before* you make a major business purchase or decision.

Figure 10-4: Lebovic's Ten Commandments of Home-Based Business Accounting

Estimated Taxes

It is a common misassumption that you don't need to pay quarterly estimated taxes, that you can settle your score with the IRS before April 15 and leave it at that. However, you *do* need to pay quarterly estimated taxes if you are showing a profit, unless you are paying adequate withholding tax on the salary you pay yourself.

Many people base the amount of their estimated tax on their previous year's earnings. A fourth quarter estimate-of-your-estimate might even indicate that you can reduce your fourth quarter tax payment instead of waiting until April to take a refund. "It's like getting your refund *now*," suggests Lebovic.

If you keep in touch with your accountant, you can avoid two end-of-year surprises that can knock the life out of your cash flow: (1) not enough money to pay for self-employment tax, and (2) tax on unemployment compensation.

Pension Planning

The days of a secure retirement check are over, unless you plan for it yourself. And plan *now*. Your best options include IRAs, Keoghs, and SEP IRAs.

Individual Retirement Account (IRA)

This is the easiest pension program to set up and is available on a pre-tax basis to any individual who is not a member of a retirement plan already.

You are allowed up to $2,000 per year, regardless of your level of income, as long as you earn at least $2,000 that year (and your spouse is not a participant in a pension plan). If your spouse is covered by a pension plan or a 401(k), you may still contribute $2000 per year to an IRA on an after-tax basis and defer taxes on the interest earned until retirement. You must fill out form 8606 each year and hold onto the annual forms until you retire.

An IRA is yours and yours alone. There are no requirements that you set one up for your employees. Keep in mind that IRAs must be deposited by April 15 even if you file your tax return on extension.

SEP IRA (Simplified Employee Pension)

SEP IRAs are profit-sharing pension plans. For sole proprietorships and partnerships, the amount allowed is based on your bottom line, with an effective maximum of 13.05 percent or $22,500, whichever is less. For corporations, the amount is based on your salary up to $150,000. Until you net about $150,000, you can usually put more into a standard IRA than into a SEP IRA.

You must put money into a SEP IRA for your employees if you put money in for yourself (a nice selling point for new hires, if you can afford it). Employees who work more than 20 hours per week are subject to contributions, regardless of their rate of pay.

SEP IRAs are easy to administer because you don't have to file any annual forms with the IRS. You don't have to put money in a SEP IRA until April 15 or the extended filing date of your tax return.

Finally, SEPs are the most popular pension option for small businesses because they represent forced savings that the individual won't touch.

Keogh

Keoghs are similar to SEP IRAs in that they are also based on a percentage of your income. Keogh profit-sharing plans use the same formulas as SEP IRAs; Keogh money-purchase plans allow for an effective maximum contribution of 20 percent. You should consult your accountant before establishing a Keogh plan.

You must put money in a Keogh for your employees if you put in for yourself. Employees who work more than 20 hours per week are subject to contributions, regardless of their rate of pay if they have worked for you in at least three of the preceding five years.

In the first year you open a Keogh, you must open with a minimum balance amount by December 31. You can then add money later, until the extended filing date of your tax return.

For tax purposes, you must file a form 5500 for the Keogh if its assets exceed $100,000.

Defined Benefit Plans

Defined benefit plans offer an opportunity for an additional contribution based on age and salary. Talk to a broker to identify all of your options. A pension attorney can also advise you. Keep in mind that these plans are customized.

Although defined benefits plans are more complex, there are many opportunities out there that you can take advantage of.

Cash Flow

Early in your business life, you will find that you absolutely *must* plan for the seasonality of the business to allow for the rise and fall of income and expense. Lebovic advises, "Plan to borrow or reserve funds to use in the low income periods. With good record-keeping, you can examine seasonal patterns and learn when these fluctuations can be expected to occur."

Profit and Loss

Don't judge whether or not you're showing a profit by what's in your checkbook, according to Lebovic, particularly when dealing with paying back loans, building inventory, and buying expensive equipment.

However, just because you're having trouble with cash flow doesn't mean you're not showing a profit, Lebovic cautions. The state of your checkbook doesn't necessarily reflect the profitability of the business for that year. Watch out for the following tax surprises: (1) If you use cash flow to build up inventory, you will not be able to deduct the inventory until you actually sell it, and (2) If you use your cash flow to purchase expensive equipment (i.e., greater than $17,500), you may show a profit without having available cash. This is because you will take more than one year to depreciate the equipment although you're out the cash from purchasing it.

Surviving an Audit

Just when you think it is time to move last year's tax information into long term storage, the letter arrives:

> **We selected your Federal Income Tax return for the year shown below to examine the items listed at the end of this letter.**

In a courteous, friendly, and annoyingly cheerful letter the IRS then gently breaks the news that you are about to face an audit. *Please call us to arrange a convenient appointment.* They don't even use the word audit in this notification, but the bottom line is clear: The IRS is looking for more money from you. If you're lucky, the amount will contain very few commas. And if you have done a respectable job of tracking your business itinerary and stockpiling receipts throughout the year in question, you will be able to maintain the integrity of your original tax filing. You may even find out, as I did, that the IRS owes *you* money.

Employee business expenses are frequent audit items. Sole proprietors and partnerships who use Schedule C will find the IRS special favorites include *car* and *truck expenses* as well as *travel, entertainment, meals,* and *lodging.* Another popular selection is *business entertainment.* But of course, the possibilities are as numerous as the lines on your tax return. And they can keep coming back for more. Generally, the IRS will not examine a taxpayer's return for issues which have been examined in one of the two prior years if the audit resulted in no additional tax. However, this repetitive audit procedure does *not* apply to Schedule C issues or to income issues. So sole proprietors, partnerships and other Schedule C users—namely, small businesses—are an easy audit target.

My first audit was conducted as a very polite, respectful two-hour business meeting between two professionals. The auditor asked questions; I responded. She asked for receipts; I provided them. She worked on her adding machine (auditors need a nice paper trail), apologized for the IRS error, and I left with the comfortable news that *they* owed *me* money.

My second audit was as horrible as the first was productive. The auditor was brand new, fresh out of training. Her desk was littered with the remains of every meeting she had conducted prior to ours. She miscalculated amounts and misplaced papers I had handed over to her only moments before. She was clueless. After four hours, she cracked and asked to wrap up the meeting. She concluded that we broke even. I realized that once again, the IRS owed *me* money. When her written summary arrived shortly afterward, I challenged it. After another three-hour meeting with her, and a conference call with her supervisor, I received another check from the IRS.

My patience had worn thin by the third consecutive year. I successfully invoked my "right" not to undergo the same exercise again, but soon learned about the loophole for Schedule C. Back I went to the IRS office to meet yet another auditor.

After working as a consultant to entrepreneurs and small businesses for over ten years, I have seen the full gamut of the "Daily Business Diary," ranging from one-word to two-word entries. Let's face it: Many entrepreneurs feel they are too busy *doing* to stop and record *what* they're doing. There always seems to be something more urgent to deal with. So they struggle along as best they can. But if you are among a growing list of successful entrepreneurs who loathe paperwork, at least incorporate a few protective techniques into your routine. Use key words, initials, memory joggers in your daily log. It's slipshod compared to the ideal—but better than nothing when you are defending your livelihood. Before your audit you will need to fill in all the blanks, then cram.

Mileage logs also make more sense when maintained on a daily basis. Your destination, purpose, and contact should clearly spell out this was *work* not play. In addition, your mileage claims and odometer readings need to match. I found that the best way to present this information was to provide an end of the month summary for my log, showing personal, business, and total miles for each month. This clarified the percentage use of each.

Most start-ups cannot afford the services of a full-time bookkeeper, but no entrepreneur can afford *not* to maintain accurate records of business transactions. If you keep the raw data on paper and in your computer you'll be able to reconstruct past events and fill in the details if you have to. If you don't save receipts, track where you traveled, document your meetings, etc., you are an easy target for any auditor. And you will have to pay, with interest and with your time. What a waste!

Before facing my first audit, I spoke with several accountants and current and former IRS employees about what to expect. One very important issue to resolve is whether you and/or your accountant should go to the audit. I believe *you* should go. And don't feel you have to bring your accountant. It may be a good tactic to say, "I'm not sure, but I will check with my accountant." In addition, no one can provide the insight and interpretation of your situation and intentions that you can. Your accountant will probably disagree with me and take one of two positions: (1) The accountant may recommend going without you, reversing my logic, or (2) the accountant may recommend that you go together. *I disagree with both strategies.* If you are a sole proprietor with straightforward tax filings, do this yourself, unless you had absolutely nothing to do with your financial records for the year in question. Harry Zarrow points out, "For personal returns without tax shelters or other complications, you can handle it." However, Zarrow strongly cautions against an individual's handling a corporation's audit:

> **In this case I recommend that the accountant go alone. The corporation can be represented most effectively by the accountant, and the accountant can deal with the IRS agent one-to-one. When additional information is needed, the accountant can go back and get it.**

Here are some suggestions for audit preparation, endurance and follow-up.

Before the Audit

◆ Keep an accurate business diary. These records will serve you well.

◆ **Prepare thoroughly for this meeting.** Treat this as you would any professional business presentation.

◆ **Discuss each item in question with your accountant.** Know the IRS rules for each item. Try to determine why questions were raised. Role-play responses to possible concerns.

◆ **Postpone it.** This is *not* the time to exercise newly acquired decision-making speed. You'll need time to prepare. Don't decide to "get it over with." You can influence the outcome in your favor by being well-organized in advance.

◆ **Keep your schedule open that day.** Your appointment may not start on time, and the length of the meeting is unpredictable. Allow sufficient time to answer every possible question and avoid a return trip.

◆ **Immerse yourself in the data prior to your audit date.** No matter how detailed your business diary is, it will be tough to remember every meeting and event if you haven't reviewed your material ahead of time. Reasons "why" will be easier to recall if you review.

◆ **Pack up your materials in an organized, easy-to-access way.** You'll probably be in a very small office, sharing the desk of the auditor, rather than in a spacious conference room.

During the Audit

◆ **Go.** If you have decided that this is the best strategy, don't chicken out at the last minute.

◆ **Start the meeting well.** First impressions count, so begin with a respectful, courteous, and attentive manner. Remember, auditors take a lot of grief in a typical day. Resist the temptation to vent about the audit immediately.

◆ **Do not leave an original copy of *anything*.** Offer to wait while your materials are copied at the IRS office, or send copies of the material in question as a follow-up.

◆ **Photocopy everything** the auditor wants to keep.

◆ **Don't let anything you pass to an auditor leave your sight.** Many papers may change hands in the course of your meeting. Be sure you leave with everything you came with.

◆ **Let the auditor decide when the meeting is over.** It's far better to answer as many questions as possible while you are there than to return, unless you truly do not know the answer.

◆ **Watch closely for signals of confusion** or "eyes glazing over." Be sure the auditor is with you in every explanation.

After the Audit

◆ **Call your accountant** and summarize the meeting.

◆ **Provide additional support documents** as soon as possible. Now *is* the time to act decisively and quickly in response to their inquiries. Follow up on every request.

◆ **Keep track** of all individuals with whom you meet or from whom you seek telephone advice. Write down their addresses and phone numbers.

After you have concluded your meeting and submitted your final support documentation, you will receive a letter from the IRS showing its findings. If you do *not* agree with the findings, you may request another meeting with a different examiner. You may also request a hearing with a member of the Office of the Regional Director of Appeals. The Appeals Officer will be an individual who has not examined your return.

Creating the Best Organization and Management Structure

- ◆ Surviving Solo
- ◆ Need Help?
- ◆ Your Organization Structure
- ◆ Special Considerations for Hiring Home-Based Workers
- ◆ Hiring Strategies
- ◆ Interviewing Techniques
- ◆ Independent Contractors
- ◆ Employees
- ◆ Interns
- ◆ Taking the Next Step

Surviving Solo

The flexibility that accompanies working alone can be hard for the truly independent entrepreneur to give up. Schedule flexibility, privacy, and control are three factors which influence the decision of many home-based business owners to work alone.

As a result, home-based business owners tend to go to the limits of exhaustion before they hire help. They wait until the last minute to accept the fact that they are wearing too many hats.

From my observations, it seems that business owners with "outside offices" are more likely than home-based business owners to hire additional personnel when they need it, at the appropriate time. "Outside office" owners tend to make staffing decisions based on a financial assessment, weighing the pros and cons of salary commitments, management responsibilities, tax implications, and other pieces of an economic puzzle. For home-based business owners, the decision whether or not to add personnel is based on business needs, but is strongly influenced by personal issues. Home-based business owners wrestle with additional concerns that are unique to their work arrangement.

Schedule Flexibility

When you work alone, you don't have to worry about any schedule but your own, your clients', and your family's. As soon as you hire someone, you'll have to formalize your work schedule and structure your time. If you have already created a *socially acceptable* work routine, hiring personnel will require less of an adjustment on your part than if you haven't. Consider this one more reason to manage your time well and to incorporate some semblance of a differentiation between work hours and leisure hours as soon as possible. What if I want to work all night long . . . change the schedule . . . meet with clients and leave the employee alone . . . take a nap . . . catch a television show . . . run a midday errand . . . goof off? The fundamental issue that pervades these concerns is this: How can I take a working arrangement that has been completely customized to my needs and ask someone else to join?

Privacy

Many home-based business owners cringe at the very thought of having someone else work in their home. It feels like an invasion of privacy for some individuals. They just can't imagine it. Will I be comfortable with someone else in my home? Will my home office look "professional" enough to inspire the best work efforts from others? How will I keep the office clean? Will I have to serve them meals? Will my kids stay out of our hair?

Control

Many entrepreneurs would rather do the work themselves than show someone else how to do it. And when the business is new, there are certainly some tasks that the entrepreneurs themselves will perform best, like start-up sales. These concerns are not unique to home-based entrepreneurs. There are, in fact, many home-based business owners who decide to grow their businesses only to the extent that they can run the company alone. Chapter 13 covers this in further detail.

Surviving solo may be fine for you. Just recognize that there are limitations to your business growth and to what any company can accomplish alone.

Need Help?

There will come a time when the volume of work in your business will make it physically impossible for you to do it all. When you begin to feel overwhelmed, and you recognize that you are working as effectively and efficiently as possible but you still cannot catch up, stop and reassess. You will need to plan to add staff.

To make this realization more comfortable for you, try to put aside the personal aspects of this decision initially. Concentrate first on the financial issues. Ask yourself: *Can I afford to pay someone?* If the answer is honestly "yes," then open your thinking to creative options for staffing. Your choices, after all, need not be limited to full-time employees. Creative job design and a clear understanding of job responsibilities may indicate that a full-time staff is more than you need. Part-time help might be all your business requires, with full-time support only during your peak periods.

Consider all of your alternative staffing options before you start interviewing prospective personnel. A wide range of choices is available. Start with a careful examination of your current needs:

1. How many hours per day, per week, do you need help?

2. Is this a seasonal need or consistent throughout the year?

3. Is special training required?

4. How much responsibility is associated with this work?

5. What tasks and responsibilities will this job encompass?

6. What kind of individual should I hire?

Next, define your requirements for your next business cycle. Are these needs immediate, or can you wait until a certain peak in your business? Your options for staffing your organization include:

- **Schedule flexibility.** Full-time or part-time, all year or for seasonal busy periods.

- **Classification options.** Employee, independent contractor, intern.

- **Virtual corporations.** Linking with other companies and their staffs—see chapter 8.

Your Organization Structure

How can your business be organized to operate more effectively? When you add personnel, what should the reporting structure be? Is it necessary to identify a chain of command, or can you keep things loose?

At the risk of over-structuring a small organization, I hesitate to recommend a full-scale organization chart for the early days of a start-up venture. On the other hand, if you can visualize distinct areas of responsibility for each individual in your company, your lines of authority will be clear too.

Job Design

The more clearly you define the jobs in your business, the more effective your employees can be in helping you meet your goals. Start by writing down all the tasks that should be handled by each job. This list of job responsibilities will identify requirements and define what will be expected of your employees. Then determine what skills and knowledge contribute to performance of the job: degree requirements, previous job experience, personal characteristics, and so on.

Clarify your strategy with the following procedure:

- **Outline an organization chart.** Do this even if some of the boxes have no names assigned or if all the boxes have your name for the moment.

- **Write a job description for each position.** Not only should you put your thoughts in writing, but you should share this job description with the incumbent. Include job duties and responsibilities, reporting relationships, and qualifications (skills and knowledge required/desired).

- **Determine the salary and/or commission structure for each job.** Determine the importance of each position in your company and its relative worth in the marketplace.

- **Benefit plans—to have or not to have?** Sometimes you can work trade-offs in salary and benefits for new hires.

◆ **Initiate incentive plans to reward excellence.** Build in a strategy to provide a "bonus" if the business, the individual, and the economy are booming.

Special Considerations for Hiring Home-Based Workers

Hiring people to work out of your home is even more difficult than hiring for outside office space. Just as there are individuals not suited to running a home-based business, there are many people who do not adapt well to working within one. There are many individuals who will not feel comfortable working in your house, no matter how formal, how separate, or how large your office is. Even if you offer a totally professional office atmosphere, your home is still your home. Before you arrange an interview with a job candidate, find out if the individual has strong feelings one way or another about home-based business. Don't waste your time with anyone who views your business as less than professional because it is home-based.

The familiar issues of zoning, privacy, security, and space need to be reconsidered when the time comes to hire. Many concerns from the early days of your business development will need to be reexamined. Consider the questions in figure 11-1.

Why are these issues important? Consider the following problem areas.

Hiring Home-Based Workers

Ask yourself the following questions about your home situation before you start interviewing job candidates to work in your home:

1. Can your home tolerate the extra cars and commotion that multiple employees will create?

2. Can your family tolerate the invasion of privacy?

3. Will you be confident about the security of your personal and business property in the hands of someone else?

4. Do you have enough physical space for more than one person to work at a time?

Figure 11-1: Hiring Home-Based Workers

Zoning

If you are not in a commercially zoned area or not in a home-based business friendly community, the extra parking requirements, traffic flow, or noise generated by having additional people coming and going from your home on a daily basis may trigger resentment from your neighbors. Be careful. Don't overlook this critical aspect of maintaining the status quo. Things are looking good for your future. Now is not the time to get slapped with a zoning violation.

Privacy

If your home is truly your castle and your personal and business information are closely intermingled, you will have trouble with a staff in your home. If you leave your checkbook lying around, give your family and friends the run of the house all day long, indulge in a co-mix of personal and business work time, or do your laundry and dishes while you are trying to break a mental block, your personal quirks will be magnified as if under a microscope when someone else works with you at home. For all the promises you may make about flexible work scheduling for your staff, they won't want to learn that some of that time will be spent watching you sort your darks and whites for the next wash cycle, pick your kids up from school, or hand-water the hemlock.

Security

Will you be out of the office while your staff is in? This is your worst security risk. Your staff will need keys to your home. Kind of a creepy thought if you don't know the individuals well. You will need to exercise extreme caution in hiring. In addition, you need not lead them into temptation by allowing access to personal financial records, your grandmother's silver, or your jewelry.

Space

You may feel comfortable using your dining room table to collate handouts or stuff envelopes, but will everyone else? You should be able to offer desk space to people who work in your home, or they may feel like gypsies. Sharing your desk will be awkward for all of you, even with the best intentions. Allow a work area for each individual. It doesn't need to be elaborate, just a little space to call their own.

Hiring Strategies

Be on the lookout for good people all the time—even before you need them. It takes a long time to find the right "fit," and the more options you have to choose from when the time comes, the better off you'll be.

Your best bet is to look long and hard before you hire, according to Ellen Silverman. "I'm very flexible *after* I hire someone," she said. "Then they have access to my kitchen. If their kids can't go to school that day, they use my family room."

Four basic sources can be used to meet your staffing needs: friends and family, newspaper ads, referrals, and employment agencies.

Friends and Family

Ellen Silverman strongly recommends against hiring friends and family. Silverman tried this in her early days of running her business and experienced nothing but problems. She hired a friend's child, but found that when things didn't work out as planned it was very awkward for her. It is also hard to fire a relative or to have a serious business performance review with a family member.

Others have found that friends and family, provided they have the right skills, are their best bet. Many of us hire *only* people we know very well or relatives. What better source of staff members who will personally care about your success and want to work to build the business? But you do have to approach the issue objectively.

Whenever we hire people we know, we optimistically hope to resolve all potential personnel or personal problems. We'd rather try extra hard to make it work than train a stranger. But to make it work, the job itself needs to be just as clearly defined as it would be for someone you don't know. Furthermore, problems have to be addressed immediately and must not be allowed to fester. The stakes are too great if you don't work things out right away.

Finally, if problems are insurmountable, you have to know when it is time to un-hire (firing is too harsh a word, and firing a relative or friend can be painful). Handle the un-hiring diplomatically and with sensitivity to your long-term relationship. Insure that no permanent damage is incurred.

Newspaper Ads

Your weekly papers could provide a better resource than larger daily publications. Carefully structure the ad, but don't mention "home-based" in the ad for security reasons. And don't conduct a first interview in your home.

Hiring Friends and Family
1. Clearly define job responsibilities.
2. Address problems immediately.
3. Resolve differences as soon as possible.
4. Un-hire when you can't reach a solution.

Figure 11-2: Checklist for Hiring Friends and Family

Hiring through newspaper ads can be an extremely time-consuming process. If you have the time, it is less expensive than using an agency. But you could end up wasting time interviewing a lot of rejects. It will distract you from your business. Even if you prescreen candidates over the phone to reduce the number of in-person interviews, the process is tedious. Silverman also does not recommend hiring from newspaper ads. She recommends referrals and agencies as your best resources.

Referrals

Business associations and community organizations can be a good source of leads for finding people who are looking for work or job changes. As large corporations downsize daily, it seems the pool of available talent is better than ever. By putting the word out locally, you'll be able to get leads from sources you are familiar with. Background, character, and reference checks are less complicated with this route.

Employment Agencies

This may seem to be an expensive alternative to newspaper advertising for job opportunities, but the time you save is worth the expense. Agency fees are based on a percentage of the salary you will pay your employees. Use agencies for help with full-time or part-time employees rather than independent contractors and interns.

An employment agency can prescreen candidates for your job according to your criteria. The agency can ask about the individual's concern about home-based business and check references before you schedule an interview. You only need to interview candidates who pass the initial screening and reference checks. Finally, you can conduct these interviews at the agency's office, not in your home.

Interviewing Techniques

Many people assume they already know the answers to some of the questions they will ask job candidates. As a result, they try to save time by stating—rather than asking for—information. Sometimes they even give away the anticipated response by including the answer in the question. *"You were in that job for three years. The owner of that company is a personal friend of mine. You liked the job, right?"* If you program the answers to your questions into the questions themselves, you leave yourself locked into obtaining less data.

Open-ended questions will give you the best information about any job candidate. Open-ended questions are structured so that the respondent cannot answer "yes" or "no," but must provide some detail in the answer. Any interviewer can obtain the maximum amount of information from a conversation through this technique.

Remember:

1. Ask open-ended questions.

2. Listen more than you talk.

3. Overcome personal prejudgments and distractions.

4. Don't interrupt. Hear the other person out.

5. Ask questions for clarification. Never assume you have understood everything.

6. Summarize, paraphrase, and interpret correctly.

Every time you interview someone for a job, you are trying to acquire massive amounts of data in a single structured conversation. The following list of suggested questions should get you started. Add your own specific job related questions—about relevant experience and credentials—to this list. Note that some questions apply to all job candidates; others are specific to the type of individual you need.

Suggested Interview Questions

If you are placing newspaper ads and screening job candidates on your own, prepare a checklist of questions to prescreen prospective candidates on the phone prior to scheduling a personal interview. Additionally, prepare questions that you will ask during the first personal interview.

If you are using the services of an employment agency, the agency should ask some fundamental questions about work experience and job attitudes during the agency's prescreening interview. However, you will still need to cover the following issues personally, even if the agency has already introduced the topic:

Checklist of Suggested Interview Questions

General (for prescreening)

◆ My business is home-based. Have you ever worked in a home-based business before?

◆ Do you have any concerns about working in a home-based business?

◆ What concerns do you have?

◆ Tell me about your most recent work assignments.

◆ Why did you decide to apply for this position?

Independent Contractors

◆ What type of work assignments are you most proficient in? Most comfortable with?

◆ How would you characterize your style of work?

◆ What are your most significant accomplishments?

◆ Tell me about other businesses you have worked with. What did you like best? Least?

◆ Tell me about the other assignments you are working on now. What are your schedule requirements? What conflicts might arise?

Employees

◆ How was the _____ as a place to work?

◆ What was the most difficult part of your last job?

◆ What kind of position would you like to hold in five years?

◆ Tell me about the worst boss you ever had . . . and the best.

◆ What do you think you'll most enjoy about this job? Least?

◆ What kind of people drive you nuts? Work well with you?

◆ What kinds of work situations are most comfortable for you? Least?

◆ What would you like my company to provide for you for growth and development?

Interns

◆ In what ways do you think your current program of study will help you with this job?

◆ How can this job help you in your present curriculum? How can it help you later?

◆ What are your career interests upon graduation?

◆ What has high school/college done for your development?

◆ What are your toughest problems in school now?

◆ What types of teachers do you work best with?

Figure 11-3: Checklist of Suggested Interview Questions

Independent Contractors

Your greatest flexibility is with part-time independent contractors. You can negotiate flexible work arrangements. They can help you handle specialized project work. They can be hired when you need them and not during your slow periods. In addition to offering freedom from accounting paperwork and tax payments as discussed in chapter 10, independent contractors usually have their own home offices and prefer not to work from your office. If an independent contractor works for you at your client's location, you can still keep the client's main files at your own home office while your independent contractor maintains the day-to-day records and correspondence.

When you hire independent contractors, you can have the benefit of working with someone who comes to you trained, experienced, and ready to hit the ground running. What you might pay in higher fees is compensated in not paying for training time.

Employees

Your biggest commitment, both financially and personally, is to a full-time employee. All the issues defined in the chapter on taxation come into play. Paperwork rules. Schedules have to be agreed upon. Benefits will have to be discussed. This is enough to send many entrepreneurs into a constant state of personal overload. They'll do anything rather than deal with paperwork.

Interns

Your least expensive alternative is interns. Commitment is more than personal. The commitment of interns is to their education and their degree program. You are simply a means to an end. But what a significant end!

Interns are students in a degree-related program who work part-time for a company to earn credit and experience in a business position related to their field of study. They are not paid a salary or benefits by the company, but they do receive full or partial academic credit for their work. You can make arrangements for intern positions in your business by working with local high schools or colleges. Your contact will be someone in the department related to the field of your work, e.g., Marketing, Journalism, Accounting.

The school or college will require documentation from you in order to decide if your job qualifies for an internship. You will need to define your job in detail. In addition, you will be asked to describe how this job offers an opportunity for a student to learn valuable job skills related to the course of study.

Taking the Next Step

Home-based business owners have all the same employment options as any other small business owner. Put aside preconceived notions that you cannot have someone else work with you at home. Get over that privacy hang-up. Hire a housekeeper or cleaning personnel. Add structure to your schedule (it really won't kill you). Move beyond the personal and into the professional.

Insurance and Other Financial Planning Concerns

- ◆ Insurance Considerations

- ◆ Attaining Financial Security

- ◆ Succession Planning

Insurance Considerations

You should contact your insurance agent as soon as you start your business to verify that your basic homeowner's policy covers fundamental liability issues related to the business. "Your homeowner's policy, regardless of the company that underwrites it, is designed to protect the homeowner and a little bit of your business contents," insurance broker Audrey Kessler explains. Kessler has counseled many home-based business owners as well as corporate moguls. "From a liability standpoint, the protection is extended to the homeowner, not the business." Many home-based business owners fail to recognize that business-related losses may not be covered under their homeowner's and auto insurance policies.

As soon as *anyone* comes to your home for a business-related purpose, his trip and fall can become *your downfall.* In addition, if you maintain inventory or purchase expensive business equipment, you may need to extend your coverage. If these potential hazards are not listed under your basic homeowner's policy, additional riders, endorsements, and/or policies are available. A business pursuits endorsement, for example, under your homeowner's policy can provide additional protection. This endorsement permits the insured to run a home-based business for a small additional premium. You want to be sure that your homeowner's policy covers you if a person is injured at your residence while there for business reasons. "Every time you run a business from your home, you open up a can of worms," said Kessler. "It's either 'pay now' (for additional insurance coverage) or 'pay a lot later' (after an uncovered loss)."

Your insurance agent will ask you a series of questions for underwriting purposes, to determine what type of coverage is most appropriate for you, and to identify special insurance coverage needs. If you exceed the insurer's basic guidelines, you will need to arrange for separate coverage for your business, either through the business pursuits endorsement on your homeowner's policy or with an additional commercial policy. Guidelines are primarily focused on the amount of business equipment you own, visitors coming to the home for business, deliveries of business-related packages or materials, and workers in the home. Figure 12-1 lists many of the questions your insurance agent should ask you to determine the coverage you need.

As your business gets off the ground, your next concerns will include your professional reputation, the information and data you deal with, the inventory you store, and the people who work for you.

Insurance Coverage Questions

Your insurance agent should ask you at least the following questions to identify the appropriate level of insurance coverage for your home-based business.

What is the nature of the business? Describe the business.

Describe the products and/or services you provide. Be specific about how these products and services are produced.

Do you create or manufacture a product at your home?

Do any employees work at your home?

Is there an area of the house dedicated to the business?

Do customers/clients come to your house for appointments, meetings, or conferences?

Do you receive frequent deliveries from UPS, vendors, manufacturers, or other sources addressed to your business?

Do you use your car for business?

Do you have special equipment, business supplies, and/or products for your business? What would you estimate the value of your business property and equipment to be?

Do you handle special data or records that must be protected for you or your clients?

Do you maintain inventory for your own business or for your clients?

Do you have any business property that is being used off-premises?

Are you a professional practitioner?

Figure 12-1: Insurance Coverage Questions

General Liability Insurance

If you manufacture or sell a product, have clients come to your home office, or have off-premises operations—just to mention a few scenarios—you may want to protect your business against lawsuits arising from slips and falls, product liability, and so on. (Remember, your homeowner's policy only protects the homeowner, not the business.)

Professional Liability

This is important for many professional practitioners. Professional liability is defined as "failure to perform," where because of your professional advice or actions, someone suffers financially or physically. It is also called malpractice insurance or errors and omissions. Examples of candidates for professional liability insurance are listed in figure 12-2.

Professional Liability Insurance

Are you a professional practitioner? Is there any possibility that a client/customer could incur financial or physical harm as a result of your advice or design? You should consider professional liability insurance if you are a(n):

accountant

attorney

insurance agent

financial planner

doctor (including psychologist)

engineer

architect

interior decorator

computer analyst

nurse or other health care professional

teacher or tutor

security consultant

real estate salesperson

publishing professional*

*If you have exposure to published materials and intellectual properties, printing, trademarks, and copyrights, or if you are in the business of "naming names" or quoting people, talk to your agent about specific coverage requirements.

Figure 12-2: Professional Liability Insurance

Workers' Compensation

In most states, the law requires that you have Workers' Compensation if you have anyone working for you—on the books or off. This applies whether the individual(s) work in your home or in their own or if they are on the road, regardless of age. Personal liability does not cover your employees. Check with your insurance agent about personal and commercial coverage. Your agent will be able to arrange for the appropriate amount.

Automobile Insurance

If you use your car, truck, or van for business, let your agent know. Your agent will determine whether you need a personal or commercial automobile policy. Using your car to transport *you* is usually not a problem. But if you are a mason, electrician, mover, caterer, or other service that transports tools or equipment for work, you will need a commercial automobile policy. If you have a sign on the car and/or have employees using the car, you will need a commercial policy. Using a car for these purposes could result in denial of a claim if you do not have a commercial policy.

Business Equipment and Property

Homeowner's policies include varying amounts of property insurance protection. They all, however, contain a limit for business property. "Some policies offer a minimum $2,500 coverage for business property on premises," according to Audrey Kessler. "Property" includes office equipment and supplies, but the "on-premises" provision of the homeowner's allowance will not cover portable technology like your laptop computer or cellular phone if damage or theft occurs on the road. Your agent may need to arrange for property coverage for business property over the limit or for business property that is kept off premises.

Business Data

This includes such data as accounting books, drawings or other paper records, electronic data processing tapes, wires, records, disks, or other software media. This is not covered under your homeowner's policy. If you have any files that need to be re-created (e.g., if you are an accountant, attorney, realtor, insurance agent, software designer) you'll need special coverage in order to get the data covered. You may be able to protect limited amounts of data by purchasing a fireproof cabinet, but a smart move is to add valuable papers coverage.

A Basic Business Owner's Policy (BOP)

This type of policy contains business property and business interruption coverage, liability, and many incidental coverages that are important to your business. Not all businesses are eligible for a BOP, but if your business qualifies it could cost as little as $300 for a good package. "It's like a homeowner's policy for a business," said Kessler. Many features are built in, but additional features can be included as you need them. Optional endorsements of a BOP include:

- **valuable papers coverage** for business data described above

- **electric data processing coverage** for the software and hardware packages you own or store

- **non-owned and hired car coverage** for your delivery staff and drivers

- **employee dishonesty coverage** for those slips and falls from grace

BOP packages differ by carrier, but many incidental coverages can be added including:

- **health and disability insurance,** which should be strongly considered (see below)

- **life insurance** if you have dependents, are a single parent, or are the financial head of your household

- **business interruption insurance** to protect you from situations beyond your control that could force you to temporarily close your business

Disability Insurance

Disability insurance is designed to protect your income if you are unable to continue working for an extended period of time. Unfortunately, disability insurance is difficult to obtain for home-based business workers. "A disability is difficult to monitor in a home-based business," said Alyce Hackett, a certified financial planner. Many insurance companies are reluctant to provide this coverage because they cannot discern if a disabled individual is still working or is truly incapacitated. Insurance companies pay for the latter, not the former.

You will need to search the different insurance companies to find disability insurance if you decide you want it. Get a broker to help you. If you have a separate exterior entrance to your office, according to Alyce Hackett, that may help. Obtaining disability insurance will still be difficult, but you might have an advantage.

Financial planning for a disability is not something the typical entrepreneur wants to dwell on while enthusiastic and energetic about a new venture. On the other hand, without financial planning you can leave yourself open to major problems later on. Loss of steady income can be devastating for most families. "Women can be the worst offenders," said Hackett, "especially if their spouse's income is the greater of the two." Sometimes people fail to recognize the significance of the combined total income on the day-to-day operation of the household, as well as the business. Today more than ever, it often takes two incomes to survive. For a home-based business owner who is able to coordinate child care with the business, the cost of child care must be factored into the cost of disability. Not only will there be a loss of income but also the added expense of a housekeeper or nanny to handle the day-to-day routine.

Personal disability is only one potential cause of loss of income from a home-based business. If you have children, or if you are responsible for elderly relatives, you already know what happens when someone gets sick or needs undivided attention. Usually, the home-worker is the one to take time off and take charge. When these situations occur randomly, for short intervals, most business owners can push ahead and make up for lost time. But in the case of an extended illness, it will be more difficult to insulate the business from impact. You will have to provide a cushion for yourself— in addition to your retirement planning, not instead of it—in case of emergency.

Attaining Financial Security

With the help of a good financial planner, you can establish a plan to save for unexpected periods of lost income, extraordinary expenses, and unanticipated time off. In addition, you can set up a strategy to reach your financial goals realistically.

Alyce Hackett starts by listing all the options and alternatives for an individual. "Then one by one we explore the pros and cons of each option. We examine 'what if' scenarios and plan for a number of possibilities." Hackett recommends that home-based business owners consult with a financial planner when they first start their business. It is also important to reassess your financial position if you experience steady changes in your business or if your personal situation changes. A financial planner will look at your unique situation and prioritize your needs based on anticipated income, your age, the type of business you are engaged in, your inventory, your general health, and how much you contribute to family needs with the income from this business.

Figure 12-3 summarizes Hackett's suggestions for financial planning.

Succession Planning

What is your vision for the long-term future of your business? Do you hope that the same little hands that played on your computer and messed up your filing system will one day take over? Not every succession succeeds, unfortunately. If your partner or children are interested in keeping your business going after you're gone (one hopes into a happy retirement), you still need to plan for a transition if you want the business to carry on smoothly.

Hackett's Habits for Financial Planning

Honestly assess your personality.

Honestly consider your personality when you make your initial projection of income. "Be honest with yourself about *you*," she cautions. "What *effort* are you going to invest in this business, and does your projected income reflect this?"

Establish financial goals that consider your business and personal needs.

Do you have pre-college-age children you need to begin saving for? Are you ready to plan for your retirement? Would you like to see steady growth for your business?

Keep your financial goals and time span in sight whenever you make important decisions.

If you want your business to grow, there may be a benefit to taking out a loan instead of dipping into savings. Assess your risks and your expenditures as well as the timing.

Have an emergency fund in the bank.

Put 3-6 months of income in the bank in case of an emergency. (Hackett recommends using a money market fund for fast access.)

Always maintain a balanced portfolio.

You can't afford to be all risk-oriented or invested too heavily in one area. Closely examine your:

◆ time horizon

◆ needed return

◆ risk tolerance

Figure 12-3: Hackett's Habits for Financial Planning

What happens if your family has no interest in maintaining the business without you? Is an employee, or an outside party, a possibility? Many people operating a business have to face this issue. Yes, this may be unpleasant to think about but it's your responsibility to face. Your partnership agreement or operating agreement, depending on your business structure, will force you to deal with these issues when you form the business. Be sure to add to these parameters, drawn up early in your business life cycle, as you learn more about the shape and focus of your business and the people best suited to build your legacy.

Using Revocable Living Trusts

Distributing personal property by will is complex enough. Add a business to the mix and matters become infinitely more complicated. Consider this fair warning: If your family and friends have suffered through the growth of this business with you, you do not want to burden them with problems later. You especially want to avoid probate.

If your will is contested, it might take a year to resolve issues that could have been clarified up front. Many business owners today avoid this dilemma by setting up a living trust, which enables a trustee to take over the day after you die. And if you are incapacitated, the living trust enables you to achieve a smooth transition in your management structure.

Do you want to protect your business against disability or death? Consider a living trust. A living trust is any trust created in your life. *(Note: A trust is defined as a legal entity that holds property for the benefit of others.)*

Irrevocable Living Trust

This is a living trust that is not part of your estate. It can't be altered once it is created and signed.

Revocable Living Trust

Only you can change the terms of this trust.

Many individuals select the alternative of revocable living trust because they retain control of the trust assets. You are the trustee—usually, if you are in good mental health—and make all the decisions about the assets. You can also be the beneficiary and receive income from the trust.

Setting up a trust is not an inexpensive activity. Costs vary by location. Assume that about $500 to $3500 will be the fee to prepare all legal documents, which also include a will and durable power of attorney. If you secure a durable power of attorney, then someone else can handle the nontrust assets in your name if you should become incompetent. Should you become incompetent without a living trust and a power of attorney, your family and associates cannot take over for you without court approval. This can be needlessly time-consuming for all concerned and can also be harmful to the business.

When the Time Comes to Move . . .
or Move Out

- ◆ When Your Business Grows
- ◆ Assess Your Situation
- ◆ Interim Solutions to Your Space Problems
- ◆ Conventional Office or Bigger Home?
- ◆ Buy, Lease, or Rent
- ◆ Workstyles and Lifestyles Reconsidered
- ◆ A Personal Decision

When Your Business Grows

If rapid growth is in the picture for your business, make sure it's what you truly want. What was your initial vision for your business? When you formulated your long-term and short-term business goals, did expansion factor into your plans? Rapid growth will become an all-consuming activity. Building a bigger business will dominate your life and your work. Are you ready for this transition?

Preparation for your business growth is as important as preparation for start-up. Remember those long hours and heavy financing requirements? You're in for Round Two when your business successfully takes off. Make sure that growth is profitable for you at this time. Control it. Plan for it. Identify your needs.

Assess Your Situation

When you estimated the cost of setting up your business and building it through your first year, you probably felt that you needed a crystal ball to do your pro formas. Original estimates are often the most difficult to prepare because you are dealing with so many unknowns.

Generating your next series of financial projections will be more comfortable because you have a track record to work with. When your business takes off quickly, you have real data to manipulate for your next set of projections. It is important to honestly assess the reality of rapid growth, considering the personal and financial commitment growth entails. You may decide to put on the brakes until you feel ready to handle it. Or you may find that it is time to accelerate.

As you weigh your options, consider the impact of your business growth in the following areas:

Your Marketing Strategy

◆ Will the business grow in new areas or through existing product/ service lines?

◆ Is your market segment the same or will you target new areas?

◆ What competition will you face if you expand?

◆ How will you challenge your competition and gain an advantage?

Your Financial Strategy

◆ How much will it cost to expand or modify your marketing strategy, enhance or change your product/service line, produce and distribute your line, and so on?

◆ Can you finance this expansion yourself, or will you need help? What options are available to you now?

◆ How long will it be until you see a profit from this growth?

◆ How can you support this growth? How much money will you need for new equipment, supplies, and the like?

Your Operations

◆ Will new equipment requirements cause your space to become cramped?

◆ How many desks will you need? What equipment, technology, and facilities will be required?

◆ How much additional office space will you need to expand?

Your Organization Structure

◆ How many people will be needed to staff this growth? Estimate the number of employees, independent contractors, and interns— part-time and full-time.

◆ What type of training will be needed for you and your staff? How much time will it take to bring your staff up to speed?

◆ Will you need to change your salary structure, commission plans, and/or benefits as your staff grows?

◆ Is it time to formalize some of the informal aspects of your management structure (job descriptions, for example)?

Perhaps the most important consideration of growth for a home-based business is personal and more difficult to determine. *Do you, your family, and your staff have the stamina to take on the challenge . . . again?*

Interim Solutions to Your Space Problems

When you first start to feel the pinch of tight quarters, you may not need to rush into changing locations immediately. You may be better off exploring interim solutions to your space problems before you panic.

Consider the options listed below to evaluate your long-term need.

Join an Office Suite Arrangement

These arrangements have become available throughout the country as a cost-effective alternative to renting your own office space. In addition to an office, desk, shelves, and phone, you will usually have shared use of a receptionist, copy machines, word processing services, conference rooms, and other equipment. Fees and schedules differ, but many arrangements include a monthly fee for a furnished office and receptionist and separate charges for all other services based on frequency of use. Try an arrangement like this before you commit to a long-term lease on office space if you are ambivalent about leaving home.

Borrow a Conference Room from a Larger Small Business

You may find that your home office works for most of your needs with a few exceptions, such as occasional large group meetings. If you have been networking, you will have made contact with other small-business owners who have outside office space. You may be able to work out an arrangement to use their space for your occasional needs. Conference rooms are rarely used all day long (unless the company has also outgrown its space) and may be available for scheduled intervals during the day or evening. Explore the possibility of renting this space on a hourly basis or barter through services for use of the room.

Borrow an Office from a Colleague

You may find that your business busy hours differ from those of your friends and associates. If your schedules do not coincide, you may be able to negotiate for use of their office space when they aren't around. An offer to pay some amount of hourly or daily rent will be advised.

Use the Offices of Professional Associations

Membership may have its privileges. Sometimes these not-for-profit facilities far outclass anything available in the real world where you have to actually pay for furniture and furnishings.

Conventional Office or Bigger Home?

Ellen Silverman, founder of Ellen Silverman Advertising, has operated her successful marketing and advertising business both in and out of her home for over fifteen years. When her business began to take off, she sought outside office space. But as it turned out, in the long run, a home office was the best solution for her company. For Silverman and many other companies long past the start-up stage, there is still no place like home.

Growth of your business doesn't necessarily mean that the business needs to move out of your home to meet additional demands for space. Many home-based businesses set the goal of adding home space over moving out. Assess your decision to seek additional room by the same detailed, logical, financial approach you would use to determine whether it would make more sense to remodel your existing home or move to a larger home.

Silverman made her decision to move her office out of her home when her business began to encroach on personal living space. The business overwhelmed the house. "Three people were working in the dining room. I couldn't entertain and I couldn't relax," she said. She also had two grown children living at home. With money in the bank and a steadily increasing business, Silverman took the advice of family and business associates who encouraged her to rent office space. In retrospect, Silverman remembers a great sense of accomplishment and fulfillment at that time. "I proved I could do it. I could drive along the highway and see my sign."

However, Silverman's business took a big financial hit after almost three years in rented space. The business had grown to six people, but the recession hit hard. Silverman had to reassess the direction and scope of the business. She decided to return to her house, scale down the company, and build back up step-by-step.

Other home-based business owners have decided to add space in their current home rather than move or move out. This is the approach I took when my office began to overrun the kids' play area in the basement at the same time that our growing family needed more room. The solution was to add a first-floor office and larger family room at the same time. While living and working through construction is an experience I would never want to repeat, there is no doubt this was the best solution for us. After seven years of looking out the basement window at the ankles of passersby, I truly appreciate my current ground-level vantage point.

Buy, Lease, or Rent

The decision to buy, lease, or rent is as personal as it is financial. If your financial projections indicate that you are capable of paying rent for outside office space, even considering seasonal fluctuations in your business cycle, or delicate economic conditions, that's only part of your concern. Signing a lease requires a personal commitment to make this work. Can you find a place you like—almost as much as home—and does it suit the needs of your business?

If you rent your home or apartment, you may have more flexibility in terms of where you move, but less flexibility in terms of timing. Many urban home-based business owners choose to rent an additional apartment in the same building as their primary residence to gain additional space. This approach has the potential to introduce a brief "commute" (e.g., an elevator ride) into the routine, but maintains the advantages of a home-based business in many regards.

When you aren't certain about location, size, or business needs, a short-term lease or rental agreement offers a safe alternative to the long-term commitment of a mortgage.

Until you are certain of the direction of your business, be careful not to get stuck with payments you may not be able to meet.

Workstyles and Lifestyles Reconsidered

Try not to lose sight of your initial business inspiration as your business grows. If your personal situation has changed since you formed your business and decided to base it at home, you should reassess. Factors that may alter your point of view include:

Change in Your Marital Status

If you were not married when you started the business, consider if your spouse can adapt—or if you can adapt—to the business at home. If you were married and aren't now, can you manage with less personal contact each day? This depends, of course, on how the separation came about. Do you need daily contact with other people? Will you be able to get it through networking or clients? Watch out for isolation and insulation.

Arrival of Children

"Arrival" can mean birth, adoption, or, in today's boomerang society, adult children returning home to live. Can you tolerate the additional commotion? How well can you block out background noise? Will you welcome the company or begrudge the intrusions? Can you remain focused?

Changing Ages of Your Children

Some home-based workers tolerate toddlers better than preteens and teenagers. The constant flurry of activity that accompanies older children may drive you nuts. Telephone calls, drop-in visitors, sports gear, shuttle requests to and from after-school activities. . . . The list is endless. Even with a separate room, insulated walls, and private business phone lines, the heightened pace of your household at this stage of your children's lives will either invigorate or exasperate you. The first time Green Day echoes through your office walls while you're on a corporate conference call may be the last. On the other hand, for many parents this is the most important time to be home—or at least accessible. Monitoring that after-school frenzy may give you a sense that you're heading off future problems you might otherwise be forced to face as a result of lack of supervision.

Do you remember the list of pros and cons of home-based business set forth in chapter 2—and the warning that some characteristics of home-based work may be viewed as positive or negative, depending on your perspective? Reconsider these issues as your business grows and your needs change. How do you feel about these concerns today?

Dealing with Daily Survival Issues

Have you had your fill of minutiae? Are you ready to scream every time you are the one emptying the wastebaskets and running to the post office? If you're a big picture person and miss distraction-free hours of corporate strategic planning in a conference room (that someone else has furnished and cleaned), it may be time to return to the big business fold.

Technology Updates

Have you honestly been able to stay up-to-the-minute in your field? Are you actively involved in professional organizations that provide the latest and greatest tips in your area of specialization? Do you keep up with trade publications, business contacts, and networking groups?

Flexible Work Schedule

Have you been able to impose self-discipline, or is a lack of formal schedule having a negative effect on your productivity? Does your 3:00 P.M. break time with your children mean your workday falls apart? Or do you fall into the opposite extreme—you just can't *stop* working? Have your odd work hours turned you into an odd person?

No One to Pass the Buck to

Are you miserable without someone to delegate to? Are you overwhelmed with the responsibility of acting out too many roles in your business? Is the home office making it more difficult for you to learn to delegate?

Co-workers

Are you lonely? Does a schedule of breakfast, lunch, and/or dinner networking events leave you unfulfilled? Do you still miss gathering around the coffee machine and arranging spontaneous lunches?

Child Care

If child care responsibilities are impossible for you to delegate during your business hours, and you cannot work around this, it is time to reconsider your arrangement. If you set up an office in your home to spend more time with your family, but neither the business nor your family is getting a fair share of your efforts, it is time to readjust. You may need to draw more clearly defined lines between family time and work time.

A Personal Decision

"For too many years," said Ellen Silverman, "I let too many people tell me what to do next." When her advertising agency became successful, building an even bigger business seemed to be a logical next step. Sometimes, however, the personal price of fast business growth is too high. If your business growth creates a lifestyle that runs counter to your personal goals, you may end up feeling miserable.

Silverman let her business grow to the point where her home could no longer accommodate it. She rented outside office space. Now she has decided that she will limit her business growth in the future rather than move the office out of her present home. She has no regrets. She feels she can build her business to $1 million comfortably in her home. Her goals today reflect a conscious decision to regulate the growth of her business to fit a structure she's happy with. With her vision of controlled growth, Silverman has decided that quality, not quantity, counts most. Her goal is to maintain a small base of profitable clients. She also hopes to concentrate her time and efforts on sales and marketing, conceptualizing and creative work. She plans to maintain a small staff for implementation and follow-through.

"You've got to like to get up in the morning. You have to know what success means to you," said Silverman.

The definition of success is truly personal.

References for Your Present and Future Needs

- ◆ Government Resources
- ◆ Organizations and Associations
- ◆ Women and Minorities Assistance
- ◆ Procurement Assistance
- ◆ Patents, Trademarks, and Copyrights

Government Resources

U.S. Small Business Administration (SBA)
409 Third Street, SW
Washington, DC 20416
(800) 827-5722

The SBA serves small businesses directly through a wide variety of programs. Counseling provided for businesses starting up includes business-plan preparation, workshops, and individual counseling. The SBA offers publications on virtually all aspects of small business needs. (See Appendix A for the SBA office nearest you.)

SBA Small Business Answer Desk—(by phone only)
(800) 827-5722

The Answer Desk is the main point of contact for general inquiries about the services available through the SBA. Included is information on other resources within federal, state, and local government agencies and the private sector. The Answer Desk will provide information on specific issues as well as direct inquiries to the appropriate person or department.

SBA On-line
General access—(800) 697-4636
D.C. area access—(202) 401-9600

This on-line electronic information service can be accessed with a computer and a modem. You are provided with immediate access to information on SBA programs, SBA field offices, business development services, government contracting opportunities.

SBA Office of Economic Development
409 Third Street, SW, Suite 8200
Washington, DC 20416
(202) 205-6657

Existing and prospective small businesses can get help in improving management and operational skills through programs and services offered within the SBA and other federal departments and agencies. Types of available assistance include:

◆ workshops and seminars for prospective business owners

◆ management counseling

◆ management courses, conferences and clinics

◆ minority and women's assistance

◆ individual counseling

◆ management-related publications (Call the Small Business Answer Desk—(800) 827-5722 for information on how to order.)

The following services are offered through SBA district and field offices or through SBA-affiliated programs:

Small Business Development Centers (SBDC) coordinate federal, state, local, university, and private resources for counseling and training small business owners. Services include management and technical assistance and training, and advice on marketing, finances, production, and organization. (See Appendix A for SBDC listings by state.)

Small Business Institutes (SBI) offer intensive university-based management training and counseling programs. Contact your local SBA office (Appendix A) to participate in the program.

Business Information Centers (BIC) use the latest information and telecommunications technology to provide small businesses access to market research databases, business planning software, and other information helpful to starting and building a business. Individual counseling is offered in conjunction with SCORE (below). Contact your local SBA office (Appendix A) or call the Small Business Answer Desk (800) 827-5722 to locate the BIC in your area.

Service Corps of Retired Executives (SCORE) are local volunteer groups that provide problem-solving assistance to small businesses. SCORE tries to match counselor experience with client needs. To find the SCORE office in your area call (800) 634-0245.

Office of Advocacy
409 Third Street, SW, Mail Code 3114
Washington, DC 20416
(202) 205-6531

The Office of Advocacy is composed of experts in law and economics whose task is to ensure that legislation and regulations that may affect small businesses are examined carefully to minimize hardship and maximize the benefit to small firms. The office is supported on the local and state levels by regional advocates who help identify new issues and problems of small businesses by monitoring the effect of federal and state regulations and policies on the local business communities within their regions.

Veterans Affairs Office
409 Third Street, SW, 6th Floor
Washington, DC 20416
(202) 205-6773

By arrangement between the SBA and the Department of Veterans Affairs, special business ownership training is available to eligible veterans. The Veterans Affairs Office provides professional and technical assistance, specialized subject matter workshops, and pre-business and start-up counseling. The Veterans Affairs Office also publishes information specifically for the small business owner who is a veteran. Call the Veterans Affairs Office directly or the toll-free Small Business Answer Desk, (800) 827-5722, for publications and information on financing.

> U.S. Department of Commerce (DOC)
> 14th Street between Constitution Avenue and E Street, NW
> Washington, DC 20230
> (202) 482-2000

The Department of Commerce encourages, promotes, and serves the nation's interest in commerce. Both national and international issues are represented in a wide scope of departments. Specific areas that are addressed include scientific and technological infrastructure, economic analysis, census information, consumer affairs, minority business development, and international trade, to name a few.

Contact your local DOC (see Appendix A) for programs and services available in your area. Note: DOC programs dedicated to women and minority owned businesses are described in the section below entitled "Women and Minorities Assistance."

Organizations and Associations

Organizations and associations are among the most valuable private-sector resources that offer help to small businesses. There are two categories—(1) general business organizations with memberships consisting of all types of businesses, and (2) trade associations, which focus on a specific industry and are organized to work out common problems and promote themselves as a group.

Besides providing excellent networking opportunities, these organizations and associations work to protect the interests of their membership by monitoring developments in legislative and regulatory environments at federal and state levels. In addition, some groups work to educate the public and often provide advertising to promote general use of a product or service as opposed to use of a specific brand or company.

Organizations and associations can offer help in directing small businesses to sources of loans, venture capital, and start-up capital. Memberships can include Small Business Investment Companies (SBIC) and Certified Development Companies (CDC). (See chapter 6—"Financing Your Venture.")

General Business Organizations

U.S. Chamber of Commerce
1615 H Street, NW
Washington, DC 20062
(202) 659-6000

Chambers of Commerce exist at national, state, and local levels. The U.S. Chamber of Commerce works with state and local chambers to help businesses succeed. It provides an important link between national business interests and the federal government. It is the world's largest federation of businesses and associations with the primary mission of enhancing the free enterprise system. More than 96 percent of the Chamber's members are small businesses with fewer than 100 employees; 71 percent of these have fewer than 10 employees. The Small Business Center is the focal point for Chamber involvement with small business concerns. The Chamber provides a variety of services and publications, with new information offered on an ongoing basis.

State chambers coordinate local programs statewide and represent the state business community to the state and federal government. (See Appendix A for state listings.)

Local chapters meet the needs of businesses by offering various programs that address general areas of interest to local businesses. Programs offering start-up assistance, business loans, equity capital, management training, and problem-solving often are available through a local Chamber of Commerce.

Small Business Center
(202) 463-5503

The Small Business Center of the U.S. Chamber is the primary source of information on small business issues for its members, Congress, the administration, the media, and others.

Publications include a monthly newsletter entitled *U.S. Chamber Watch on Small Business Legislation and Regulation* with a column highlighting prominent issues in the administration and on Capitol Hill. Also available is a booklet called *Concerns of Small Business* that answers questions most commonly asked by business owners. Information on SBA loans, government agencies, and legislative issues is also available to members.

Office of Membership Grassroots Management
(202) 463-5604

Grassroots Action Information Network (GAIN) is a vehicle for Chamber members to communicate their opinions to members of Congress as well as for tracking relevant business issues. Background information and updates on issues tracked by the U.S. Chamber are available to participants.

Alliance of Independent Store Owners and Professionals (AISOP)
3725 Multifoods Tower
Minneapolis, MN 55402
(612) 340-9855

AISOP consists of 3,500 members, most of whom are independent small-business owners whose mission is to protect and promote fair postal and legislative policies for small-business advertisers. Reasonable third class mail rates are important to members to promote business and contact customers in their trade areas. Affordable mail rates for advertising are critical in enabling members to compete with larger businesses that advertise in print and on radio and television. AISOP monitors postal rates and regulations, sales taxes, privacy issues, and pertinent environmental legislation.

American Entrepreneur Association (AEA)
2392 Morse Avenue
Irvine, CA 92714
(714) 261-2325
Membership information
(800) 421-2300; in California call (800) 352-7449

AEA publishes *Entrepreneur*, a monthly magazine with articles of interest to would-be entrepreneurs and small-business owners. Members of the organization receive the magazine *Entrepreneur* each month, as well as discounts on operations manuals and free counseling. There are more than 250 start-up operations manuals available for purchase. These include step-by-step instructions on starting and running a business.

Coalition for Responsible Franchising
933 Alden, Suite 100
Buffalo Grove, IL 60089
(708) 520-1809

The coalition is a nonprofit organization dedicated to preserving a positive business environment and promoting an increased understanding of the dynamics and value of franchising. The coalition undertakes activities to encourage sound public policy that will maintain and grow productive franchise relationships.

Edward Lowe Foundation
P.O. Box 8
Cassopolis, MI 49031
(616) 445-4200/4244

This foundation was established in 1985 to adopt the mission of fostering and promoting small business and entrepreneurship. It seeks to represent the interests of the small business community and provides services and programs to assist small businesses.

Employee Benefit Research Institute (EBRI)
2121 K Street, NW, Suite 600
Washington, DC 20037-1896
(202) 659-0670

EBRI is a nonprofit research organization dedicated to research and education on issues which include health care, retirement, child care, flexible benefits, 401(k) arrangements, and other benefit programs. Publications include Employee Benefit Notes, EBRI Issue Briefs, EBRI's Benefit Outlook, EBRI Washington Bulletin, Quarterly Pension Investment Report, and Fundamentals of Employee Benefit Programs.

International Franchise Association (IFA)
1350 New York Avenue, NW, Suite 900
Washington, DC 20005-4709
(202) 628-8000

IFA is dedicated to enhancing and safeguarding the business environment for franchisees and franchisers around the world. IFA is a resource center for current and prospective franchisees, franchisers, the media, and the government. IFA has promoted programs that expand opportunities for women and minorities in franchising (see "Women and Minorities Assistance" below). IFA offers an extensive catalog of publications available by calling this number: (800) 543-1038. The *Franchise Opportunity Guide* lists every franchise opportunity in the U.S., along with the person to contact. Other publications offer information on buying a franchise, financing, franchising a business, and legal issues in franchising.

National Association of Development Companies (NADCO)
4301 N. Fairfax Drive, Suite 860
Arlington, VA 22203
(703) 812-9000

NADCO is the trade group for Certified Development Companies (CDC). These community-based nonprofit organizations promote small business expansion and job creation through the U.S. Small Business Administration's 504 loan program. This program offers fixed, low-interest loans to qualified existing businesses for the purchase of fixed assets. This funding is guaranteed by the SBA. Call the NADCO number listed above for the CDC in your state.

National Association for the Self-Employed (NASE)
2121 Precinct Line Road
Hurst, TX 76054
(800) 232-6273

NASE is comprised of small business owners having generally fewer than five employees. The association offers over 100 benefits that include federal and state representation, business equipment discounts, travel-related discounts, a toll-free business consultant hotline (listed above), and small business publications. NASE also offers a range of insurance products and conducts membership research to determine and report small business concerns.

National Association of Small Business Investment Companies (NASBIC)
1199 N. Fairfax Street, Suite 200
Alexandria, VA 22314

NASBIC coordinates and promotes activities of over 400 small business investment companies (SBIC) nationwide. SBICs are privately capitalized, owned, and managed investment firms licensed by the SBA that provide equity capital, long-term financing, and management assistance to small businesses.

The actual assistance is provided by individual SBICs. A directory listing over 400 SBICs is available from NASBIC for $10.00 by writing to: NASBIC Directory, P.O. Box 4039, Merrifield, VA 22116.

National Association of Manufacturers (NAM)
1331 Pennsylvania Avenue, NW, Suite 1500
Washington, DC 20004-1780

NAM is a membership-based association representing 12,500 manufacturers nationwide, more than 9,000 of which are small businesses.

National Business Association (NBA)
5025 Arapaho Road, Suite 515
Dallas, TX 75248
(800) 456-0440

The NBA provides small-business owners and entrepreneurs with benefits and services in the areas of business, lifestyle, health, and education. These benefits include group health, dental and disability insurance, travel discounts, informative publications, and business services.

National Federation of Independent Businesses (NFIB)
53 Century Boulevard, Suite 205
Nashville, TN 37214
(615) 872-5800

The NFIB is a nonprofit organization dedicated to supporting the American free enterprise system. The guiding principal of NFIB is to determine, by opinion of its membership, policy positions on legislative and administrative issues affecting small and independent businesses.

National Small Business United (NSBU)
1155 15th Street, NW, Suite 710
Washington, DC 20005
(202) 293-8830

NSBU is a private, nonprofit organization representing more than 65,000 small-business owners through the U.S. Emphasizing bipartisan advocacy. NSBU works with members of Congress and other elected and appointed officials to improve the economic climate for small business survival and growth.

Puerto Rico Commerce Development Administration
P.O. Box S-4275
San Juan, PR 00905
(809) 721-3290

The administration serves the needs of small and medium-sized businesses of Puerto Rico. (Also listed in the section entitled "Women and Minorities Assistance.")

Small Business Survival Committee (SBSC)
1320 18th Street, NW
Washington, DC 20036
(202) 785-0238

SBSC is a 40,000 member nonprofit, nonpartisan advocacy organization. Members of SBSC represent a diversity of small businesses and enterprises across America.

National Association for the Cottage Industry (NACI)
P.O. Box 14850
Chicago, IL 60614
(312) 472-8116

This 30,000-member group provides information to cottage workers (i.e. workers producing goods in the home) through a bimonthly newsletter and semiannual conferences.

National Association of Home-Based Businesses (NAHBB)
10451 Mill Run Circle, Suite 400
Owings Mills, MD 21117
(410) 363-3698

The NAHBB was founded in 1984, and works with home-based entrepreneurs in over 200 classifications of businesses. The association works to support and develop start-up and existing businesses by counseling members in business and marketing plan preparation as well as other business needs. Services include the Home-Based Business Information Superhighway on the Internet.
(http://www.USAHome-Business.com).

Trade Associations

Advertising Mail Marketing Association
1333 F Street, NW, Suite 710
Washington, DC 20004-1108
(202) 347-0055

American Bankers Association
1120 Connecticut Avenue, NW
Washington, DC 20036
(202) 663-5000

American Electronics Association
1225 Eye Street, NW, Suite 950
Washington, DC 20005
(202) 682-9110

American Financial Services Association
919 18th Street, NW, Third Floor
Washington, DC 20006
(202) 296-5544

American Forest and Paper Association
1111 19th Street, NW, Suite 700
Washington, DC 20036
(202) 463-2700

American Health Care Association
1201 L Street, NW, Eighth Floor
Washington, DC 20005
(202) 842-4444

American Institute of Certified Public Accountants
1455 Pennsylvania Avenue, NW, Suite 400
Washington, DC 20004
(202) 737-6600

American Insurance Association
1130 Connecticut Avenue, NW, Suite 1000
Washington, DC 20036
(202) 828-7100

American Petroleum Institute
1220 L Street, NW, Suite 900
Washington, DC 20005
(202) 682-8000

American Retail Federation
701 Pennsylvania Avenue, NW, Suite 710
Washington, DC 20004
(202) 783-7971

American Society of Travel Agents
1101 King Street
Alexandria, VA 22314
(703) 739-2782

American Trucking Association
430 First Street, SE
Washington, DC 20003
(202) 544-6245

Association of American Publishers
1718 Connecticut Avenue, NW, Suite 700
Washington, DC 20009
(202) 232-3335

Associated Builders and Contractors, Inc.
1300 North 17th Street
Arlington, VA 22209
(703) 812-2000

Associated General Contractors of America
1957 E Street, NW
Washington, DC 20006
(202) 393-2040

Automotive Parts and Accessories Association
4600 East-West Highway
Bethesda, MD 20814
(301) 654-6664

Automotive Service Association
P.O. Box 929
Bedford, TX 76095-0929
(817) 283-6205

Computer and Business Equipment Manufacturers Association
1250 Eye Street, NW, Suite 200
Washington, DC 20005
(202) 737-8888

Electronic Industries Association
2001 Pennsylvania Avenue, NW
Washington, DC 20006
(202) 457-4900

Food Marketing Institute
800 Connecticut Avenue, NW
Washington, DC 20006
(202) 452-8444

Independent Insurance Agents of America
412 First Street, SE, Suite 300
Washington, DC 20003
(202) 863-7000

Independent Petroleum Association of America
1101 16th Street, NW, Second Floor
Washington, DC 20036
(202) 857-4722

Information Industry Association
555 New Jersey Avenue, NW, Suite 800
Washington, DC 20001
(202) 639-8262

International Association for Financial Planning
Two Concourse Parkway, Suite 800
Atlanta, GA 30328
(404) 395-1605

National Association of Convenience Stores
1605 King Street
Alexandria, VA 22314-2792
(703) 684-3600

National Association of Desktop Publishers
426 Old Boston Street
Topsfield, MA 01983
(800) 874-4113

National Association of Home Builders
1201 15th Street, NW
Washington, DC 20005
(202) 822-0200

National Association of Realtors
777 14th Street, NW
Washington, DC 20005
(202) 383-1000

National Association of Truck Stop Operators
P.O. Box 1285
Alexandria, VA 22313-1285
(703) 549-2100

National Association of Wholesaler-Distributors
1725 K Street, NW, Suite 710
Washington, DC 20006
(202) 872-0885

National Lumber and Building Materials Dealers Association
40 Ivy Street, SE
Washington, DC 20003
(202) 547-2230

National Restaurant Association
1200 17th Street, NW
Washington, DC 20036
(202) 331-5900

Printing Industries of America, Inc.
100 Dangerfield Road
Alexandria, VA 22314
(703) 519-8100

Travel Industry Association of America
1133 21st Street, NW
Washington, DC 20036
(202) 293-1433

Women and Minorities Assistance

All resources available to small businesses are available to women- and minority-owned businesses. However, some states give special consideration and offer special programs to these firms.

The Small Business Association defines minorities as those who are socially or economically disadvantaged. Socially disadvantaged individuals are those who have been subject to racial or ethnic prejudice or cultural bias because of their identity as members of a group, without regard to individual qualities. Social disadvantage can also be determined on a case-by-case basis for those who feel they are socially disadvantaged, (e.g., the physically handicapped). Economically disadvantaged individuals are those whose ability to compete in a free enterprise system has been impaired because of diminished capital and credit opportunities. Economic disadvantage has to do with the barrier that social disadvantage has placed in the way of an individual's participation in business and employment.

Listed below are organizations that specialize in promoting women- and minority-owned businesses. The sections titled "Associations and Organizations" and "Procurement Assistance" in this chapter contain additional references.

> Office of Minority Enterprise Development
> U.S. Small Business Administration
> 409 Third Street, SW
> Washington, DC 20416
> (800) 827-5722

The main objective of this office is to foster business ownership by socially and economically disadvantaged individuals and to promote the competitive viability of such firms. A major program toward this goal is the 8(a) Business Development Program. Under this program, SBA acts as a prime contractor and enters into contracts with other federal departments and agencies, negotiating subcontracts with small companies in the 8(a) program. Most subcontracts are awarded on a noncompetitive or limited-competition basis.

For more information about the 8(a) program and eligibility requirements, call the Small Business Answer Desk at (800) 827-5722.

> Office of Women Business Ownership (OWBO)
> U.S. Small Business Administration
> 409 Third Street, SW
> Washington, DC 20416
> (202) 205-6673

The OWBO is the primary advocate for the interests of women business owners. This office provides assistance to start-up and existing women-owned businesses through services and programs including prebusiness workshops; technical, financial and management information; and information on selling to the government. (See the section titled "Procurement Assistance" for additional information on government contracts.)

The OWBO also sponsors the Women's Network for Entrepreneurial Training (WNET). This program matches successful entrepreneurial women (mentors) with women business owners (protégées) whose companies are ready to grow. Mentors meet one-on-one with their protégées over a period of a year to provide guidance through the growth process.

Call the OWBO directly or the toll-free Small Business Answer Desk (800 827-5722) for further information.

Minority Business Development Agency (MBDA)
U.S. Department of Commerce
14th Street between Constitution Avenue and E Street, NW
Washington, DC 20230
(202) 482-4547

The MBDA is a bureau of the U. S. Chamber of Commerce created to help minority businesses. The agency's goal is to help businesses effectively participate in the economy by overcoming disadvantages that have limited them in the past. Management and technical assistance and information on contract opportunities with the government are provided through a network of local Minority Business Development Centers. For information on the center in your area, call or write to the MDBA's office in Washington, D.C.

National Association of Women Business Owners
1377 K Street, NW, Suite 637
Washington, DC 20005
(301) 608-2590

NAWBO is a membership-based national organization representing the interests of women entrepreneurs in all types of businesses. Through over 50 local chapters, the organization offers networking opportunities and monthly programs that address a wide range of business issues.

Women's Franchise Network (WFN)
International Franchise Association
1350 New York Avenue, NW, Suite 900
Washington, DC 20005

The WFN, part of the International Franchise Association, was established to promote and foster opportunities in franchising to women. Call the hotline number, (202) 628-8000, extension 7788, for information on membership and upcoming WFN events.

National Association of Women's Yellow Pages (NAWYP)
P.O. Box 6021
Mobile, AL 36660
(334) 660-2752

The NAWYP has 25 member directories across the country reaching one million women. The NAWYP is a tool for women-owned businesses, national corporations, and small businesses alike. For information on starting a directory or national advertising rates, call (708) 679-7800.

> National Association of Investment Companies (NAIC)
> 1111 14th Street, NW, Suite 700
> Washington, DC 20005
> (202) 289-4336

NAIC is a trade association representing minority enterprise investment companies that invest exclusively in small businesses owned by socially or economically disadvantaged entrepreneurs.

> National Association of Minority Contractors (NAMC)
> 1333 F Street, NW, Suite 500
> Washington, DC 20004
> (202) 347-8259

The NAMC is a trade association designed to address the needs of minority contractors nationwide. Services include legislative, procurement, and information bulletins; networking opportunities through 45 affiliates and chapters nationwide; and educational and training seminars.

> National Business League (NBL)
> 1511 K Street, NW, Suite 432
> Washington, DC 20005
> (202) 737-4430

NBL is a national federation with the goal of achieving economic independence for minority Americans. The NBL works to expand minority business participation in franchise ownership, transportation, telecommunications, and high-tech and energy-related fields. Managerial and technical assistance are available for small business owners as well as workshop training and seminar programs.

> U.S. Hispanic Chamber of Commerce (USHCC)
> 1030 15th Street, NW, Suite 206
> Washington, DC 20005
> (202) 842-1212

The USHCC represents over 400,000 Hispanic-owned firms nationwide. As the premier national Hispanic business network in the U.S., the Chamber advocates the business interests of Hispanics and develops minority business opportunities with major corporations and all levels of government. Networking capabilities, referral services, training, and technical assistance are available through over 220 local chamber corporate partners nationwide.

> Latin American Management Association (LAMA)
> 419 New Jersey Avenue, SE
> Washington, DC 20003
> (202) 546-3803

LAMA is a national trade association dedicated to the goal of advancing opportunities promoting the interests of the Hispanic and minority business community.

> Puerto Rico Commerce Development Administration
> P.O. Box S-4275
> San Juan, PR 00905
> (809) 721-3290

The Administration serves the needs of small and medium-sized businesses of Puerto Rico. (Also listed in the section titled "Associations and Organizations.")

Procurement Assistance

The Small Business Act of 1953 states that a fair proportion of government procurement should be placed with small firms. For small business owners with a product or service of interest to federal agencies, procurement can be a source of income. Small businesses should be interested in two types of procurement: (1) small business set-asides that are procurement opportunities required for all contracts under $10,000 or a certain percentage of an agency's total procurement expenditures and (2) the SBA 8(a) program in which small businesses and minority-owned and operated businesses are admitted to the program and can negotiate on special contracts.

A small business owner has the opportunity to become a prime contractor, a subcontractor, or a supplier to a prime contractor. Any businessperson wanting to do business with the federal government must learn procurement regulations and procedures. Procurement information can be obtained through SBA district and regional offices (see Appendix A for SBA listings by state) and GSA Business Service Centers (see below).

Note: In some states, women are considered minorities for procurement purposes. A publication entitled *Doing Business with the GSA* describes the types of products and services that the government buys and explains the process of selling to the government. Included is a special section on procurement programs for small businesses. Contact the nearest Business Service Center (listed below) for a copy.

General Services Administration (GSA)
18th and F Streets, NW
Washington, DC 20405
(202) 708-5082

Among the GSA's duties is responsibility for the federal government's procurement of supplies, disposal of property, stockpiling of strategic materials, management of the government's automatic data processing resources program, and operation of the Business Service Centers (BSC).

Business Service Centers promote the participation of businesses, especially small and disadvantaged firms, in government contracting. Information and counseling are provided in developing the government market potential for products and services, procuring contracts, and purchasing surplus property. BSCs also distribute federal directories, publication lists, references and regulations, and a variety of technical publications concerning contracts and bidding forms, specifications and standards, and specialized purchasing programs.

Federal Supply Schedules are available through the BSCs. These schedules list goods and services that government agencies wish to purchase. In addition, small businesses may apply to be listed on GSA schedules as suppliers of goods and services to the federal government.

Business Service Centers are located in the following cities:

Atlanta	(404) 331-5103
Boston	(617) 565-8100
Chicago	(312) 353-5383
Denver	(303) 236-7408
Fort Worth	(817) 334-3284
Kansas City	(816) 926-7203
Los Angeles	(213) 894-3210
New York	(212) 264-1234
Philadelphia	(215) 656-5525
San Francisco	(415) 744-5050
Seattle	(206) 931-7956
Washington, D.C.	(202) 708-5804

Each agency of the federal government with significant procurement authority has an Office of Small and Disadvantaged Business Utilization (OSDBU). The OSDBU is responsible for ensuring that a certain percentage of products and services are purchased from small businesses, small disadvantaged businesses, and women-owned business enterprises according to federal regulations. In addition, an equitable share of the total prime contracts awarded by that agency must be awarded to these small firms.

Identifying Government Contract Opportunities

Commerce Business Daily (CBD), published by the Department of Commerce, is the most common method of contract advertisement. The CBD publishes government procurements and contracts of $25,000 or more. Contact the Government Printing Office at (202) 783-3238 to order a subscription.

Bidders' Mailing List is maintained by each government department and agency at the national level and identifies solicitations for goods and services. Businesspersons must apply to be placed on the list by completing Standard Form 129. Bidders' mailing lists are specific to each department or agency (i.e., there is no master list of all federal agencies offering procurement contracts). Contact the Office of Small and Disadvantaged Business Utilization of the concerned department or agency through information provided by the nearest GSA business service center (listed above).

Note: For local procurement opportunities, *Bidders' Mailing Lists* are also maintained by federal government offices in your area. Contact your nearest SBA office (Appendix A) to apply to be on its lists.

Procurement Automated Source System (PASS) is a computerized listing of firms maintained by the SBA. Government procurement offices and prime contractors have access to PASS to help them identify small businesses qualified to provide goods and services for contracts and subcontracts. Small firms can register their company at no cost by obtaining a PASS form from any SBA office (Appendix A) or by calling the Small Business Answer Desk at (800) 827-5722.

Note: SBA field offices can put you in touch with SBA procurement center representatives, commercial marketing representatives, and SBA procurement advisors.

Figure 14-1: Identifying Government Contract Opportunities

In addition, the OSDBU provides publications on how to do business with various government agencies. For information on specific agencies with OSDBU offices or procurement problems or questions, contact the GSA business service center nearest you.

Patents, Trademarks, and Copyrights

Patents and Trademarks

Patents give their owners the right to exclude others from manufacturing, using, or selling an invention throughout the U.S. If the invention is a process, a patent gives the owner the right to exclude others from using, selling, or importing into the U.S.

products made by that process. Information on patents, including patent applications, is available by writing to:

Patent and Trademark Office
U.S. Department of Commerce
Washington, DC 20231
(703) 557-4636

A publication entitled *General Information Concerning Patents* is available from the Government Printing Office, Washington, DC 20402. Call (202) 783-3238 to order by phone.

A trademark is a unique symbol, design, name, slogan, or sound used in trade to distinguish the goods and services of one party from those of another. Registration is not necessary for trademark protection, but it does give the registrant priority. Other benefits include the right to use the registered trademark symbol with the mark. Trademarks are registered at the national level with the Patent and Trademark Office (above). A publication entitled *Basic Facts About Trademarks* is available by calling (703) 557-4636.

Copyrights

Registration is not necessary to claim copyright of an original literary, dramatic, musical, or artistic work. However, registration does provide certain benefits in the event of infringement. Details on how to register a copyright can be obtained by writing to:

Copyright Office
Library of Congress
Washington, DC 20231
(202) 707-3000
To order copyright forms, call (202) 707-9100.

Appendix A

SMALL-BUSINESS RESOURCES

STATE OFFERINGS

ALABAMA

Small Business Development Center
University of Alabama at Birmingham
Medical Towers Building
1717 Eleventh Avenue South
Suite 419
Birmingham, AL 35294
(205) 934-7260

SBA District Office
221 Eighth Avenue North
Suite 200
Birmingham, AL 35203-2398
(205) 731-1344

Export Assistance Center
2015 Second Avenue North
Suite 302
Birmingham, AL 35203-0131
(205) 731-1331

Alabama Development Office
Small Business Office of
Advocacy/Minority Business
Enterprise
401 Adams Avenue
Montgomery, AL 36130-4106
(205) 242-0400

Alabama Small Business
Development Consortium
University of Alabama at Birmingham
Medical Towers Building
1717 Eleventh Avenue South
Suite 419
Birmingham, AL 35294
(205) 934-7260

ALASKA

Small Business Development Center
University of Alaska at Anchorage
430 West Seventh Avenue
Suite 110
Anchorage, AK 99501
(907) 274-7232

SBA District Office
222 West Eighth Avenue
Room 67
Anchorage, AK 99513-7559
(907) 271-4022

Export Assistance Center
222 West Eighth Avenue
Room 67
Anchorage, AK 99513-7559
(907) 271-6237

Department of Commerce and
Economic Development
State Office Building
9th Floor
333 Willoughby Avenue
Juneau, AK 99811-0800
(907) 465-2500

ARIZONA

Small Business Development Center
Arizona SBDC Network
2411 West 14th Street
Room 132
Tempe, AZ 85281
(602) 731-8720

SBA District Office
2828 North Central Avenue
Suite 800
Phoenix, AZ 85004-1025
(602) 640-2316

Export Assistance Center
2901 North Central Avenue
Suite 970
Phoenix, AZ 85012-2793
(602) 640-2513

Arizona Enterprise Development
Corporation
Arizona Department of Commerce
3800 North Central Avenue
Suite 1500
Phoenix, AZ 85012
(602) 280-1341

ARKANSAS

Small Business Development Center
University of Arkansas at Little Rock
Little Rock Technology Center Building
100 South Main Street
Suite 401
Little Rock, AR 72201
(501) 324-9043

SBA District Office
2120 Riverfront Drive
Suite 100
Little Rock, AR 72202
(501) 324-5871

Export Assistance Center
425 West Capitol Avenue
Suite 700
Little Rock, AR 72201-3439
(501) 324-5794

Arkansas State Chamber of
Commerce
410 Cross Street
P.O. Box 3645
Little Rock, AR 77203
(501) 374-9225

CALIFORNIA

Small Business Development Center
California Trade and Commerce
Agency
801 K Street
Suite 1700
Sacramento, CA 95814
(916) 324-5068

SBA District Offices—San Francisco
(Regional)
71 Stevenson Street
San Francisco, CA 94105-2939
(415) 744-6402

SBA Fresno
2719 North Air Fresno Drive
Suite 107
Fresno, CA 93727-1547
(209) 487-5189

SBA Los Angeles
330 North Brand Boulevard
Suite 1200
Glendale, CA 91203-2304
(818) 552-3210

SBA San Diego
880 Front Street
Suite 4-S-29
San Diego, CA 92188-0270
(619) 557-5440

SBA San Francisco
211 Main Street
4th Floor
San Francisco, CA 94105-1988
(415) 744-6820

SBA Santa Ana
901 West Civic Center Drive
Santa Ana, CA 92703-2352
(714) 836-2494

Export Assistance Center—
Los Angeles
11000 Wilshire Boulevard
Room 9200
Los Angeles, CA 90024-3611
(310) 575-7104

Export Assistance Center—
Long Beach
One World Trade Center
Suite 1670
Long Beach, CA 90831
(310) 980-4550

Export Assistance Center—
Newport Beach
3300 Irvine Avenue
Suite 305
Newport Beach, CA 92660-3108
(714) 836-2461

Export Assistance Center—
San Diego
6363 Greenwich Drive
Suite 230
San Diego, CA 92122-5947
(619) 557-5395

Export Assistance Center—
San Francisco
250 Montgomery Street
14th Floor
San Francisco, CA 94104-3401
(415) 705-2300

California Chamber of Commerce
1201 K Street
12th Floor
Sacramento, CA 95814
(916) 444-6670

Office of Small Business
Trade and Commerce Agency
801 K Street
Suite 1600
Sacramento, CA 95814
(916) 324-1295

COLORADO

Small Business Development Center
Office of Business Development
1625 Broadway
Suite 1710
Denver, CO 80202
(303) 892-3809

SBA District Office
721 Nineteenth Street
Suite 426
Denver, CO 80202-2599
(303) 844-3984

Export Assistance Center
1625 Broadway
Suite 680
Denver, CO 80202-4706
(303) 844-6622

CONNECTICUT

Small Business Development Center
University of Connecticut
School of Business Administration
368 Fairfield Road, U-41
Room 422
Storrs, CT 06269-2041
(203) 486-4135

SBA District Office
330 Main Street
Hartford, CT 06106
(203) 240-4700

Export Assistance Center
450 Main Street
Room 610-B
Hartford, CT 06103-3093
(203) 240-3530

Office of Small Business Services
Department of Economic Development
865 Brook Street
Rocky Hill, CT 06067
(203) 258-4200

Connecticut Business and Industry
370 Asylum Street
Hartford, CT 06103
(203) 244-1900

DELAWARE

Small Business Development Center
University of Delaware
Purnell Hall
Newark, DE 19716
(302) 831-1555

SBA District Office
(302) 573-6294 (By phone only)

Export Assistance Center
(Philadelphia, PA)
660 America Avenue
King of Prussia, PA 19406-1415
(215) 962-4980

Delaware State Chamber of
Commerce
1201 North Orange Street
Suite 200
Wilmington, DE 19899
(302) 655-7221

Delaware Development Office
99 Kings Highway
P.O. Box 1401
Dover, DE 19903
(302) 739-4271

DISTRICT OF COLUMBIA

Small Business Development Center
Howard University
Metropolitan Washington SBDC
2600 Sixth Street, NW
Room 125
Washington, DC 20059
(202) 806-1550

SBA District Office
1110 Vermont Avenue, NW
Suite 900
Washington, DC 20036
(202) 606-4000

Export Assistance Center
14th and Constitution Avenue
Room 3802
Washington, DC 20230-0002
(202) 482-5777

Office of Business and Economic
Development
717 Fourteenth Street, NW
10th Floor
Washington, DC 20005
(202) 727-6600

FLORIDA

Small Business Development Center
University of West Florida
19 West Garden Street
Pensacola, FL 32501
(904) 444-2060

SBA District Offices—Coral Gables
1320 South Dixie Highway
Suite 501
Coral Gables, FL 33146-2911
(305) 536-5521

SBA District Office
7825 Baymeadows Way
Suite 100-B
Jacksonville, FL 32256-7504
(904) 443-1900

Export Assistance Center—
Clearwater
128 North Osceola Avenue
Clearwater, FL 34617-2457
(813) 461-0011

Export Assistance Center—Miami
5600 Northwest 36th Street
Suite 617
Miami, FL 33166
(305) 526-7425

Export Assistance Center—Orlando
200 East Robinson Street
Suite 695
Orlando, FL 32801-1957
(407) 648-6235

Export Assistance Center—
Tallahassee
Collins Building
107 West Gaines Street
Room 366-G
Tallahassee, FL 32399
(904) 488-6469

Bureau of Business Assistance
Florida Department of Commerce
443 Collins Building
107 West Gaines Street
Tallahassee, FL 32399-2000
(904) 488-9357

Entrepreneurship Network
(904) 488-9357 (By phone only)

Florida Chamber of Commerce
136 South Bronought Street
Tallahassee, FL 32302
(904) 425-1200

GEORGIA

Small Business Development Center
University of Georgia
Chicopee Complex
1180 East Broad Street
Athens, GA 30602-5412
(706) 542-6762

SBA District Office
1720 Peachtree Road, NW
Atlanta, GA 30309
(404) 347-2441

Export Assistance Center—Atlanta
4360 Chamblee-Dunwoody Road
Suite 310
Atlanta, GA 30341-1055
(404) 452-9101

Export Assistance Center—
Savannah
120 Barnard Street
Room A-107
Savannah, GA 31401-3645
(912) 652-4204

Georgia Chamber of Commerce
233 Peachtree Street, NE
Suite 200
Atlanta, GA 30303
(404) 223-2264

Georgia Department of Industry,
Trade and Tourism
P.O. Box 1776
Atlanta, GA 30301
(404) 656-3556

HAWAII

Small Business Development Center
University of Hawaii at Hilo
200 West Kawili Street
Hilo, HI 96720-4091
(808) 933-3459

SBA District Office
300 Ala Moana Boulevard
Room 2213
Honolulu, HI 96850-4981
(808) 541-2990

Export Assistance Center
300 Ala Moana Boulevard
Room 4106
P.O. Box 50026
Honolulu, HI 96850
(808) 541-1782

Hawaii Chamber of Commerce
1132 Bishop Street
Honolulu, HI 96813
(808) 545-4300

Department of Business, Economic
Development and Tourism
Grosvenor Center, Mauka Tower
737 Bishop Street
Suite 1900
Honolulu, HI 96813
(808) 586-2591

IDAHO

Small Business Development Center
Boise State University
College of Business
1910 University Drive
Boise, ID 83725
(208) 385-1640

SBA District Office
1020 Main Street
Suite 290
Boise, ID 83702-5745
(208) 334-1696

Export Assistance Center
700 West State Street
Statehouse Mail
Boise, ID 83720-0093
(208) 334-2470

Idaho Association of Commerce
and Industry
802 West Bannock Street
Suite 308
Boise, ID 83701
(208) 343-1849

ILLINOIS

Small Business Development Center
Department of Commerce and
Community Affairs
620 East Adams Street
5th Floor
Springfield, IL 62701
(217) 524-5856

SBA District Office
500 West Madison Street
Room 1250
Chicago, IL 60661-2511
(312) 353-4528

Export Assistance Center—Chicago
55 West Monroe Street
Suite 2440
Chicago, IL 60603-5008
(312) 353-8040

Export Assistance Center—Rockford
515 North Court Street
Rockford, IL 61103-0247
(815) 987-8123

Export Assistance Center—Wheaton
201 East Loop Road
Wheaton, IL 60187-8488
(708) 353-4332

Illinois State Chamber of Commerce
20 North Wacker Drive
Suite 1960
Chicago, IL 60606
(312) 983-7100

INDIANA

Small Business Development Center
Indiana Chamber of Commerce
One North Capitol Avenue
Suite 420
Indianapolis, IN 46204-2248
(317) 264-6871

SBA District Office
429 North Pennsylvania Street
Suite 100
Indianapolis, IN 46204-1873
(317) 226-7272

Export Assistance Center—Carmel
11405 North Pennsylvania Street
Suite 106
Carmel, IN 46032-6905
(317) 582-2300

Export Assistance Center—
Indianapolis
One North Capitol Avenue
Suite 700
Indianapolis, IN 46204
(317) 232-8800

Indiana State Chamber of
Commerce, Inc.
One North Capitol Avenue
Suite 200
Indianapolis, IN 46204
(317) 264-3110

IOWA

Small Business Development Center
Iowa State University
College of Business Administration
137 Lynn Avenue
Ames, IA 50014-7126
(515) 292-6351

SBA District Offices—Cedar Rapids
373 Collins Road, NE
Suite 100
Cedar Rapids, IA 52402-3147
(319) 393-8630

SBA Des Moines
210 Walnut Street
Room 749
Des Moines, IA 50309
(515) 284-4422

Export Assistance Center
210 Walnut Street
Room 817
Des Moines, IA 50309-2105
(515) 281-7400

Department of Economic Development
200 East Grand Avenue
Des Moines, IA 50309
(515) 242-4700

Iowa Association of Business
and Industry
431 East Locust Street
Des Moines, IA 50309
(515) 244-6149

KANSAS

Small Business Development Center
Wichita State University
1845 Fairmont
Wichita, KS 67260-0148
(316) 689-3193

SBA District Office
100 East English Street
Suite 510
Wichita, KS 67202
(316) 269-6571

Export Assistance Center—Wichita
151 North Volutsia
Wichita, KS 67214-4695
(316) 269-6160

Export Assistance Center —Topeka
400 SW Eighth Street
5th Floor
Topeka, KS 66603-3957
(913) 296-3480

Kansas Chamber of Commerce
and Industry
835 SW Topeka Boulevard
Topeka, KS 66613-1671
(913) 357-6321

KENTUCKY

Small Business Development Center
University of Kentucky
Center for Business Development
225 Business and Economics Building
Lexington, KY 40506-0034
(606) 257-7668

SBA District Office
600 Dr. M.L. King Jr. Place
Room 188
Louisville, KY 40202
(502) 582-5978

Export Assistance Center
520 South Fourth Street
Marmaduke Building, 3rd Floor
Louisville, KY 40202-2243
(502) 582-5066

Kentucky Chamber of Commerce
Versailles Road
P.O. Box 817
Frankfort, KY 40602
(502) 695-4700

Kentucky Cabinet for Economic
Development
Small and Minority Business Division
2300 Capital Plaza Tower
Frankfort, KY 40601
(502) 564-7140

LOUISIANA

Small Business Development Center
Northeast Louisiana University
College of Business Administration,
Room 2-57
Monroe, LA 71209-6435
(318) 342-5506

SBA District Office
365 Canal Street
Suite 3100
New Orleans, LA 70130
(504) 589-2354

Export Assistance Center
501 Magazine Street
Room 1043
New Orleans, LA 70130-3329
(504) 589-6546

Department of Economic Development
Office of Commerce
P.O. Box 94185
Baton Rouge, LA 70804
(504) 342-3000

Louisiana Association of Business
and Industry
P.O. Box 80258
Baton Rouge, LA 70898-0258
(504) 928-5388

MAINE

Small Business Development Center
University of Southern Maine
15 Surrenden Street
Portland, ME 04101
(207) 780-4420

SBA District Office
40 Western Avenue
Room 512
Augusta, ME 04330
(207) 622-8378

Export Assistance Center
187 State Street, #59
Augusta, ME 04333
(207) 622-8249

Maine Chamber of Commerce
and Industry
126 Sewall Street
Augusta, ME 04330
(207) 623-4568

Department of Economic and
Community Development
State House Station #59
Augusta, ME 04333-0949
(207) 287-3153

MARYLAND

Small Business Development Center
Department of Economic and
Employment Division
217 East Redwood Street
Suite 936
Baltimore, MD 21202
(410) 333-6995

SBA District Office
10 South Howard Street
Room 608
Baltimore, MD 21202
(410) 962-4392

Export Assistance Center
401 East Pratt Street
Suite 2432
Baltimore, MD 21202
(410) 962-4539

Maryland Chamber of Commerce
275 West Street
Suite 400
Annapolis, MD 21401
(410) 268-7676

Department of Economic and
Employment Development
Redwood Tower
217 East Redwood Street
Baltimore, MD 21202
(410) 333-6197

MASSACHUSETTS

Small Business Development Center
University of Massachusetts
School of Management
Room 205
Amherst, MA 01003
(413) 545-6301

SBA District Office
10 Causeway Street
Room 276
Boston, MA 02222-1093
(617) 565-5590

Export Assistance Center
World Trade Center
Commonwealth Pier
Suite 307
Boston, MA 02210
(617) 565-8563

Office of Business Development
One Ashburton Place
Room 2101
Boston, MA 02108
(617) 727-3206

MICHIGAN

Small Business Development Center
Wayne State University
2727 Second Avenue
Detroit, MI 48201
(313) 964-1798

SBA District Office
477 Michigan Avenue
Room 515
Detroit, MI 48226
(313) 226-6075

Export Assistance Center—Detroit
477 Michigan Avenue
Room 1140
Detroit, MI 48226-2518
(313) 226-3650

Export Assistance Center—
Grand Rapids
City Hall
300 Monroe Street, NW
Room 406-A
Grand Rapids, MI 49503
(616) 456-2411

Michigan Chamber of Commerce
600 South Walnut Street
Lansing, MI 48933
(517) 371-2100

Department of Commerce
P.O. Box 30004
Lansing, MI 48909
(517) 373-1820

MINNESOTA

Small Business Development Center
Department of Trade and Economic
Development
500 Metro Square
121 Seventh Place East
St. Paul, MN 55101-2146
(612) 297-5770

SBA District Office
100 North Sixth Street
Suite 610
Minneapolis, MN 55403-1563
(612) 370-2324

Export Assistance Center
110 South Fourth Street
Room 108
Minneapolis, MN 55401-2227
(612) 348-1638

Minnesota Chamber of Commerce
30 East Seventh Street
Suite 1700
St. Paul, MN 55101
(612) 292-4650

Small Business Assistance Office
500 Metro Square
121 Seventh Place East
St. Paul, MN 55101-2146
(612) 282-2103

MISSISSIPPI

Small Business Development Center
University of Mississippi
Old Chemistry Building
Suite 216
University, MS 38677
(601) 232-5001

SBA District Office
101 West Capitol Street
Suite 400
Jackson, MS 39201
(601) 965-4378

Export Assistance Center
201 West Capitol Street
Suite 310
Jackson, MS 39201-2005
(601) 965-4388

Mississippi Department of Economic
and Community Development
P.O. Box 849
Jackson, MS 39205-0849
(601) 359-3449

Mississippi Economic Council
620 North Street
P.O. Box 23276
Jackson, MS 39225-3276
(601) 969-0022

MISSOURI

Small Business Development Center
University of Missouri
300 University Place
Columbia, MO 65211
(314) 882-0344

SBA District Offices—Kansas City
323 West Eighth Street
Kansas City, MO 64105
(816) 374-6708

SBA St. Louis
815 Olive Street
Room 242
St. Louis, MO 63101
(314) 539-6600

Export Assistance Center—
Kansas City
601 East 12th Street
Room 635
Kansas City, MO 64106-2808
(816) 426-3141

Export Assistance Center—
St. Louis
8182 Maryland Avenue
Suite 303
St. Louis, MO 63105-3786
(314) 425-3302

Missouri Chamber of Commerce
P.O. Box 149
Jefferson City, MO 65102
(314) 634-3511

Missouri Department of Economic
Development
Truman State Office Building
301 West High Street
P.O. Box 1157
Jefferson City, MO 65102
(314) 751-4962

MONTANA

Small Business Development Center
Montana Department of Commerce
1424 Ninth Avenue
Helena, MT 59620
(406) 444-4780

SBA District Office
301 South Park
Room 528
Helena, MT 59626
(406) 449-5381

Export Assistance Center
(Denver, CO)
1625 Broadway, Suite 680
Denver, CO 80202-4706
(303) 844-6622

Montana Chamber of Commerce
2030 Eleventh Avenue
P.O. Box 1730
Helena, MT 59624
(406) 442-2405

Export Assistance Center
1424 Ninth Avenue
Helena, MT 59620
(406) 444-3494

NEBRASKA

Small Business Development Center
University of Nebraska at Omaha
College of Business
Administration Building
60th and Dodge Streets
Room 407
Omaha, NE 68182
(402) 554-2521

SBA District Office
11145 Mill Valley Road
Omaha, NE 68154
(402) 221-4691

Export Assistance Center
11135 "O" Street
Omaha, NE 68137-2337
(402) 221-3664

Nebraska Chamber of Commerce
and Industry
1320 Lincoln Mall
P.O. Box 95128
Lincoln, NE 68509
(402) 474-4422

Nebraska Department of Economic
Development
P.O. Box 94666
301 Centennial Mall South
Lincoln, NE 68509-4666
(402) 471-3747

NEVADA

Small Business Development Center
University of Nevada at Reno
College of Business Administration
Room 411
Reno, NV 89557-0100
(702) 784-1717

SBA District Office
310 East Stewart Street
Room 301
Las Vegas, NV 89125-2527
(702) 388-6611

Export Assistance Center
1755 East Plumb Lane
Suite 152
Reno, NV 89502-3680
(702) 784-5203

Nevada Chamber of Commerce
P.O. Box 3499
Reno, NV 89505
(702) 686-3030

Nevada State Development
Office of Small Business
350 South Center Street
Suite 310
Reno, NV 89501
(702) 323-3625

NEW HAMPSHIRE

Small Business Development Center
University of New Hampshire
108 McConnell Hall
Durham, NH 03824
(603) 862-2200

SBA District Office
143 North Main Street
Suite 202
Concord, NH 03302-1257
(603) 225-1400

Export Assistance Center
(Boston, MA)
World Trade Center
Commonwealth Pier
Suite 307
Boston, MA 02210-2075
(617) 565-8563

Business and Industry Association
of New Hampshire
122 North Main Street
Concord, NH 03301
(603) 224-5388

Business Finance Authority
New Hampshire Industrial
Development Authority
4 Park Street
Suite 302
Concord, NH 03301
(603) 271-2391

NEW JERSEY

Small Business Development Center
Rutgers University
Graduate School of Management
University Heights
180 University Avenue
Newark, NJ 07102
(201) 648-5950

SBA District Office
60 Park Place
Newark, NJ 06102
(201) 645-2434

Export Assistance Center
3131 Princeton Pike
Building 6
Suite 100
Trenton, NJ 08648-2201
(609) 989-2100

New Jersey State Chamber of
Commerce
One State Street Square
50 West State Street
Suite 1110
Trenton, NJ 08608
(609) 989-7888

New Jersey Department of Commerce
and Economic Development
20 West State Street
CN 835
Trenton, NJ 08625
(609) 292-2444

NEW MEXICO

New Mexico Small Business
Development Center
Santa Fe Community College
P.O. Box 4187
South Richards Avenue
Santa Fe, NM 87502-4187
(505) 438-1362

SBA District Office
625 Silver Avenue, SW
Suite 320
Albuquerque, NM 87102
(505) 766-1868

Export Assistance Center
625 Silver SW
Albuquerque, NM 87102-3173
(505) 766-2070

Association of Commerce and
Industry of New Mexico
2309 Renard Place, SE
Suite 402
Albuquerque, NM 87106
(505) 842-0644

Economic Development Department
P.O. Box 4187
Santa Fe, NM 87502-4187
(505) 827-0381

NEW YORK

Small Business Development Center
State University of New York (SUNY)
SUNY Plaza S-523
Albany, NY 12246
(518) 443-5398

SBA District Offices—New York
26 Federal Plaza
Room 3100
New York, NY 10278
(212) 264-4355

SBA—Syracuse
100 South Clinton Street
Room 1071
Syracuse, NY 13260
(315) 423-5383

Export Assistance Center—Buffalo
Federal Building
111 West Huron Street
Room 1312
Buffalo, NY 14202-2301
(716) 846-4191

Export Assistance Center—New York
26 Federal Plaza
Room 3718
New York, NY 10278-0004
(212) 264-0634

Export Assistance Center—
Rochester
111 East Avenue
Suite 220
Rochester, NY 14604-2520
(716) 263-6480

Department of Economic Development
1515 Broadway
51st Floor
New York, NY 10036
(212) 827-6150

Business Council of New York State
152 Washington Avenue
Albany, NY 12210
(518) 465-7511

NORTH CAROLINA

Small Business Development Center
University of North Carolina
4509 Creedmore Road
Raleigh, NC 27612
(919) 571-4154

SBA District Office
200 North College Street
Suite A2015
Charlotte, NC 28202-2137
(704) 344-6563

Export Assistance Center
400 West Market Street
Suite 400
Greensboro, NC 27401-2241
(910) 333-5345

North Carolina Citizens for Business
and Industry
225 Hillsborough Street
P.O. Box 2508
Raleigh, NC 27602
(919) 828-0758

NORTH DAKOTA

Small Business Development Center
University of North Dakota
118 Gamble Hall
University Station
Grand Forks, ND 58202-7308
(701) 777-3700

SBA District Office
657 Second Avenue North
Room 218
Fargo, ND 58108-3086
(701) 239-5131

U.S. Department of Commerce District
Office (Omaha, NE)
11133 "O" Street
Omaha, NE 68137-2337
(402) 221-3664

Greater North Dakota Association/
State Chamber of Commerce
2000 Schafer Street
P.O. Box 2639
Bismarck, ND 58502
(701) 222-0929

Department of Economic Development
and Finance
1833 East Bismarck Expressway
Bismarck, ND 58504
(701) 221-5300

OHIO

Small Business Development Center
Ohio Department of Development
77 South High Street
P.O. Box 1001
Columbus, OH 43266
(614) 466-2711

Ohio Chamber of Commerce
35 East Gay Street
2nd Floor
Columbus, OH 43215-3181
(614) 228-4201

SBA District Offices—Cleveland
1111 Superior Avenue
Suite 30
Cleveland, OH 44144-2507
(216) 522-4180

SBA—Columbus
2 Nationwide Plaza
Suite 1400
Columbus, OH 43215-2692
(614) 469-6860

Export Assistance Center—Cincinnati
Federal Office Building
550 Main Street
Room 9504
Cincinnati, OH 45202
(513) 684-2944

Export Assistance Center—
Cleveland
600 Superior Avenue East
Room 700
Cleveland, OH 44114-2650
(216) 522-4750

OKLAHOMA

Small Business Development Center
Southeastern State University
517 University
Durant, OK 74701
(405) 924-0277

SBA District Office
200 North West 5th Street
Suite 670
Oklahoma City, OK 73102
(405) 231-5521

Export Assistance Center—
Oklahoma City
6601 North Broadway Extension
Building 5
Oklahoma City, OK 73116
(405) 231-5302

Export Assistance Center—Tulsa
440 South Houston Street
Room 505
Tulsa, OK 74127-8913
(918) 581-7650

Oklahoma State Chamber of
Commerce and Industry
4020 North Lincoln Boulevard
Oklahoma City, OK 73105
(405) 424-4003

Oklahoma Department of Commerce
6601 North Broadway Extension
Building 5
Oklahoma City, OK 73116
(405) 843-9770

OREGON

Small Business Development Center
Lane Community College
99 West Tenth Street
Suite 216
Eugene, OR 97401
(503) 726-2250

SBA District Office
222 South West Columbia Street
Suite 500
Portland, OR 97201-6605
(503) 326-2682

Export Assistance Center
121 SW Salmon Street
Suite 242
Portland, OR 97204-2911
(503) 326-3001

Economic Development Office
775 Summer Street NE
Salem, OR 97310
(503) 986-0197

PENNSYLVANIA

Small Business Development Center
University of Pennsylvania
The Wharton School
423 Vance Hall
3733 Spruce Street
Philadelphia, PA 19104-6374
(215) 898-1219

SBA District Offices—Pittsburgh
960 Penn Avenue
Pittsburgh, PA 15222
(412) 644-2780

SBA—King of Prussia
475 Allendale Road
Suite 201
King of Prussia, PA 19406
(215) 962-3827

Export Assistance Center—
(Philadelphia, PA)
660 America Avenue
King of Prussia, PA 19406-1415
(215) 962-4980

Export Assistance Center—
Pittsburgh
1000 Liberty Avenue
Room 2002
Pittsburgh, PA 15222-4194
(412) 644-2850

Department of Commerce
Office of Small Business
400 Forum Building
Harrisburg, PA 17120
(717) 783-8950

Pennsylvania Chamber of
Business and Industry
One Commerce Square
417 Walnut Street
Harrisburg, PA 17101
(717) 255-3252

PUERTO RICO

Small Business Development Center
University of Puerto Rico at Mayagüez
Building B, Second Floor
Box 5253—College Station
Mayagüez, PR 00681
(809) 834-3590

SBA District Office
Citibank Tower
Suite 3201
252 Ponce de Leon Avenue
Hato Rey, PR 00918
(809) 766-5572

Export Assistance Center
Federal Building
Room G-55
Carlos Chardon Avenue
Hato Rey, PR 00918
(809) 766-5555

Department of Commerce
P.O. Box S—4275
San Juan, PR 00905
(809) 724-7373

Chamber of Commerce of Puerto Rico
100 Tetuán Street
Old San Juan, PR 00901
(809) 721-3290

RHODE ISLAND

Small Business Development Center
Bryant College
1150 Douglas Pike
Smithfield, RI 02917-1284
(401) 232-6111

SBA District Office
380 Westminster Street
Providence, RI 02903
(401) 528-4561

Export Assistance Center
7 Jackson Walkway
Providence, RI 02903-3623
(401) 277-2601

Greater Providence
Chamber of Commerce
30 Exchange Terrace
Providence, RI 02903
(401) 521-5000

SOUTH CAROLINA

Small Business Development Center
University of South Carolina
College of Business Administration
1710 College Street
Columbia, SC 29208
(803) 777-4907

SBA District Office
1835 Assembly Street
Room 358
Columbia, SC 29201
(803) 765-5376

Export Assistance Center
1835 Assembly Street
Suite 172
Columbia, SC 29201-2440
(803) 765-5345

South Carolina Chamber
of Commerce
1201 Main Street
Suite 1810
Columbia, SC 29201
(803) 799-4601

Enterprise Development, Inc.
P.O. Box 1149
Columbia, SC 29202
(803) 737-0888

SOUTH DAKOTA

Small Business Development Center
University of South Dakota
School of Business
Patterson Hall 115
414 East Clarke Street
Vermillion, SD 57069
(605) 677-5498

SBA District Office
101 South Main Avenue
Suite 101
Sioux Falls, SD 57102-0527
(605) 330-4231

Export Assistance Center
(Omaha, NE)
11135 "O" Street
Omaha, NE 68137-2337
(402) 221-3664

Governor's Office of Economic
Development
711 East Wells Avenue
Pierre, SD 57501-3369
(605) 773-5032

Industry and Commerce Association
of South Dakota
P.O. Box 190
Pierre, SD 57501
(605) 224-6161

TENNESSEE

Small Business Development Center
Memphis State University
South Campus
Getwell Road
Building One
Memphis, TN 38152
(901) 678-2500

SBA District Office
50 Vantage Way
Suite 201
Nashville, TN 37228-1500
(615) 736-5850

Export Assistance Center—Knoxville
301 East Church Avenue
Knoxville, TN 37915-2572
(615) 545-4637

Export Assistance Center—Memphis
22 North Front Street
Suite 200
Memphis, TN 38103-2190
(901) 544-4137

Export Assistance Center—Nashville
404 James Robertson Parkway
Number 114
Nashville, TN 37219-1505
(615) 736-5161

Department of Economic and
Community Development
320 Sixth Avenue North
Nashville, TN 37243
(800) 872-7201

Tennessee Association of Business
611 Commerce Street, Suite 3030
Nashville, TN 37203-3742
(615) 256-5141

TEXAS

Small Business Development Center
Dallas County Community College
1402 Corinth Street
Dallas, TX 75215
(214) 565-5831

SBA District Offices—Corpus Christi
606 North Carancahus
Suite 1200
Corpus Christi, TX 78476
(512) 888-3333

SBA—El Paso
10737 Gateway West
Suite 320
El Paso, TX 69935
(915) 540-5155

SBA—Fort Worth
4300 Amon Carter Boulevard
Suite 114
Fort Worth, TX 76155
(817) 885-6500

SBA—Harlingen
222 East Van Buren Street
Room 500
Harlingen, TX 78550
(210) 427-8533

SBA—Houston
9301 Southwest Freeway
Suite 550
Houston, TX 77074-1591
(713) 773-6500

SBA—Lubbock
1611 Tenth Street
Suite 200
Lubbock, TX 69401
(806) 743-7462

SBA—San Antonio
7400 Blanc Road
Suite 200
San Antonio, TX 78216-4300
(210) 229-4535

Export Assistance Center—Austin
410 East 5th Street
4th Floor
Anson Jones Building
Austin, TX 78701-3706
(512) 320-9604

Export Assistance Center—Dallas
2050 North Stemmons Freeway
Suite 170
Dallas, TX 75258-9998
(214) 767-0542

Export Assistance Center—Houston
500 Dallas Street
1 Allen Center
Suite 1160
Houston, TX 77002-4802
(713) 229-2578

Texas Department of Commerce
816 Congress Avenue
P.O. Box 12728
Austin, TX 78711
(512) 472-5059

Texas Chamber of Commerce
900 Congress
Suite 501
Austin, TX 78701-2447
(512) 472-1594

UTAH

Small Business Development Center
University of Utah
102 West 500 South
Suite 315
Salt Lake City, UT 84101
(801) 581-7905

SBA District Office
125 South State Street
Room 2237
Salt Lake City, UT 84138-1195
(801) 524-3209

Export Assistance Center
324 South State Street
Suite 105
Salt Lake City, UT 84111-8321
(801) 524-5116

Community and Economic
Development
324 South State Street
Suite 500
Salt Lake City, UT 84111
(801) 538-8700

Utah State Chamber of Commerce
Association
c/o St. George Area Chamber
of Commerce
97 East St. George Boulevard
St. George, UT 84770
(801) 628-1658

VERMONT

Small Business Development Center
Vermont Technical College
P.O. Box 422
Randolph, VT 05060-0422
(802) 728-9101

SBA District Office
87 State Street
Room 205
Montpelier, VT 05602
(802) 828-4474

Export Assistance Center
(Boston, MA)
World Trade Center
Commonwealth Pier
Suite 307
Boston, MA 02210-2075
(617) 565-8563

Vermont Chamber of Commerce
P.O. Box 37
Montpelier, VT 05601
(802) 223-3443

Vermont Department of Economic
Development
109 State Street
Montpelier, VT 05602
(802) 828-3221

VIRGINIA

Small Business Development Center
Commonwealth of Virginia
Department of Economic Development
1021 East Cary Street
11th Floor
Richmond, VA 23219
(804) 371-8253

SBA District Office
400 North Eighth Street
Room 3015
Richmond, VA 23240
(804) 771-2617

Export Assistance Center
Federal Building
400 North Eighth Street
Room 8010
Richmond, VA 23240
(804) 771-2246

Virginia Chamber of Commerce
9 South Fifth Street
Richmond, VA 23219
(804) 644-1607

Office of Small Business and
Financial Services
Virginia Department of Economic
Development
P.O. Box 798
Richmond, VA 23206
(804) 371-8252

WASHINGTON

Small Business Development Center
Washington State University
College of Business and Economics
Kruegel Hall, Room 135
Pullman, WA 99164-4727
(509) 335-1576

SBA District Offices—Seattle
915 Second Avenue
Room 1792
Seattle, WA 98174-1088
(206) 220-6520

SBA—Spokane
601 West First Avenue
Spokane, WA 99204-0317
(509) 635-6844

Export Assistance Center—Seattle
3131 Elliott Avenue
Room 290
Seattle, WA 98121-1047
(206) 553-5615

Export Assistance Center—Spokane
808 West Spokane Falls Boulevard
Room 625
Spokane, WA 99201-3333
(509) 353-2992

Business Assistance Center
Department of Community, Trade
and Economic Development
919 Lakeridge Way SW
Suite A
Olympia, WA 98504-2516
(206) 753-5632

Association of Washington Business
P.O. Box 658
1414 South Cherry
Olympia, WA 98507-0658
(206) 943-1600

WEST VIRGINIA

Small Business Development Center
West Virginia Development Office
1115 Virginia Street
East Charleston, WV 25301-2406
(304) 558-2960

SBA District Office
168 West Main Street
Clarksburg, WV 26301
(304) 623-5631

Export Assistance Center
405 Capitol Street
Suite 807
Charleston, WV 25301-1727
(304) 347-5123

West Virginia Chamber of Commerce
1000 Kanawha Valley
P.O. Box 2789
Charleston, WV 25330
(304) 342-1115

Development Office
Department of Commerce
Capitol Complex
M-146
Charleston, WV 25305
(304) 558-2234

WISCONSIN

Small Business Development Center
University of Wisconsin
432 North Lake Street
Room 423
Madison, WI 53706
(608) 263-7794

SBA District Office
212 East Washington Avenue
Room 213
Madison, WI 53703
(608) 264-5261

Export Assistance Center
517 East Wisconsin Avenue
Room 596
Milwaukee, WI 53202-4588
(414) 297-3473

Department of Development
Division of Economic Development
123 West Washington Avenue
P.O. Box 7970
Madison, WI 53707
(608) 266-1018

Wisconsin Manufacturers and
Commerce
501 East Washington Avenue
P.O. Box 352
Madison, WI 53701-0352
(608) 258-3400

WYOMING

U.S. Small Business Administration
Caspar District Office
Federal Building
Room 4001
100 East B Street
P.O. Box 2839
Caspar, WY 82602-2839
(307) 261-5761

Export Assistance Center
(Denver, CO)
1625 Broadway
Suite 680
Denver, CO 80202-4706
(303) 844-6622

Division of Economic and Community
Development
2301 Central Avenue
Barrett Building
4th Floor North
Cheyenne, WY 82002
(307) 777-7284

Appendix B

Sample Business Plan Outline

I. Introductory material

  A. Cover sheet

  B. Statement of purpose

  C. Contents

II. Summary

  A. Business description

    1. Name

    2. Location and plant description

    3. Product

    4. Market and competition

    5. Management expertise

  B. Business goals

  C. Summary of financial needs and application of funds

  D. Earnings projections and potential return to investors

  E. "Exit" Strategy—You must describe to a potential investor exactly how he will be repaid on his investment. Repayment may come from operations, refinancing, or selling stock to others.

III. Market analysis

  A. Description of total market

  B. Industry trends

  C. Target market competition

IV. Products or services

  A. Description of product line

  B. Proprietary position: patents, copyrights, and legal and technical considerations

    C. Comparison to competitors' products

    D. Opportunities or plans for expanding or redesigning product or service lines

    E. Projected changes in sales mix, cost, and profit

V. Manufacturing process

    A. Materials

    B. Sources of supply

    C. Production methods

VI. Market strategy

    A. Overall strategy

    B. Pricing policy

    C. Sales terms

    D. Method of selling, distributing and servicing products

    E. Ongoing evaluation

VII. Potential risks and pitfalls

    A. Critical risks your business faces

    B. Problems that may hinder/prevent plan execution

    C. How to avoid or offset problems

VIII. Management plans

    A. Form of business organization

    B. Board of directors composition

    C. Officers: organization chart and responsibilities

    D. Resumes of key personnel

    E. Staffing plan/number of employees

    F. Facilities plan/planned capital improvements

    G. Operating plan/schedule of upcoming work for next one to two years

IX. Financial data

    A. Financial history (last five years)

    B. Five-year financial projections (first year by quarters; remaining years annually)

        1. Profit and loss statements

        2. Balance sheets

3. Cash flow chart

4. Capital expenditure estimates

C. Explanation of assumptions underlying the projections

D. Key business ratios

E. Explanation of use and effect of new funds

F. Potential return to investors compared to competitors and the industry in general

Creating a Business Plan

Whether the business plan is developed for personal use or for review by outside investors, it is a critical document for defining your business. By writing a business plan, you will avoid overlooking details as you concentrate on the bigger picture of building and operating your own company.

Introductory Material

This is a brief introduction of your company and your mission. If you are submitting the business plan to request financing, include the dollar amount requested, terms and timing of the loan, and the type and price of securities.

Summary

In a business plan, your company's goals, strategy, and critical success factors belong up front. Therefore, your summary should be carefully written to reflect the enthusiasm and confidence that propelled you into starting your own business in the first place.

Market Analysis

The market analysis should highlight the opportunities for your company to achieve its goals. Some of the following questions should be answered:

◆ To whom are you trying to sell?

◆ What are the trends in your target market?

◆ Who are your customers?

◆ What are the customers' product/service preferences and reasons for purchasing?

Products or Services

This section should fully describe each product or service, including any brand names and unique features. Analyze competitive advantages and disadvantages. Your company's customers may be the final users or may resell to someone else. In the latter case, you should know the identity of the ultimate consumer as well as your immediate customer.

Manufacturing Process (If Applicable)

Where and by what technology you will manufacture your product. Include materials to be used, sources of supply, production methods, storage issues, delivery of finished products, etc.

Market Strategy

Name the customer groups your business will target. Identify the product or service attributes that your company will emphasize to generate sales. List advertising or promotional strategies to gain recognition and distinguish your company's products or services.

Potential Risks and Pitfalls

Things rarely proceed exactly according to plan. Build in flexibility by developing contingency plans to meet crises and likely problems.

Management Plan

Key managers and owners, along with their qualifications (e.g., education, skills, experience) should be defined here. Include job descriptions to clarify duties and responsibilities. In addition, name the members of the board of directors (including affiliations and experience) as well as any outside consultants.

Financial Data

Financial data quantify in dollar terms a business's past performance and expected future operation. Financial statements and projections must be consistent with the business plan's descriptions of your marketing assumptions and strategy, the execution process, and the external funds needed.

Appendix C

Sample Marketing Plan Outline

A marketing plan is used to identify a marketing strategy for partners, management, or potential investors. The length and detail of the marketing plan will vary according to the complexity of the marketing situation. The following outline would be used to market a major product. However, your personal plan may not need all of these functions. A shortened version of this, included in your business plan, may be all you need.

Executive Summary of the Plan

The executive summary summarizes marketing activities and schedules, budgets, planned expenditures, estimated sales and revenues, marketing profit and loss, and future "break-even," plus sales goals for the next two to five years.

Product or Service

The product or service plan describes the product or service in detail and justifies the need for the product. It includes:

- The consumer need you plan to satisfy
- Competitive advantages
- Infringement protection
- Characteristics of potential buyers and their persuadability
- Potential sales volume and profits

Market Research

Market research summarizes all the marketing, product, and competitive information gathered through statistical data, consumer and trade surveys, pre-test results, etc. and presents the rationale for the plan. It also creates the foundation for and acceptance of the marketing objectives.

Naming, Packaging, and Pricing the Product or Service

This aspect of the plan presents the marketing and imagery objectives and strategies to achieve each of the desired elements, e.g., name, art/design, color images, need, associations, quality/standards, etc.

Marketing Objectives

Marketing objectives list major goals for the year's plan, such as: unit and dollar sales, services to be offered, product distribution channels, consumer product familiarity and trials, marketing costs as a percent of sales revenues, etc.

Marketing Strategies to Achieve Objectives

This part of the plan details the individual strategies for the marketing, selling, advertising media and creative (art, design, copy) processes, and promotional plans to achieve those goals. Marketing strategies include sales force and territory expansion, sales training, level of advertising and promotion, reducing ineffective activities, changing product pricing, packaging, copy themes, etc.

Marketing Plan

The marketing plan details implementation of the strategies, including estimated sales, approved spending budgets as a percent of sales, detailed advertising and promotional schedules, sales drives with estimated costs versus budgets by marketing periods (weekly or monthly), etc. This schedule of cost versus budget data can be compared to overall business cash flow by period and cumulatively throughout the year. Note: This section should also include copies of the proposed advertisements, radio/TV commercials, promotional materials, brochures, publicity, etc.

Measuring Success (or Failure)

Statistical tables provide the means for reporting the performance of various aspects of the plan. Decisions regarding necessary plan changes can be made by reviewing sales, expenditures, and the effectiveness of individual activities.

References

Chapter 1

Aburdene, Patricia, and John Naisbitt. *Megatrends for Women*. New York: Villard Books, 1992.

Edwards, Paul and Sarah. *The Best Home-Based Businesses for the 90s*. New York: G.P. Putnam's Sons, 1994.

Hall, Daryl Allen. *1101 Businesses You Can Start from Home*. New York: J. Wiley & Sons, 1995.

Holtz, Herman. *How to Succeed as an Independent Consultant*. New York: John Wiley & Sons, 1983.

Kilborn, Peter T. "Women and Minorities Still Face 'Glass Ceiling'." *The New York Times*, 16 March 1995: A22.

Lonier, Terri. *Working Solo: The Real Guide to Freedom & Financial Success with Your Own Business*. New Paltz, NY: Portico Press, 1994.

Popcorn, Faith. *The Popcorn Report*. New York: HarperCollins, 1992.

Radin, William. *Breakaway Careers—The Self Employment Resource for Freelancers, Consultants and Corporate Refugees*. Hawthorne, NJ: Career Press, 1994.

Start Your Own Temporary Help Agency. Amsterdam. San Diego, CA: Pfeiffer & Company, 1994.

"Women-Owned Businesses: The New Economic Force," *NFWBO, 1994 Biennial Membership Survey*, NFWBO 1995.

Chapter 2

Bhide, Amar. "How Entrepreneurs Craft Strategies That Work." *Harvard Business Review,* April 1994: 151.

Covey, Stephen R. *First Things First*. New York: Simon & Schuster, 1994.

———. *The Seven Habits of Highly Effective People*. New York: Simon & Schuster, 1989.

Griessman, B. Eugene. *Time Tactics of Very Successful People*. New York: McGraw-Hill, 1994.

"Influencing Others: Psychologists Identify Central Skills." *The New York Times,* 18 February 1986: C15.

Mackenzie, R. Alec. *The Time Trap*. New York: McGraw-Hill, 1972.

Chapter 3

Arden, Lynie. *Franchises You Can Run from Home*. New York: John Wiley & Sons, 1990.

Aronoff, Craig E., and John L. Ward, eds. *Family Business Sourcebook: A Guide for Families Who Own Businesses & the Professionals Who Serve Them.* Detroit: Omnigraphics, 1991.

Eyder, David. *Starting & Operating a Home-Based Business.* New York: John Wiley & Sons, 1990.

Serwer, Andrew E. "Trouble in Franchise Nation." *Fortune,* 6 March 1995.

Chapter 4

Brauer, Roger L. *Facilities Planning: The User Requirements Method.* 2d ed. New York: AMACOM, 1992.

Chapter 5

Cronin, Mary J., Ph.D. *Doing Business on the Internet: How the Electronic Highway Is Transforming American Companies.* New York: Van Nostrand Reinhold, 1993.

Kent, Peter. *The Complete Idiot's Guide to the Internet.* Indianapolis, IN: Alpha Books, 1994.

Small, Ned. *Navigating the Internet with Windows '95.* Indianapolis, IN: Sams.net, 1995.

Smith, Richard J. *Navigating the Internet.* Carmel, IN: Sams Publishing, 1994.

Chapter 6

DeThomas, Art. *Financing Your Small Business.* Grant's Pass, OR: Oasis Press, 1992.

Diener, Royce. *How to Finance a Growing Business.* Santa Monica, CA: Merritt Publishing, 1995.

Flanagan, Lawrence. *The Money Connection.* Grant's Pass, OR: Oasis Press, 1993.

Gladstone, David. *New and Revised Venture Capital Handbook.* Englewood Cliffs, NJ: Prentice-Hall, 1988.

Leshco, Matthew. *Government Giveaways for Entrepreneurs II.* Maryland: Information USA, 1994.

Loeb, Marshall. *Lifetime Financial Strategies.* New York: Little, Brown and Company, 1996.

Chapter 7

AMA Complete Guide to Small Business Marketing. Chicago: American Management Association, 1995.

Baker, Wayne E. *Networking Smart: How to Build Relationships for Personal and Organizational Success.* New York: McGraw-Hill, Inc.

Holtz, Herman. *Priced to Sell: The Complete Guide to More Profitable Pricing.* Chicago:

Upstart Publishing Company, 1996.

Levine, Michael. *Guerrilla P.R.* New York: HarperBusiness, 1993.

Levinson, Jay Conrad, and Charles Rubin. *Guerrilla Marketing OnLine—The Entrepreneur's Guide to Earning Profits on the Internet.* New York: Houghton Mifflin, 1995.

Linneman, Robert E., and John L. Stanton, Jr. *Making Niche Marketing Work—How to Grow Bigger by Acting Smaller.* New York: McGraw-Hill, 1991.

McKenna, Regis. *Relationship Marketing: Successful Strategies for the Age of the Customer.* Boston: Addison-Wesley, 1991.

Myers, Gerry. *Targeting the New Professional Woman: How to Market and Sell to 57 Million Working Women.* Chicago: Probus Publishing Company.

Winninger, Thomas J. *Price Wars: A Strategy Guide to Winning the Battle for the Customer.* Rocklin, CA: Prima Publishing, 1995.

Chapter 8

Ross, Marilyn and Tom. *Big Ideas for Small Service Businesses: How to Successfully Advertise, Publicize, and Maximize Your Business or Professional Practice.* Buena Vista, CO: Communication Creativity.

Porter-Roth, Bud. *Proposal Development: How to Respond and Win the Bid.* Grants Pass, OR: Oasis Press, 1993.

Chapter 9

Davidson, Robert L., III. *The Small Business Partnership Kit.* New York: John Wiley & Sons, 1993.

Diamond, Michael R. and Julie L. Williams. *How to Incorporate.* New York: John Wiley & Sons, 1993.

DuBoff, Leonard D. *The Law (in Plain English) for Small Businesses—Second Edition.* New York: John Wiley & Sons, 1991.

Friedman, Robert. *The Complete Small Business Legal Guide.* Chicago: Dearborn Financial Publishing, 1993.

McQuown, Judith H. *INC. Yourself—How to Profit by Setting Up Your Own Corporation.* New York: Harper Business, 1992.

Nicholas, Ted. *The Business Agreements Kit.* Chicago: UPSTART Publishing, 1995.

Steingold, Fred S. *The Legal Guide for Starting and Running a Small Business.* Berkeley, CA: Nolo Press, 1995.

Chapter 10

Bernstein, Peter W., ed. *The Ernst and Young Tax Guide.* New York: John Wiley &

Sons, published annually.

Cooke, Robert A. *Doing Business Tax-Free.* New York: John Wiley & Sons, 1995.

H & R Block Income Tax Guide. New York: Collier Books, published annually.

J.K. Lasser Institute. *J.K. Lasser's Your Income Tax.* New York: Macmillan, published annually.

Schnepper, Jeff A. *How to Pay Zero Taxes.* 13th ed. New York: McGraw-Hill, 1996.

Chapter 11

Burton, Terence T., and John W. Moran. *The Future-Focused Organization: Complete Organizational Alignment for Breakthrough Results.* Englewood Cliffs, NJ: Prentice-Hall PTR, 1995.

Cook, Kenneth J. *AMA Complete Guide to Strategic Planning for Small Business.* Lincolnwood, IL: NTC Business Books, 1995.

Chapter 12

Business Insurance—6th Edition. Dearborn. R&R Newkirk. Chicago: Dearborn Financial Publishing, 1995.

Chapter 13

Cook, Robert J. *Leasing Office Space You Can Afford.* Chicago: Probus Publishing Company, 1993.

Chapter 14

Caplan, Suzanne. *A Piece of the Action: How Women and Minorities Can Launch Their Own Successful Businesses.* New York: AMACOM, 1994.

Jenkins, Michael D., & the Entrepreneurial Services Group of Arthur Young & Company. *Starting & Operating a Business in New Jersey.* Grants Pass, OR: Oasis Press, 1989.

Littman, Barbara and Michael Ray. *The Women's Business Resource Guide: A National Directory of Over 600 Programs, Resources, and Organizations to Help Women Start or Expand a Business.* Eugene, OR: The Resource Group, .

Novick, Lawrence. *How to Start a Business in the State of New Jersey.* Holmdell, NJ: L. N., 1992.

SCORE. *Starting & Managing Your Own Business in New Jersey.* Published by SBA and updated annually.

General Interest

Adamson, David. *Walking the High-Tech Highwire: The Technical Entrepreneur's Guide to Running a Successful Enterprise.* New York: McGraw-Hill, 1994.

Alcorn, Pat. *Success & Survival in the Family Owned Business.* New York: McGraw-Hill, 1982.

Allen, Marc. *Visionary Business: An Entrepreneur's Guide to Success.* Novato, CA: New World Library, 1995.

Arden, Lynie. *The Work-at-Home Sourcebook.* Boulder, CO: Live Oak Publications, 1994.

Bond, William J. *Home-Based Catalog Marketing: A Success Guide for Entrepreneurs.* New York: McGraw-Hill, 1994.

Bratline, Anita F. *Diary of a Small Business Owner.* New York: AMACOM, 1996.

Bygrave, William D. *The Portable MBA in Entrepreneurship.* New York: John Wiley & Sons, 1994.

Drucker, Peter. *Innovation & Entrepreneurship.* New York: Harper & Row, 1985.

Havania, David. *Home Business Made Easy.* Grant's Pass, OR: Oasis Press, 1992

Kolbe, Kathy. *Pure Instinct: Taking Advantage of Untapped Talents at the Workplace.* New York: Random House, 1993.

Leaptrott, Nan. *Rules of the Game: Global Business Protocol.* Cincinnati, OH: Thompson Executive Press, 1996.

Loden, Marilyn. *Feminine Leadership (or How to Succeed in Business Without Being One of the Boys).* New York: Time Books, 1985.

May, Bess Ritter. *Starting and Operating a Business after You Retire.* Garden City Park, NY: Avery Publishing Group, 1993.

Meade, Jeff. *Home Sweet Office—The Ultimate Out-of-Office Experience: Working Your Company Job from Home.* Princeton, NJ: Peterson's, 1993.

Naisbitt, John. *Megatrends Asian: Eight Asian Megatrends that Are Reshaping Our World.* New York: Simon & Schuster, 1996.

Rockham, Neil, Lawrence Friedman, and Richard Ruff. *Getting Partnering Right: How Market Leaders Are Creating Long-Term Competitive Advantage.* New York: McGraw-Hill, 1996.

Silver, David A. *Enterprising Women: Lessons from 100 of the Greatest Entrepreneurs of Our Day.* New York: AMACOM, 1994.

Slywotzky, Adrian J. *Value Migration: How to Think Several Moves Ahead of the Competition.* Boston: Harvard Business School Press, 1996.

Stark, Peter B. *It's Negotiable: The How-to Handbook of Win/Win Tactics.* San Diego, CA: Pfeiffer and Company, 1994.

Stolze, William J. *Start up: An Entrepreneur's Guide to Launching and Managing a New Business.* 3d ed. Hawthorne, NJ: Career Press, 1994.